Why I Wrc

MW00861435

Why I Wrote This Poem

62 Poets on Creating Their Works

3/30/23

Edited by WILLIAM WALSH

[signature]

To Dana,

I hope you enjoy this vast collection
of poetic voices, each with their
own story and reason
for becoming a poet.

My best to you,

Bill Walsh

McFarland & Company, Inc., Publishers

Jefferson, North Carolina

Library of Congress Cataloguing-in-Publication Data

Names: Walsh, William J., 1961– editor.
Title: Why I wrote this poem : 62 poets on creating
their works / edited by William Walsh.
Description: Jefferson, North Carolina : McFarland & Company, Inc., Publishers, 2023 |
Includes bibliographical references and index.
Identifiers: LCCN 2022052511 | ISBN 9781476684055 (paperback : acid free paper) ∞
ISBN 9781476647401 (ebook)
Subjects: LCSH: American poetry—21st century. | Poetry—Authorship.
| BISAC: LITERARY CRITICISM / Poetry
Classification: LCC PS617 .W49 2023 | DDC 811/.608—dc23/eng/20221103
LC record available at https://lccn.loc.gov/2022052511

British Library cataloguing data are available

ISBN (print) 978-1-4766-8405-5
ISBN (ebook) 978-1-4766-4740-1

Front cover images © 2023 Shutterstock

Printed in the United States of America

McFarland & Company, Inc., Publishers
Box 611, Jefferson, North Carolina 28640
www.mcfarlandpub.com

This book is dedicated to Frances McGuffey,
my senior English teacher at Southaven High School
in Southaven, Mississippi. Ms. McGuffey introduced me to a
world of literature through Shakespeare, Tolkien, and Eliot,
but most especially, to John Steinbeck and *Tortilla Flat*.

Acknowledgments

I would like to thank the poets included in this anthology for their time and effort in helping to create this book. Each poet has worked tirelessly, and I am indebted to them. I would like to thank my friends and family who stood with me as I talked about this project, but especially Donna Little, Wayne Glowka, and Mark Roberts for their friendship and encouragement, as well as the support of Reinhardt University. I owe a debt to the poets and publishers for granting permission to reprint these poems and essays. I would also like to thank my student editors who read early versions of the essays, as well as the final line edits: Nikki Bowen, Elizabeth Day, Angela Drury, and Olivia Ruzicka. These four students are some of the finest editors I have worked with on any project. Without them, this anthology would not have reached its full potential.

Table of Contents

Introduction

I began compiling and editing this anthology before the Covid outbreak, which, as we all know, essentially shut down the world. Could any of us have imagined what we would go through with the changes in our daily lives? I cannot recall in my life such dramatic, and often, polarizing transformations.

Recently, I watched a television show, *1968*, which made me realize how we often forget that the world is changing all the time and opposing forces are always clashing, like the tectonic plates, always pushing against each other until the forces erupt. Each generation has its issues as they push for the changes they believe are needed, just as it was in 1968. It's part of our job as poets to capture those moments. In our case: the pandemic, the murder of George Floyd and the riots in our major cities, the government listening to our cellphone conversations and emails, Facebook friends destroying one another over different political views, and much more.

Included in this anthology is Nikki Giovanni, a poet who was on the frontlines back in 1968 and who documented the pain, suffering, and outrage at the *system* with her poem "My Poem." At the time she was just twenty-five years old and considered a young poet, and now you can hear her frustration echoed fifty-five years later by today's protesters and contemporary poets. Her 1968 lines resonate, and a reader might never guess that they were penned five decades ago:

> I am 25 years old, black female poet
> asking nigger can you kill
> if they kill me it won't stop the revolution....

> My phone is tapped my mail is opened
> they've caused me to turn on all my friends....

> and if I never see a peaceful day or do a meaningful black thing
> it won't stop the revolution....

In the February 7, 2017, issue of *The Conversation*, senior lecturer at the University of East London, Tim Atkins, wrote "Five Protest Poets All

1

Demonstrators Should Read," where he stated that in 1968, "as demands for greater human rights and fewer governmental wrongs grew, the bloody violence that was meted out by the army and police saw an increasingly strident, anguished, and collective response in verse." How much different is this than what we see today? It's eerily similar.

What has changed the most in everyone's life is technology. In 1968, one of the high-tech offerings was a Kodak Instamatic 814 camera priced at $140, which in 2023 dollars would be approximately $950, about the price of a nice cell phone. It took weeks and sometimes months for photos to be taken, processed and developed, then sent out into the public eye for the average person to see images of what was occurring in the world. But now, live-streaming offers the world instantaneous connection and instantaneous outrage. Could anyone back in 1968 have imagined crystal clear video and photos, not to mention Zoom sessions on our laptops or cell phones? All you had to do back in 1968 was drop the film cartridge in and shoot. Then wait for your photos. Now our cell phones have more processing power than the Apollo spacecraft that landed on the moon. With this instant access to news and the "happenings" of the world, we have the ability for an immediate response.

With our modern technologies, our opportunity to connect with the entire world is greater than ever before. This privilege extends to poets, who have spoken-word, easily-accessible poetry websites, virtual readings, and craft discussions—a wealth of outlets to express themselves to readers around the globe. What better time to be a poet writing about the world than now?

The world turns to the poet to speak the truth about the world, and the poet speaks for their generation, which is one of the initial ideas behind this anthology, to allow the poet a forum to discuss how and why a particular poem was written. For a number of years, I thought about an anthology where poets write about one of their poems—maybe their favorite or most iconic poem, or perhaps one that was seminal in their mind or career. Through a series of events, I wrote a narrative first-person essay for *Georgia Backroads*, a fine magazine that caters to Georgia, the past and present. The essay was about how I came to write my poem "Brook Trout Along the Ellijay." My efforts were popular with the editors, and I even received a few fan letters. This occurred as I was beginning to mold this project into shape and discuss it with fellow poet, William Wright. It was also influenced by other books, such as James Dickey's *Self-Interviews*, where he discusses the impetus of his poems. In 1997, Jay Parini and Robert Pack followed a similar concept in their *Introspections: American Poets on One of Their Own Poems*. That was twenty-five years ago. With the exception of David Baker and Stephen Dunn, *Why I Wrote This Poem* is filled with an entirely new group of poets.

There are sixty-two poets represented in the anthology, all from vastly different backgrounds, cultures, and lifestyles. Sixty-two is a strange number. Why not simply sixty? I wish I could have included two hundred, which was quite possible given the strength of contemporary poetry. You might ask why so-and-so is not in this collection. Many poets were asked to be included, but to my surprise, many declined, because they simply did not have the time to write an essay. Some ignored my invitation. Some committed but never delivered. The number of poets included was arbitrary. It was primarily based on the word count by the publisher, which I exceeded despite my best efforts. After 60 poets were completed, two more arrived late. There was no way to say no. Hence, the word count increased, as well. To me, that was really never a consideration—the final length was what it was. Included in this anthology are big rock star names, poets on the rise in mid-career, and a few up-and-coming younger poets. Is this everyone who should be included in the book? No. Not by a long shot. Because of the health and need for poetry, I could have included, as I said, at least 200 poets. Perhaps a second volume will be considered. I firmly believe that this anthology, albeit a microcosm, is a fair and balanced representation of contemporary poetry in 2023. It has been a labor of love, two years in the making, and I hope each reader finds it as enjoyable and informative as I have.

Kim Addonizio

Cigar Box Banjo

Blind Willie Johnson could coax
music from a single string. God plucked a rib
and found a woman. Concert aria
in the gypsy song, long groan
of orgasm in the first kiss, plastic bag
of heroin ripening in the poppy fields.
Right now, in a deep pocket of a politician's brain,
a bad idea is traveling along an axon
to make sure the future resembles a cobra
rather than an ocarina.
Still there's hope in every cartoon bib
above which a tiny unfinished skull in
its beneficence dispenses a drooling grin.
The heart may be a trashy organ,
but when it plucks its shiny banjo
I see blue wings in the rain.

Cigar Box Banjo Reflection

For "Cigar Box Banjo," I first had in mind a project to write poems about different musical instruments. I had been immersed in playing harmonica and listening to the blues, that quintessential and foundational American music. Some friends had loaned me their banjo—a five-string, resonator banjo, surprisingly heavy—and I was fooling around with it, thinking I might buy one. Online, I discovered cigar box instruments. In early America, African slaves had brought their traditional instruments or recreated them from what was at hand. In the mid–19th century, many of the early country blues players, who were often Black and too poor to afford an instrument from the store, made their own. An empty cigar box, a broomstick or length of wood, a wire or two taken from the porch screen, and they, too, found a way to bring forth the music inside them. Blues legend Buddy Guy started out on a cigar box guitar. So did another legend, Jimi Hendrix, using rubber bands for strings. As far back as the Civil War, you could find soldiers playing cigar box fiddles. Cigar box banjos were made, too, and people are still crafting them today.

I didn't yet know what I wanted to say about a cigar box banjo, but I had banjos on my mind, and I liked the sound of that for a title. I don't always, or even often, start with a title. Sometimes it's the last thing I write, after the poem is pretty much done. But I had come up with this project for myself. Most of my projects start out with the hope of becoming an entire book, and if I'm lucky, I end up with a small handful of decent poems. Having a project is a good way to get a poem started, even if you never actually finish the project. Having a physical object in mind is also useful. Maybe the object is something in your immediate environment, like a banjo. It could be a lamp, a kitchen table, a ceiling fan, the sight of a tree or factory out the window. Or something you remember from your childhood: an autographed baseball, a stuffed lion ripped apart by your dog, your grandmother's false teeth in a glass on the bathroom counter. It could be something that calls to mind a dark time in your life, or someone else's. Coffin. Crack pipe. Divorce papers. A simple noun, a named thing, can be a door, a portal, a wormhole in space.

I'd been reading poet Terrance Hayes, some of whose work had shown me a very specific strategy: Use a title to generate words that will become the end-words of lines in your poem. If you were to write a poem called "Spring," you'd have words like *spin, ring, sip, grin, sprig, grips*. It's basically the old word/dice game, *Perquackey*. So, I made list of words from my title:

Air	narc	airbag
car	ago	coax
bar	raccoon	corn
boxcar	divorce	noir
rain	job	boar
garb	rib	jar
grin	jargon	bingo
acorn	boxing	—and a few more.

Now I had a subject, a kind of formal principle, and some language. The challenge became how to go more deeply into the expansive place that is the imagination. Any formal principle is a kind of restriction, a challenge. Writing poetry is a beautiful problem, one that lights up your brain. Right away your neurons are excitedly sending little chemical or electrical texts to each other as you try to figure out the next word, the next idea.

Your brain is on fire with possibilities. When you put out that fire, by finishing the poem, you go looking to start another one. More light.

I started messing around, writing lines that ended with some of the words, hoping to find a direction. Wandering, listening, trying to tune in. While Googling early cigar box instruments, I'd read about Blind Willie Johnson. Johnson, at the tender age of five, had made his own one-string cigar box guitar. I'd often listened to his haunting "Dark was the Night (Cold was the Ground)," which sounded to me like a spare, mournful piece of wordless lament. Someone had described the guitar technique of that song being an outgrowth of his early playing. I came up with a couple of lines, really only a line and a half:

> Blind Willie Johnson could coax
> music from a single string.

That felt like a good beginning, even if he hadn't played the banjo. Maybe I could write about Johnson, born in 1897, blinded at seven years old. Too poor to find a place to live after his house burned down, sickened by malaria or possibly pneumonia, refused care at a hospital, dead at forty-eight, buried in Beaumont, Texas. Gospel singer, songwriter, preacher. A man whose music not only reached many on earth, but was also included on the so-called Golden Record sent out into the universe on the Voyager space probes. I looked at my word list. I tried to imagine my way into this man's life, so alien to my own, so many years ago. Maybe he could sit outside in the night *air,* drinking whiskey from a *jar,* and listen to the *rain.* But nothing felt right. I was stuck, and I'd barely begun.

I can't remember how long it took to get this far—probably a couple of days of work. Play. Fooling around. Maybe this portal, the Terrance Hayes *Perquackey* door, wasn't going to budge. But I wasn't ready to give up and look for another one.

I stared at my word list again.

Acorn.

There's an old saying about mighty oaks growing from acorns. That struck me as a bit like Blind Willie Johnson's music coming from one string; the string was a small thing, but profound music could come from it. Just because I'd started with Blind Willie didn't mean the poem had to be about him. I didn't have to tell his story; I had to see where the language led me. I didn't know what my poem might end up being about, but that word had given me a possible direction. *Bingo.*

I thought about Eve, born of Adam's *rib.* I thought about pigs and *bacon,* diamonds and *carbon,* and *corn* in toothpaste (it contains Sorbitol, derived from corn). I wrote some lines, including these:

> Inside the acorn,
> oak that will one day cleave the barn.
>
> Like the pig, why be born
> only to end up as bacon?

Then I took out most of the lines I'd just written, starting with the acorn and the barn-cleaving oak—which was briefly the barn-shading oak, but either way, it seemed too obvious and easy. The mighty oak was something anyone might think of. Though Allen Ginsberg famously said, "First thought, best thought," "first thought" usually turns out to be "boring, cliched thought." The interesting ones come when you dig underneath the loose soil, below the kind of phrases and metaphors you already know and start to work your way through the hard clay beneath. So, I kept digging.

> In every trash can, the raccoon
> That will one day upend it.
>
> With this ring
> I will soon thee divorce.

Eventually, after a lot of writing best left in the trash can and sealed off from foraging raccoons, I got to something I felt fairly happy with. A week or so later, on rereading, I saw it needed more work. This is how things go in writing. You start digging, and once you get into the rhythm of it, you feel like you're flying. Your poem is growing like a beautiful hallucinatory flower before your eyes. Then, you leave it alone, come back in a week or a month to see how it's doing, and realize you've got to clear away some weeds and maybe add some compost. You see that it's all process. You and the world have changed, slightly, in the time you've been away. You have a new relationship with the words you've written so far. Now, the poem asks you to look again, to engage again with something you'd thought you were done with.

Mostly, I saw that my piece needed a better ending. Endings are difficult, because they come out of the decisions you've made along the way, and if you've made a false move somewhere, you may have to backtrack to figure out where you went wrong. Toward the end of my latest draft, I had something about the heart plucking its banjo, and a last line I could not get right. A couple of discarded versions:

> But sometimes, if given a banjo,
> it makes everything sound like rain.
>
> The heart plucks its little banjo
> and turns your blood to rain.

In my drafts, there are two pages of what the heart might make from the rain. Blue roses (inspired by Jim's nickname for Laura Wingfield in

The Glass Menagerie). Also, blue horses, dirty snow, dresses, rivers, tigers. Tremors. Diamonds. Kindness. Chaos. Lilies. Keyholes. Jewelry. Hail. Crystals. Cathedrals. Fireworks. Miracles. Bells.

I finally gave up on what the rain might make. I started again with a series of "I see..." statements—a change of syntax, a different approach. At last, I arrived at a line that felt simple but resonant—a single string that could vibrate into the silence after the poem ended:

I see blue wings in the rain.

A few years later, I still like the imagery and sounds created by those seven syllables. The process, again. Sometimes, after thinking a poem is finished, you may realize that you were wrong. You have to feel your way through a poem, as well as think your way, and then, when you're fairly satisfied, you have to get dissatisfied again and ask for more. You have to be willing to let go of ideas and directions after struggling to make them work. And you have to be willing, for a while, to make some noise that, with enough faith and struggle, may turn into a well-made song, blue horses in the river, tigers in the lilies, cathedrals of dirty snow.

David Baker

Nineteen Spikes

Then the storm came. It raked our world with terrible teeth.
Then dissolved—like a calcium spike—back into bone—

I see what you mean. But your barn's not really a barn.
Old lady just sat there—married to the guy fifty years—

Wash your doorknob. Your hands. Triage your mail.
I had a nightmare I was living my present life—

Can't touch my nose. It's called *resorption*. What?
It throbs like crickets in my ears. Your BP was *what?*—

No touching. COVID petals. She said wash your hands.
It took his body hours to work down through the corn—

The quicksand weight of it. Her in her folding chair.
Him with a new auger for the bin. He sort of spilled out—

So the viburnum's full of little pink blooms. Bees in orbit.
With their spikes, their barbs—poisons—perfumes—

Then the hail-balls, jagged as kidney stones, half a foot of rain.
Trees seemed to blow up—then the whole thing, whoosh—

Some natural forms are so successful they're viral.
Calcium nodes on your clavicle. I see them everywhere—

How small can they get? How big? Any size explodes—
Is it gas? You mean the barn? Is it gas? A heat storm—

Barn = a non–SI metric unit of area equal to 10^{-28} m^2 (or 100 fm^2)—
To quantify interaction of a nucleus with an electric field gradient—

And branchlets are pithy, many-angled, winged. *Liquid-Ambar styraciflua.* Surrounded by rusty hairy bracts—

Looks like a tiny naval mine. Between 80 and 120 spikes.
Terminal barbs. A special form of moored contact mine—

And equipped with a plummet. He fell right through.
The spikes on the outer edge of the virus particles—

Give coronaviruses their name. Sweet gum. Storax.
Redgum. Star-leaved alligator-wood. Limpet mine—

In place of torpedoes, the silos carry twelve charges.
I heard my heartbeat in my bones. A positive "kill rate"—

Airbnb. *Missile Silo Fixer-up Now Swanky Bachelor Pad.*
Storm shelter; a storage bin; your "ultimate" safe room—

Each virus is a single pleomorphic spherical particle—
Satin-walnut—with bulbous surface projections—

I see what you mean. Wash your hands. Like that really helps.
Leaves ripped clean off. It's coming back. I know—

Writing in Peril

When I saw a bright color depiction of the COVID-19 virus for the first time, it struck me like a storm—how beautiful it was, how unspeakably familiar it felt to me.

The storm came in the late afternoon, after an early spring morning of stillness and surprising warmth. It pushed across the trees, first a breathing sound, then movement, shaking up high, then hard and harder rain and roaring winds ripping through the trees and down to the ground-level plants. Big limbs broke or were torn and fell in the sheering wind, and the weird, slow-motion-explosion blooms of the viburnum growing along one side of my backyard were shaken hard, but they stayed put.

The storm came as a whirlpool of corn, pulling down the man where he had fallen to suffocate there. It came as a virus over me, through me, in 1993, and was unidentified for many months but shook me hard for several years. It recurred, such a slow-motion terror, four years ago.

This poem is about why. It is a conceptual poem. I mean that "Nineteen Spikes" began not as a story or an event, not as image or phrase, not music, not information, but as an idea. Those others are my usual ways of starting a poem, with a sound, an occurrence, a detail, a fact. But this time: a concept, and the concept is simple.

A single COVID-19 virus particle looks very much like a viburnum bloom. Or to expand the image a bit: like a viburnum bloom with bees circling it. It looks very much like the seed-ball of a sweetgum tree. It looks very much like a naval explosive mine, the kind that floats and is meant to damage or destroy submarines and ships.

It is a single sphere with a number of spikes or protruding arms, tiny adhesive triggers. And those COVID spikes, aren't they like the triggers on those mines? Or like sharp calcium deposits that recur and vanish back into a collarbone or shoulder? My orthopedic surgeon calls that vanishing "resorption." And my infectious-disease doctor calls the onset of a serious illness like mine—chronic fatigue/immune deficiency syndrome, or myalgic encephalomyelitis—a "viral storm."

I wanted to let all those similarities and likenesses orbit the single, elusive body of the poem. We never quite see the subject at hand, only the pieces around it, in orbit.

This is a hard poem to read. I realize that. It's in pieces, the syntax, the stories, even the tone. It doesn't quite focus, or rather it keeps shifting from microscopic to "normal" to over-sized images and details. It's hard to get a handle on the thing. That's what it's like to suffer from a hard illness or to be in the midst of a storm or to try to comprehend grave danger or the natural peril of host bodies. That's certainly what it's like to witness and be part of a global pandemic, at the mercy of a virus whose methods we hardly understand, whose effects can vary monumentally, whose trajectory is terrifying, and whose future is beyond our knowing for now, maybe ever.

Everything happens in the poem many times. There are nineteen couplets, each made of two monostichs that often terminate with a spiky dash. Sometimes the syntax or meaning of one of those lines is continued in the next line or several lines later. Things recur, are picked up, are refreshed or reused in a kind of syntactic or conceptual mutation.

When the farmer fell into his own silo, next to his barn, he was pulled down into the corn-grain and died of asphyxia. The rescuers—even with help and equipment from a nearby Air Force base—couldn't get to him in time. This happened nearby and in the autumn before the COVID onset. And maybe even an ear of corn, with its cylindric cob and all those orbiting kernels, has a shape a bit like the virus?

Everywhere in the poem I am looking for likenesses of that shape and behavior. Some natural shapes, as the poem says, are particularly vital or viable, aren't they? A helix. A tree. A layer or stratification. A sphere with spikes.

As for the voice of "Nineteen Spikes," I realize that we are—and our voices are—actually made of many, many others. I wanted the poem to be as many-voiced as the stories, as all the viral pieces. Someone talks, a doctor diagnoses, someone else observes, a farmer reports, and someone wonders to himself. In gathering material, I referred to information from the CERN Writing Guidelines on Nuclear Testing. For instance, a barn, as we know, is a farm building and is often situated near a silo; but a "barn" is also a unit of measurement at the subatomic level, used especially in the designing of nuclear weapons. Likewise, a silo is a tall cylindrical farm building made for storage of grains, but it is also a chute in the ground or on a submarine for storing and launching missiles. I read books on trees and articles about warfare, COVID, and my own disease. And throughout, I tried to let those languages percolate, overlap, and work their ways into my language—whatever my language is.

Of course, none of this makes "Nineteen Spikes" any better or worse. And part of the rigorous pleasure of reading a poem is engaging yourself with its complexities and even its obscurities. There's plenty more for you to discover and add on your own to this poem.

So, about the writing itself. The concept for my poem came as soon as I saw the COVID depiction. I took a few quick notes—mostly likenesses, the first being the sweetgum. This was early March 2020, the same month I first got sick, myself, so many years earlier. My viburnum started blooming in early April, and so I added that to my list that also included naval mines by then. The wind and rainstorm occurred mid–April. I didn't know the form or the movement or the phrasing of the poem, not yet, but just kept taking notes. As I did, a phrase would emerge, and some information seemed necessary to weave into the poem, and the phrases began to feel like long lines—monostichs—and at some point, I knew the poem had to be halting, phrasal, and plural-voiced, and full of peril, poison, and blossoming.

Once I started working on the poem, itself, I had a draft in two or three slow days. I liked discovering that spiky dash at the end of several phrases, clauses, and every couplet. None of this actually "ends," does it? I spent about a month writing and negotiating with phrasing and constantly moving the pieces around. All of this was during the quarantining. Both the beauty and conundrum of a non-narrative or non-linear poem are that things can happen in many different orders. But it had to start with the storm, and it had to end with the non-ending of recurrence or relapse, a continual contagion.

A poem is not for what we already know. It is for what we don't know. Perhaps it becomes its own way of knowing, as W.H. Auden said, or a means of finding out. Or, maybe better, a poem is a way of staying alive, alert, and grateful for the persistence of never knowing for sure.

❧

Aliki Barnstone

Scripture for Coronavirus

we wait for the apex of the curve which won't be noonday
sunlight but the city's nadir for at the apex the most will stop
breathing as if the earth went dark at noon and the next day
will be like the day after winter solstice the second darkest day
of the year and the apex will roll like sunlight that leaves
shadows in the East first yet lingers another hour to the West
and still another hour further West where the curve still
climbs toward the apex and more and more will gasp for air
and grow feverish in the hour light lingers on fallow fields
and there will be no shade from the heat at noonday for those

in the midlands who believed the false prophet's lies blindly
and blind they cursed reporters who bore the facts to the light
and they will drive toward the too bright lights of the hospital
and they will pray I shall call upon God and be saved for evening
and morning and at noon I will complain and murmur and God
will hear my voice though the megachurch worship music
did not transport them to health and the miracle healings
were fake news and the minister who exhorted his flock
to break the law of sinners and test fate or faith was the wrong
kind of angel to lead their prayers and they spoke the word

with blood on their upraised hands and guns on their hips
and they did not heed the word they disdained that foretold
the virus's apex and how to shelter from the storm that steals
away breath the ruthless wind beating against the lungs' walls
for divine vitality dwells in the cells and matter waits
for science's revelations and as they lie dying on a gurney
the healer will hover above them in a precious mask and still
they will mutter what a bad deal and the doctors are elitist
crooks and it was all rigged whatever it was and when blue-
gloved hands reach for instruments gleaming on a stainless
steel tray at last they will pray for another kind of salvation

15

On Writing "Scripture for Coronavirus": E Pluribus Unum

At the beginning of the pandemic, I invited friends to join me for a daily Zoom poetry game. I've been playing the poetry game ever since I was a little girl in Vermont, gathered around the fireplace with my family and Ruth Stone and her three daughters. I play with my friends, my university students and with the K–12 students I worked with when I traveled around Missouri as the state's poet laureate. It's simple—we come up with a list of words together, decide how long we'll write, and then use any, all, or none of the words. Then we read to each other. Its magic is ubiquitous. People are surprised by the poems they write; people who don't consider themselves poets are surprised that they can write at all. There's an uncanniness—words that appear in several people's poems that weren't on the list, a kind of telepathy, a sense that by writing in the company of others, we've entered a communal, synergistic space. The pandemic iteration of the poetry game differs from the past in that, while not everyone comes every session, we have made coming together to write a practice, a practice that we agree has not only proved generative but is saving our lives, or at least our psychic lives.

My notebook reveals that I'd started playing the poetry game with friends at about the same time my daughter returned to Missouri from New York City. She grieved having lost the life she'd built there. (She was determined and lucky and rebuilt it better by midsummer of 2020.) I witnessed how rapidly the situation in the City became dire, how droves of people left—if they could. The night before she flew, my brave and independent daughter said in a low voice, "It's scary here, the streets empty, sirens wailing at all hours." For a month, we'd been watching Andrew Cuomo's daily briefings. On April 3, the day I wrote the first draft of "Scripture for Coronavirus," he said: "what we're looking at now is the apex, top of the curve, roughly at the end of April…. Which means another month of this. The apex, the recent number is you could need 110,000 COVID beds … 37,000 ventilators" (Andrew Cuomo). This language was daily—the curve, the apex, the numbers of hospital beds, ventilators, PPE, healthcare workers needed, the numbers of infected and dead, the refrigerator truck morgues parked next to the hospital.

Meanwhile, here in the Midwest, while many people anticipated shortages and stocked up on supplies, the denialism deepened the trauma. Trump is a hate and death cult leader who brainwashed people into making masks a political statement—and a religious one, for some. A terrifying percentage of evangelicals believe that Trump is the chosen one who will bring on the rapture. I've heard from several friends that they've been asked firmly to leave their churches because they don't support Trump. I find this kind of religious extremism troubling and enraging, not because I don't believe in God, but because I do. I read the Bible and—though it's probably a waste of my mental energy—at points of particular pressure, its verses come to me and refute a version of a selfish God hellbent on laissez faire capitalism, guns, controlling women's bodies, and who demands the devout science against miracles to prove their faith (when by definition faith is not based on proofs).

The day I drafted "Scripture," my daughter had tested negative for COVID-19 after quarantining for two weeks. I started writing a sonnet about the trays of food I'd left outside her door during her quarantine, but the words we came up with, particularly "apex," "doctor," and "stainless steel," led me in a different direction and I abandoned those lines and any semblance of received form. I began, "we wait for the apex of the curve," and rushed on writing urgently, no punctuation, transcribing the rabble of voices I heard, the political, the scientific, the religious and biblical. Governor Cuomo talked every day about flattening the curve, reminding us that when you reach the top of mountain, it takes time to come down. The visual image of the mountain and the upward climb of cases and deaths combined in my mind's eye with time passing and sunlight that goes dark from East to West, just as the pandemic spread from coast to heartland. The shadow of the pandemic would extinguish the light here in Missouri, and people would sicken and die here, too, regardless of their beliefs.

After the initial drafts, I researched some of the phrases that had come to me as scripture—"darkness at noon," a recurrent celestial phenomenon at cataclysmic moments in the Bible, as well as the comforting trope of divine protective shade from the noonday heat in Psalms and Isaiah. The image is the same but has two opposite emotional resonances. I was particularly struck by Amos 8:9 when God declares, "I will make the sun go down at noon and make the dark in broad daylight" and wove into my own poem echoes of these verses: "there will be no shade from the heat at noonday for those// in the midlands who believed the false prophet's lies blindly / and blind they cursed reporters who bore the facts to the light." I want to say I appropriated the language of Trumpers, evangelicals, megachurches, etc., and used it ironically against them—as they so often use ours against us, but that's not quite right. The language of culture belongs to us all and I want to steal it back, as Alicia Ostriker might say, and reconstitute it to name my vision and experience.

At the same, I was teaching Muriel Rukeyser's poem sequence, *The Book of the Dead*, in my Environmental Literature and Introduction to Women's Literature courses. Written before the term was coined, the book is a work of docu-poetry that gives voice to victims of the Hawk's Nest

Tunnel disaster, one of the worst failures of industry to protect its workers. The construction company did not provide protective equipment and the workers breathed in silica and developed fatal lung disease. Three-fourths of the workers were Black people seeking work during the Great Depression and they sickened and died, leaving their loved ones to mourn—and to tell their stories. In the poem "Merle Blankenship," Merle recounts:

> "I wake up choking, and my wife
> rolls me over on my left side;
> then I'm asleep in the dream I always see:
> the tunnel choked
> the dark wall coughing dust"

I don't see this dream as personifying the Earth. Instead, Merle's dreamscape metaphor aligns the human with the Earth, reveals a primal sense that harming the earth harms our own health. In Greek, the word for breath, *pneuma*, means wind. The poem imagines humanity as part of the natural world. I heard the wind both as breathing and taking away breath: "how to shelter from the storm that steals/ away breath the ruthless wind beating against the lungs' walls."

I say "I heard" because when I state that I researched or explain in detail where my lines come from, I don't want you to think that I added these phrases mechanically. I follow the music, the rush spurred by our list of words, sun and shade marking time, breathlessness and breathiness, the poetry of the Bible and prose of slogans, my own rage and fear—the desire to live. I write down what I hear before the crossback into wordlessness. Then I back it up with research, which helps me refine and edit and surprises me at once. For example, in "Scripture for Coronavirus," I added "and there will be no shade from the heat at noonday" in the third draft, which resonated with the curve and the sunlight and shadow marking time on the landscape; the line suggests that those who follow false prophets unwittingly risk leaving God's shelter. I have an impulse to soften my own harsh interpretation of that line because I am, personally, tenderhearted. But this poem is not tender, and as Emily Dickinson famously wrote, "When I state myself, as the Representative of the Verse—it does not mean—me—but a supposed person" (L268). Poems are both reflective of their author's self and separate from it. As such this poem has a life of its own as an angry, alternative scripture for the pandemic, driven by the foreseen epidemiological outcome of viral mendacity—the misinformation, propaganda, and lies.

As I was putting the finishing touches on this essay, the U.S. Capitol was attacked and I would like to end by addressing the issues of lies and predictability, given that the insurrection was incited by misinformation and that the coup attempt, I would argue, was predictable. Of course, predictably, the virus did spread from the coasts to the center of the country, which doesn't make my poem prescient or prophetic. The poem rejects such quasi-religious terms, though it employs them ironically and observationally. The events I envisioned were based on reported facts and the findings of experts. The political scene I describe in the lines below was also foreseeable:

> they spoke the word / with blood on their upraised hands
>   and guns on their hips
>
> ....
>
> [they] believed the false prophet's lies blindly / and blind
>   they cursed reporters who bore the facts to the light
>
> ....
>
> and still / they will mutter what a bad deal and the doctors
>   are / elitist crooks and it was all rigged whatever it was

The spread of the virus was not surprising, just as the terrorist attack on the U.S. Capitol was not.

The difference between the language of scientific and statistical probability and that of religious and political tyranny is that the former is based on facts and the latter is based on lies and propaganda, and propaganda depends on clichés, slogans, and the kind closing down and abuse of language that Orwell pithily sums up in *1984* in the three legendary slogans of the Party that are written on the wall of the Ministry of Truth: "WAR IS PEACE / FREEDOM IS SLAVERY / IGNORANCE IS STRENGTH" (4). One of ironies of *1984* is that its predictive qualities are based on Orwell's knowledge of history, particularly of Nazi Germany, just as Margaret Atwood's *The Handmaid's Tale* is. Atwood states that there's "nothing in the book that didn't happen, somewhere" (Allardice).

These works are warnings. Tyrannical regimes are unimaginative; they imitate each other, employing the same playbook, updated to utilize new technology for the same ends, as we can see in historian Timothy Snyder's succinct *On Tyranny: Twenty Lessons from the Twentieth Century.* The ninth lesson is "Be kind to our language":

> "Be kind to our language. Avoid pronouncing the phrases everyone else does. Think up your own way of speaking, even if only to convey that thing you think everyone else is saying. Make an effort to separate yourself from the internet. Read books.... The effort to define the shape and significance of events requires words and concepts that elude us when we are entranced by visual stimuli.... We take this collective trance to be normal. We have slowly fallen into it [59–61]."

At last, too late to forestall the violence, pundits are calling a "coup attempt" the coup attempt Trump himself told us for years that he'd stage. As crucial as they are, we need more than facts and journalism in order to counter what the pundits are finally calling "The Big Lie"—because now, predictably, we're all using those terms, too. If we are to "avoid pronouncing the phrases everyone else does," we need language that transports us and takes us into the untranslatable via language that is multivalent and opens up possibility.

The poetry game nurtures and expands the language because we are engaged in a common journey to the ineffable. The lists of words we come up with are spells that give us courage to explore unknown regions, to be guided by and influenced by our friends, our companion travelers, to dare to go beyond our craft and knowledge and to try new moves, to listen to the freshly drafted poems of others that convey other worlds, and to be surprised again and again in the village of our own making. It's not my individual poem or the individual poems of my friends who play the poetry game with me—anybody can play—just reading a book is playing. It's letting go of the myth of the solitary artist. It's taking on the mantle of meaning-maker and passing it on with generosity and love. It's writing in community, participating in something larger than oneself, and doing the cultural work through the language of art and dissent.

Works Cited

Allardice, Lisa. "Interview: Margaret Atwood: I'm not a prophet. Science fiction is about now." *The Guardian*. 20 Jan 2018.

"Andrew Cuomo New York Coronavirus Briefing Transcript April 1." *Rev*, May 6, 2020, www.rev.com/blog/transcripts/andrew-cuomo-new-york-coronavirus-briefing-transcript-april-1.

Orwell, George. *1984*. 1949. Signet. 1961.

@realDonaldTrump. "The FAKE NEWS media (failing @nytimes, @NBCnew, @ABC, @CBS, @CNN) is not my enemy, it is the enemy of the American People!" *Twitter*. 18 February 2017. (Trump's Twitter account was suspended but as of May 2022 it was back on)

Snyder, Timothy. *On Tyranny: Twenty Lessons from the Twentieth Century*. Tim Duggan Books. 2017.

Erin Belieu

With Birds

It's all *Romeo and Juliet*—
hate crimes, booty calls, political
assassinations.
Who's more Tybalt than the Blue Jay?
More Mercutio than the mockingbird?
The ibis pretending to be a lawn ornament
makes a vain and stupid prince.
Birds living in their city-states, flinging
mob hits from the sky, they drop their dead
half chewed at my gates. But give anything
even once lice-riddled wing and suddenly
we're symbolic, in league with the adult
collector of teddy bears, the best-addressed-
in-therapy pinned like a kitty-cat calendar in
every cubicle. Pathetic, really. With birds,
make no exception.
                    All right. It's possible
I'll give you this morning's
mourning doves, there on the telephone
wire, apart from the hoi polloi—
something in their pink, the exact shade
of an aubade. And shouldn't we recall
that keen pheromonal terror, when dawn
arrives too bright, too soon? Let's hope we
never muster what God put in the goose's
head. For this,
                    you keep the doves.

Notes on "With Birds"

My back deck is anchored by a magnificent live oak. She's hundreds of years old, with branches that span the length of a house in each direction. She also serves as the village meeting place for all the wildlife in my neighborhood who live in her enormous canopy. I can be found most mornings sitting at my patio table beneath her, peacefully contemplating the wild things as they go about their business above me.

But one morning a couple years back, I was startled by the juicy THWACK of something hitting my deck. I looked over to find a large chunk of decapitated snake carcass where it had landed two feet from me. One of the barred owls who hang out in my tree had apparently dropped its breakfast. While a variety of slithering things is something you get used to if you live in north Florida, this was a bit much, even for my typical sangfroid in the face of full-contact nature.

I'll spare you the details of cleaning up the mess, but once I was settled back at my table, I began thinking about all the bird life I witness daily from under my tree. And I felt a poem calling to me.

Typically, it's a good feeling when you hear a poem calling. But in this case, I thought, "Oh no! Please God, not a 'bird poem'!" Because I'm always wary of tropes and images that tempt poets into the stock footage of lyric clichés. Waves, stars, moons, autumn leaves, flowers, etc.—all those things that are so astonishingly beautiful that humans have put them in their poems again and again. And again. And again.

Which is to say, it can be extremely difficult to reanimate thoughts and images that poets have been writing about for thousands of years. And, what do I urgently need to say about birds that writers like Catullus or Dickinson or Hardy haven't already brilliantly observed?

The number one truth of poem making is that clichés—both in thought and language—are the ultimate poetry killers. Even the most gorgeous noise is exactly that—noise. I compare the pretty, empty sounds some poems make to the kind of pleasantly bland music massage therapists play when you're lying on the table. It's music that's designed not to distinguish itself. This vague, forgettable quality is not what poets want for their poems.

My challenge then was to write something both true and surprising with birds as my subject. After all, surprising language in a poem is pointless if it isn't also something a reader encounters and says, "Ahh. Yes. I hadn't exactly seen/thought about it that way."

With these considerations in mind, I decided I would brave writing a poem about birds. But I first made a list of all the words I wouldn't use (and having some formal strictures when writing a free verse poem is most often useful to keep the poem from being flabby). My list included all those words that people immediately associate with birds—sky, wings, flight, nest, feathers, beak—and so on.

My list assured me I was much more likely to avoid clichés if I took the subject's greatest hits off the table. Then, I considered what people seem to typically think about birds—the way we humans so often project our romantic notions onto them. I mean, who can resist these beautiful creatures that can actually fly? How extraordinary they are! But this led me to consider what I also know to be true of birds after observing them most days for many years, especially after having just cleaned up one's gruesome mess.

One thing I know about birds is that they fight viciously, and they fight a lot. They also mate with similar frequency and intensity, or at least the male birds spend a lot of time strutting about and whooping at the top of their lungs. There's frequently some ruckus going on up in my tree, and it reaches such a screeching pitch sometimes that I've yelled at them more than once to knock it off.

This initial observation led me to thinking of human romance and violence that have similar dramatic intensities. Hence, the poem's opening comparison to *Romeo and Juliet,* the most famous of romantic and violent plays in English. It tickled me to realize how aptly some of the birds I encounter in my live oak mirrored the characters Shakespeare imagined for us.

Then, my mind turned to how often we sentimentalize birds, projecting onto them cheap emotion, shaping them to fit what we wish them to represent. Humans have a difficult tendency toward self-delusion and not a little dishonesty, qualities that distinguish us from the other animals and which cause us no end of personal trouble, so human history suggests.

You may notice in this section of the poem I do allow myself a single word that was originally on my list of language I'd forbidden myself—the word *wing.* I thought about whether or not I could truly justify using that word for quite a while—whether I had actually earned its use in the poem—and finally decided I'd said something with that image that I hadn't heard anyone else put into words before.

But despite my resolve to capture birds as the complicated, often unlovely creatures they are, I was surprised to discover the speaker in my poem is ultimately, if grudgingly, affected by the beauty of the mourning doves that appear at the poem's end. Not all romance is inherently bad, I suppose. And the poem acknowledges this while also alluding to one of the most memorable moments in Shakespeare's play—when Romeo and Juliet wake after having spent the night together. I thought this ending fit my poem perfectly as there's a very old type of poem—called an aubade—which is a morning song written on the occasion of lovers parting at dawn. You really can't get more romantic than that.

So, my poem ended up teaching me something about what I actually feel and think on this particular subject. It's essential to a poem for a writer not to pre-think and plot it too much if you want to avoid clichés (please do) and discover in the writing something you and the reader didn't already know. I trust language and the unconscious mind to take me somewhere new and interesting, and I don't worry too much about letting go of that control. Once you get used to not being in charge of your poem, letting the imagination wander as it will, I think you'll find this is actually the best, most satisfying part of writing.

Richard Blanco

Looking for The Gulf Motel
Marco Island, Florida

There should be nothing here I don't remember....

The Gulf Motel with mermaid lampposts
and ship's wheel in the lobby should still be
rising out of the sand like a cake decoration.
My brother and I should still be pretending
we don't know our parents, embarrassing us
as they roll the luggage cart past the front desk
loaded with our scruffy suitcases, two-dozen
loaves of Cuban bread, brown bags bulging
with enough mangos to last the entire week,
our espresso pot, the pressure cooker—and
a pork roast reeking garlic through the lobby.
All because we can't afford to eat out, not even
on vacation, only two hours from our home
in Miami, but far enough away to be thrilled
by *whiter* sands on the *west* coast of Florida,
where I should still be for the first time watching
the sun set instead of rise over the ocean.

There should be nothing here I don't remember....

My mother should still be in the kitchenette
of The Gulf Motel, her daisy sandals from Kmart
squeaking across the linoleum, still gorgeous
in her teal swimsuit and amber earrings
stirring a pot of *arroz-con-pollo*, adding sprinkles
of onion powder and dollops of tomato sauce.
My father should still be in a terrycloth jacket
smoking, clinking a glass of amber whiskey
in the sunset at the Gulf Motel, watching us
dive into the pool, two boys he'll never see
grow into men who will be proud of him.

There should be nothing here I don't remember....

24

My brother and I should still be playing *Parcheesi*,
my father should still be alive, slow dancing
with my mother on the sliding-glass balcony
of The Gulf Motel. No music, only the waves
keeping time, a song only their minds hear
ten-thousand nights back to their life in Cuba.
My mother's face should still be resting against
his bare chest like the moon resting on the sea,
the stars should still be turning around them.

There should be nothing here I don't remember....

My brother should still be thirteen, sneaking
rum in the bathroom, sculpting naked women
from sand. I should still be eight years old
dazzled by seashells and how many seconds
I hold my breath underwater—but I'm not.
I am thirty-eight, driving up Collier Boulevard,
looking for The Gulf Motel, for everything
that should still be, but isn't. I want to blame
the condos, their shadows for ruining the beach
and my past, I want to chase the snowbirds away
with their tacky mansions and yachts, I want
to turn the golf courses back into mangroves,
I want to find The Gulf Motel exactly as it was
and pretend for a moment, nothing lost is lost.

Memory as Homeland

Continent, city, country, society:
the choice is never wide and never free.
And here, or there.... No. Should we have stayed at home,
wherever that may be?
—Elizabeth Bishop, "Questions of Travel"

I figuratively started writing this poem (well, all my poems) while I was still in the womb. Let me explain. My mother, seven months pregnant with me, left Cuba with my father and brother, arriving as exiles to Madrid, Spain, where I was born. Forty-five days later we immigrated and eventually settled in Miami, Florida, where I would be raised. Only a few weeks old, I belonged to three cultures, three cities, three countries, and yet to none. To my mind, the dominant theme of my poetry, as a whole, dates back to that perplexing genesis of mine. It's said that every poet is writing one poem their entire life. Meaning every poet is haunted by some fundamentally personal and complex question; and each poem is an attempt to answer some part of that question, which can never be completely answered. Every poem I write in some way asks me to ask myself and others that proverbial question that obsesses me, *what is home?* And explore the multitude of meanings which that tiny, one-syllable word encompasses. Here is the story of how one of those poems came to life, like the birth of a star adding to the constellation of my body of work, trying to map my mythology of home across the abyss of the night sky that is the bare white page at my desk.

In 1999, I accepted my first creative writing professorship and had to trade the palm tree pompoms of my native Miami for Connecticut's stately maples, and I watched them turn from green to red to dead, bare branches that I pitied as lonely as me for three winters long in my windows. I abandoned for Brazil's sultry waterfalls, until my awe for them misted away and they became simply waterfalls as common as tears. Which I exchanged for the rage of Guatemala's volcanoes, as temperamental as my madness at the thought of drifting aimlessly all my life. Which I soothed with the tempered marble of D.C.'s monuments, a resplendence that ultimately dulled me. Which is to say: I spent five wander-lost years culturally misplaced and emotionally homeless. Which is why I moved back to Miami—my home city—in 2005, expecting to step right back into the life I had (never) left behind. I spent the first few months frequenting all my former haunts and stomping grounds, feasted on Cuban sandwiches and guava *pastelitos* at La Carreta, baptized myself again in the aqua waters of Surfside Beach, and danced again shirtless in the storm of disco lights at Twist. Everything seemed the same, yet not quite the same, as if I was living in a fuzzy hologram of my life's memories. Something felt off about the spices, the music, the color of the ocean. Had these changed while I was away; did I just remember them wrong? Or had I changed? And if so: why, how?

Those questions were variations of my same, life-long question: *What is home?* My poetic muse at the time asked me to ponder the old adage: *you can't go back home.* I refused to believe it, certain that I could return to some place where my life was not a hologram. While paging through an old photo album, I thought: *That's it—that's the place—Marco Island—yes!* Since childhood, and well into my young adulthood, all my family could afford was a yearly weekend vacation on the shores of the sleepy island off the west coast of Florida, at the Gulf Motel, only a couple of hours from Miami. Surely nothing there had changed from what I remembered: a few similar motels dotting a spare main street; one mom-and-pop grocery store; barely any footprints on the sugar-white sands along miles of empty beaches; and the unobstructed views of the Gulf's timid waters from the balcony of the Gulf Motel. I talked up my memories to my boyfriend Mark (who would become my husband) and enticed him to treat me to a weekend getaway. We packed our SUV and headed down Route 41, west toward memory lane. Surely everything was the same, even though I hadn't been there in over twenty years.

Of course, nothing was the same: a concrete curtain of condos twenty-plus stories high along the shore; chain restaurants and gas stations with neon signs blaring at every corner; souvenir shops stocked with plaster-made coral and cheap sunglasses; canals carved through the island for "waterfront" McMansions crowded against each other. The Gulf Motel was nowhere to be found as I surveyed street after street (mis)guided by memory. *What was I thinking?* Worse than a hologram, I felt completely erased, as if my past had never happened. Displaced, distraught, angry, resentful—I began cussing like a sailor: *What the fuck? How dare they? Goddamn capitalism. This is bullshit.* Mark was taken aback by my reaction. *Calm down. Damn, you sound just like your mother talking about Cuba,* he said, a comment that was lost on me at the moment. *Fuck that! Let's get out of here,* I mouthed back, made a U-turn and headed east back to Miami. As soon as I got home, I started penning the first draft of this poem, unleashing all my vitriol on the page. A few days later I shared it with Mark who said, *That's the worst poem you've ever written.* His response put me on the defensive: *No, it's not. It says exactly what I want to say ... what I feel,* I blurted out. Almost as soon as I heard those words leave my mouth, the golden rule of writing began echoing in my mind: *show, don't tell ... show, don't tell ... show, don't tell.* But I ignored it, knew I was ignoring it, and continued to ignore it.

Serendipitously, about three months later I began working with the visual artist John Bailly on a collaborative project that involved my poems and his paintings in a co-creative dialogue with each other. In one particular canvas, John had drawn out a line from that first draft of the poem that I had given him: *There should be nothing here I don't remember.* For weeks, the painting haunted me for reasons I didn't consciously understand. Eventually, I instinctually came to realize that single line was the only one worth keeping; it held the essence of what I needed to ask and discover by showing my life to myself and to others, instead of simply telling it. And so, I tossed out my first draft and began anew by scribbling that line at the top of a blank page. (*There should be nothing here I don't remember.*) As I wrote on, the line kept coming back as a refrain. (*There should be nothing here I don't remember.*) And I kept responding to it, stanza after stanza, trying to decipher what that abstract, telling line meant by recalling tangible, tactile, sensory details that allowed me to re-experience my memories of the Gulf Motel, diving deeper into the emotional core of the poem, its gravitas, its raison d'être. I finished the poem in one three-hour sitting, titled it "Looking for The Gulf Motel," and never looked back to revise a single word.

However, over the past eight years since then, I have continued *looking back* at the poem in various related contexts. As I like to say, *my poems are smarter than I am.* They *know things* about myself, my creative process, and poetry itself, which I eventually discover much later, in retrospect, as I read them to myself or share them with others, astonished by their reactions. My poems continue to teach me long after they're written. As regards "Looking for The Gulf Motel," it's since donned on me that the real emotional center of the poem was not anger, but my fear at the prospect of contending with my lack of human agency against the inevitability of change and loss, just as my mother did when she left Cuba (as Mark observed). Marco Island was figuratively the same island of my mother's long-lost Cuba. What's more, I had to face my mortality for the first time in my life, and I struggled with surrendering to it. This reinforced for me Richard Hugo's view that, *In truth, the writer's problems are usually psychological, like everyone else's,* as he noted in his classic book, *The Triggering Town.* Indeed, it was that dive into my subconscious that allowed me to revise my emotions, which in turn enabled me to consciously revise that vexed first draft of the poem. I've come to trust that the truest poems emerge when our subconscious feelings connect with the conscious mind through the synapses of language.

I believe that's what happened when writing "Looking for The Gulf Motel," which I now regard as one of the most important poems I've ever written. So much so, that it became the gateway *and* the title poem of the new collection which it spawned. Over its lifetime, the poem has revealed to me yet another dimension of my endless questioning of home, of that *one poem* I've been writing all my life since I was in the womb—and am still writing. That question Elizabeth Bishop and I seem to have posed all our lives, respectively: ... *home,/ wherever that may be?* Writing this poem taught me that I can't ascertain my sense of home by merely claiming or reclaiming it in the physical, three-dimensional world, which is constantly and necessarily changing. But rather, perhaps the only true home I can keep coming back to are the sensory memories of those long-lost worlds I've stored in my mind and body. Memory: where I can experience my life at the Gulf Motel over and over again, exactly as it was, or how I want it to have been, and will forever be in this poem. Memory: the ultimate homeland where I can perpetually and immutably exist.

David Bottoms

Under the Vulture-Tree

We have all seen them circling pastures,
have looked up from the mouth of a barn, a pine clearing,
the fences of our own backyards, and have stood
amazed by the one slow wing beat, the endless dihedral drift.
But I had never seen so many so close, hundreds,
every limb of the dead oak feathered black.

And I cut the engine, let the river grab the jon boat
and pull it toward the tree.
The black leaves shined, the pink fruit blossomed
red, ugly as a human heart.
Then, as I passed under their dream, I saw for the first time
its soft countenance, the raw fleshy jowls
wrinkled and generous, like the faces of the very old
who have grown to empathize with everything.

And I drifted away from them, slow, on the pull of the river,
reluctant, looking back at their roost,
calling them what I'd never called them, what they are,
those dwarfed transfiguring angels
who flock to the side of the poisoned fox, the mud turtle
crushed on the shoulder of the road,
who pray over the leaf-graves of the anonymous lost,
with mercy enough to consume us all and give us wings.

Under the Vulture-Tree on the Wakulla River

Back before my daughter was born, I used to do a lot of fishing. This poem, "Under the Vulture-Tree," is from the time when I lived in Tallahassee, Florida, while I was working on a Ph.D. at Florida State University. I used to go fishing there about twice a week. I had a little aluminum boat that I loved to run up and down my two favorite rivers—the St. Mark's and the Wakulla. I don't think I ever caught a fish out of either of those rivers, but I loved to sit in that boat just before dawn, drag a wad of dead worms behind me, and pretend I was some kind of twentieth-century John James Audubon. Anyway, one morning, I was on the Wakulla River, and all around me there was nothing but jungle—about as much jungle as you could find in the panhandle of Florida in the 20th century. It might help to remember that two of those old Johnny Weissmuller Tarzan movies were filmed there, along with a movie called *The Creature of the Black Lagoon.*

So, I came around a bend in the river, and on the right bank the jungle opened up. There was this one black tree stuck right in the middle of the clearing. It looked like someone had taken a huge piece of black construction paper and snipped out the silhouette of a full-grown oak tree and pasted it there, and it gave me a strange feeling. I cut my trolling motor and drifted a little closer and saw that it was some kind of fruit tree. It was speckled with little pink fruit. When I passed just under the tree, I felt very strange because I saw these pink things were not fruit, but heads. They were the heads of vultures. I'd come on a buzzard roost, and they were literally packed shoulder to shoulder in the tree. I could hardly see light between them.

I thought, "Well, here's a river and a tree and a bunch of vultures. If you can't make a poem out of this, you should just give up." When I got home, I remembered something I'd read about vultures actually being revered in some cultures, and I started to see the vultures in a different way. The whole thing became sort of my re-evaluation of the American buzzard. I wrote the poem pretty quickly, I think, and sent it to Peter Davison at *The Atlantic.* In a couple of months, his response came back. It was very enthusiastic, but he said I didn't need the first stanza, which was pretty much about getting the boat on the river and getting the poem going. I said, "Fine, scratch it." And when the poem appeared in *The Atlantic*, the first stanza was gone.

Earl Sherman Braggs

Sandy Columbine Hook Parkland

And when one day a field of Colorado blue columbine flowers
wilted into never,
what once was a picture-perfect School Picture taking Day
angled flat-out into the camera lens of something without a name.

Tintype tinted without overtone, no contrast, too vanished out
to photo-copy school colors.
School uniforms of dress-coded labels, we've since been instructed
to   *Iron Before Washing.*   We don't know why, but why
knows the spelling of each, our names. Introspection, time doesn't
afford. News-day grief is so brief these days.
And it should come as no surprise, we are surprised that we live.

One day after the next, to the milk shaking voice of something sour,
we listen to the echoes of too many echoes not to notice the smell.
Teachers and principals, beyond over expended, explaining
what they cannot explain. In plain view, a red fox hides her cubs
in white Colorado snow.
Nights of guarded warnings, too often, forget to fall asleep. Day light
reminds relentlessness not to re-reveal too much too soon to us.

It is not safe to say that we would rather not remember our dreams.
We count our blessings by not counting the spaces
between empty chairs. We ride school buses into the immutable
yellow haze of school morning days. No front door welcome mat,

no classroom homeroom to speak not of. *Love,* 2 consonants,
2 vowels, erased into the relenting rub of a yellow #2 pencil.
Text books
check-out the pure danger of opening the wrong page.
Library books
check us out as if we know more than they know.
Hallway lockers, all, slam sad.
Smiles, hugs, and the quote "Most likely to…."
in last year's yearbooks tell everything but the truth so help us God.

31

We dream in inverted question marks.
The reverse of why is still why.
The reverse of what is still what, but the reverse of when doesn't know
when to tell us when.
1st period, this morning, reached down to grab me,
grabbed instead the frayed seams of my no-brand-name backpack
as if metal detectors can detect or not, last night,
I completely finished reading *A Midsummer Night's Dream*.

Days in, days out quick as they are slow, we never know what is which.
Silent, a red noise circles us like moving target games at a county fair.
I know you think I should be, but I'm not afraid.
It's something more.
I know you think I should be, but I'm not despaired.
It's something more,
something heavier than the weight of waiting for the other
"something" to drop, heavier than the gravity of trying to forget
the names of towns and cities where cross hairs cross out children.

I have never been an A student, I often question a B, but
I have always turned in my homework on time. But time,
these days, seems no more to care
about homework assignments to be done at home.
Now-a-days we get full credit for everything, anything
by just showing up the day after the latest network news.

Baby Sister, 14, and her baby brother, killed again yesterday
in Parkland, Newtown, CT.

A terrible ear it takes to want to hear nothing more than
more gun music.
Arm elementary school teachers some stupid, gun music
playing politician reportedly said. Dead, can he not see us
walking, almost, already?
Can he not spell his own children's names? Can he not
see, clearly, what we see?

Little school children, less than 3½ feet tall, 1st grade,
first day of school
and every day thereafter standing, pledging allegiance,
point blank, eye to eye, facing an over-loaded handgun
in the teacher's desk, top right hand drawer, left side
divider, next to a roll-
call book that knows the spelling of each, their names.

What We Come to Know, What Comes to Know Us

"The Colorado blue columbine flower is an easy-to-grow perennial
that offers seasonal interest throughout the year." Sometimes, what seems

immaterial to the topic of discussion, becomes central to what ultimately gets talked about. This, in moving color, I learned when I started composing "Sandy Columbine Hook Parkland." Sometimes the poem teaches the composer how to compose, and sometimes the poet listens to the poem.

"Sandy Columbine Hook Parkland" takes its title by combining the tragic sites of three mass school shootings: Sandy Hook Elementary School, Newtown, Connecticut (December 14, 2012); Columbine High School, Littleton, Colorado (April 20, 1999); and Parkland, Florida's Stoneman Douglas High School (February 14, 2018). Sandy Columbine Hook Parkland, the title, is presented somewhat in the fashion of a person with a tragic four-part name. My attempt here is to show that the shooters, the targets, and the shootings themselves are all in the same (average) American family, a family related by blood left on the written and unwritten history of American battlefields. "Sandy Columbine Hook Parkland" is a poem written from the point of view of a white, male, high school junior. He is from a slightly upper-class American family, and the American Dream is just another dream he doesn't have to worry about dreaming about on any given night. For him, the American Dream is a given if he applies himself, and given to him if he doesn't. Before I speak to what and who inspired me to write "Sandy Columbine Hook Parkland," I want to talk about how I came to be in the position to be inspired to compose "Sandy Columbine Hook Parkland," a poem whose speaker is far removed from who I am.

"Earl, do not write out of what you do not know," some days, still echoes. The voice of Lynda Hull, my mentor, my graduate school professor, so many years later, still dances across my pages. The day she said that, my poem "Vietnam Revisited" was the last poem scheduled to be workshopped. One student asked, "Did you go to Vietnam?" "No, I never made it there," I almost apologized. The "I" (speaker) in "Vietnam Revisited" is an African American soldier still dressed in army fatigues, taking a Greyhound bus through rural Georgia, locked in a drunken conversation with an older African American soldier freshly back from Southeast Asia. I sent "Vietnam Revisited" out and within three to four months, it was accepted for publication in *Black Poetry of the 80s from the Deep South*.

What had happened? Did I write out of what I did not know, or did I write out of what I came to know? The latter, I came to know what I was talking about. This was proven to me one evening after a poetry reading when a Vietnam veteran came up to me to share his experiences because, as he said, they were so similar to mine (the "I" in "Vietnam Revisited"). Art is a lie. That Vietnam veteran was *touched* not by actuality, but by my words because the only essential truth in art is the emotional truth.

Walt Whitman said, "The 'I' is always another." I don't pretend to know exactly what Whitman meant by that statement. All I know is what Whitman's poetry means to me and how his approach to composition encourages me. Any "I" could be me and "I" could visit any place "I" wanted to visit without visiting any one of them. All I had to do was come-to-know who "I" was and where "I" was. Like Zen, what I came to know came to know me.

According to Phillip Levine, John Berryman once said in workshop, "You should always be trying to write a poem that's impossible for you to write." Me, speaking with unnoticed authority from the perspective of a 17-year-old upper-middle class, white boy from central Florida who had recently witnessed a mass shooting at his school is the definition of impossibility. But I can come-to-know this impossibility, embrace this impossibility, fall in love with this impossibility and write this impossible into possible. How one comes-to-know a place, a subject, a person is what John Updike called "Just Looking." When I started to "Just Look," I just smelled the Columbine blue flower, then I just walked down the speaker's school hallway. I noticed that school lockers in those situations, under those conditions, as you might imagine, slam more softly. The personification of each told me the troubled relationship between backpacks and metal detectors. I saw how the janitors were much nicer, almost sweet, and didn't yell when kids did what kids do, spill sweet drinks on newly mopped cafeteria floors. I noticed that lunchtime was still loud, but it was a hushed loudness, as if waiting to hear something louder. Walking around the campus of the speaker's school, I realized what it means to walk on eggshells, hear unintended whispers, see around corners, feel something when there is nothing to feel. When I looked into the eyes of the student's parents, I could see that each of them was more afraid than any one of their children. And after roaming those school hallways, I can say with utmost confidence that those teachers and those principals don't need to be good actors to win an Emmy for their daytime, school day roles.

So what inspired me to write "Sandy Columbine Hook Parkland"? Gun music. I was listening to the television talking heads one day and I heard gun music. Yes, some politicians talking about arming elementary school teachers, gun music. My question: How crazy is that? Yet, during the year(s) in question, among too many policy makers, it was/is a perfectly normal stance to take. So, I was primed to witness, just after the Parkland shooting, a generation of diverse school kids surface in protest. They organized and went to the Washington, D.C. Mall en masse to voice their dissatisfaction and disappointment with the power the NRA was allowed to wield from corner to corner in America. These young kids, many not even voting age, were articulate beyond anything America had seen since the children of the '60s Flower Power Movement and the parallel Black Power Movement. Watching those young people, it occurred to me who they were. They were Obama's children, children who turned thirteen during the span of Barack Obama's eight-year presidency. When those children came of age and looked at the leader of the United States of America, they saw a brilliant, articulate, caringly kind, soulfully handsome, compassionate, eloquent, African American man. The children saw and felt the teacher in President Obama's voice, and they were hungry to listen, hungry to learn. Listening to those children speak, I noticed that they were special. I noticed that Obama's Children were designed for the time, just in time. Shortly thereafter, I started composing a collection of poetry titled *Obama's Children*. *Obama's Children* was published in December 2021 by Madville Press. "Sandy Columbine Hook Parkland" was the first poem I wrote for the collection. The speaker in the poem is just an average, everyday Obama child changing America, one new convert at a time, from red to blue.

Fred Chappell

The Departures

Always as a child I felt their gaze
from ceiling corners, broken chimneys, gullies.
What did they discern? That I was vulnerable,
helpless as the white blind kitten, that anyone
will know of me what I can never know?

The more I wished myself invisible
the more obtrusive my haphazard presence.
I prayed to the Sunday-school Divinity
to allow me a painless martyrdom
and blessedness by happy accident.

Who were they, spying relentlessly?
What could they find not already known to them?
Each day they stole one of my futures.
They warned eternity to guard its shadow.
They wore dark robes of ragged spider-thread.

Now a distant bell sounds and they turn away
and do not look back, forsaking me,
disappearing into the grove that enfolds them with silence,
into a nightfall cool and windless.

They

I was not asleep.
I was not awake.
Someone was watching me as I lay in bed.
Then I woke, recalling that most interior sensation from childhood,
the feeling that I was being spied upon by judgmental eyes. The watchers
were unknown to me, but if ever I saw them, I would recognize them. They
were keeping records not only of my activities but also of my thoughts and
longings and dreams and fantasies. The watchers were not my parents but

were leagued with them in some obscure way to say stern sentences to me and about me. Sooner or later I would have to pay the price for being who and what I was.

Then I arose and dressed myself partially and went to my desk and found a pencil and 4"×6" yellow notepad and wrote three lines: "Now they have placed cameras / in the ceiling corners wherefrom as a child / I felt their disapproving gaze."

My childhood fears had come to pass. Some government agency or some criminal gang or some personal antagonist was taking notes on my behavior, keeping records to be used against me later.

Or I had watched another dumb TV spy movie before turning in last night.

The source made no difference; the feeling was vivid and, however puzzling or trivial, still meaningful. Not because it may be slightly para-noid in the usual casual way, but simply because it is vivid and refreshes memories of previous feelings so forceful they amount now, as they had when I was ten or twelve years old, to physical sensations.

Okay. Enough. Time for coffee. I would return to these few words later.

Next afternoon I read them aloud to myself. Who spoke this slightly ominous sentence? Not Fred personally, but the I-persona who speaks most lyric poems by me and many others, the mask of "I," through which words are made to sound intimate, revealing, *confessional*, though there is no impulse to confess any secret whatsoever. Fred has no impulse to confess because he had no confidentiality worth confessing, but "I" is overflowing with secret messages, with subtle warnings and intimations, suggestive half-memories and colorful fantasies, some of them unhealthy.

Alienation is a common, maybe even a standard, theme in lyric because it acknowledges and uses simultaneous, different points of view. The "I" is an observer who reports what she or he sees and thinks and feels; this particular "I" is an observer being observed, so he sees himself from two vantages at once. He is alien from whoever or whatever is watch-ing him but also from his observed self. He is a potential victim, vulnera-ble and puzzled. And he is participating in this ... game, is it? Or strange, amorphous conspiracy?

He must make clear his present situation and try to return to the ear-liest intuitions he had about this quandary. So, he cancels those first words and tries to make clear and dramatic his childhood semi-perceptions:

> Always as a child I felt their gaze
> from ceiling corners, broken chimneys, gullies.
> What did they discover? That I was frightened vulnerable,
> vulnerable helpless as my blind kitten, that everyone else anyone
> knew more about me than I could ever find? know?

Only five possible lines and already the incipient poem seems self-indulgent and a little precious. Maybe it is trying too hard to be clear, the poet fearing that no one else ever experiences these feelings, that there is no community of sympathy to which he can appeal. And maybe this special condition of feeling belongs in a psychological casebook rather than in a poem that can interest others. Maybe he is trying to portray a merely personal symptom of some sort that he alone has harbored and which is therefore trivial.

But he has felt a pressure both within himself and from outside. He has felt it as a vague, indefinable but present threat. How shall he protect himself?

He must hide; he must become invisible. He must remove himself from the purview of the watchers. And so he tries:

> The more I wished myself invisible
> the more ~~obvious~~ obtrusive my ~~unwelcome~~ haphazard presence.
> I prayed to the ~~gentle~~ Sunday-school ~~God~~ Divinity
> ~~to make me a saint though not a martyr~~
>   ~~or if a martyr, immune to pain~~
> to allow me ~~to become an unmartyred saint~~
>   sainthood minus martyrdom
> and ~~wings, without the duties of an angel~~ and blessedness by happy accident.

Here is the necessary admission of fear or, more accurately, of cowardice that is the wellspring of his obscure emotions. Trying to protect himself, this "I" must own up to being afraid of some thing or situation he cannot name.

Why is he afraid? He is in no physical danger. The watchers, whoever or whatever they may be, can do him no bodily harm. Is it just the fact or idea that merely by knowing certain of his secrets they violate him? How so? What are these secrets so important to him that he feels their revelation presents a danger?

He does not know. The only harmful result of revelation would be public embarrassment, temporary and trivial. "I" is no Bluebeard or Stalin or Iago. His secrets are of the mildest sort, so silly that most of the time he cannot recall them. Even so, they should not be revealed; their revelation would diminish him, weaken whatever power or resolve he can usually muster.

This feeling being so familiar to him generally does not signal his attention; it is merely a condition of his everyday life. Yet still there is a tinge or shade of the outré about it, something natural to him that suggests the supernatural.

Then the thought comes that this poem has already been written by himself or someone else. A common suspicion for Fred and if it is true, then he need not write the poem. If an articulation already exists, his is superfluous.

He tries to recall, and in a while, remembers a deservedly renowned poem by Walter de la Mare, "The Listeners," and so hastes to his shelves and reads it anew. In this poem, the Traveller comes to a castle and knocks upon the door. No one answers. He knows there are presences inside, but all he hears is the sound of his horse champing "the grasses / Of the forest's ferny floor." The Traveller never receives a response from inside the castle, but the poet tells us of "a host of phantom listeners … that stood," "thronging the faint moonbeams on the dark stair." He knocks again and, hearing no answer, departs. "'Tell them I came, and no one answered, / That I kept my word,' he said." Then he departs.

"The Listeners" is a wonderfully eerie poem, charged with implication and suspense. It is the story of a Quester whose quest proves futile. His quest he did not undertake upon his own initiative; it was demanded of him. They who demanded its undertaking now refuse to acknowledge his existence. Or they mock him.

De la Mare delivers his allegorical fable in terms of sounds: the Traveller's knocking, the horse champing, the shifting position, echoes within the house, this foot fitting into the stirrup, the sounds of horseshoes upon stone, and the departing, "plunging," hoofs. The most powerful and pervasive sound is silence, omnipresent and palpable, its power underlined by the noises that distress it.

"The Listeners" has undoubtedly influenced Fred's "They" in conception and perhaps in execution, but there is sufficient dissimilarity from him to resolve to continue. In both poems the question of who "they" are remains unresolved; de la Mare's poem gathers enormous force by leaving the listeners undescribed and mysterious.

"I" decides to ask the question directly:

> Who were they, then, spying relentlessly?
> What could they ~~gather~~ find they did not know already?
> ~~Why were they silent, why so disapproving?~~
> Each day they stole one of my future days.
> They warned eternity to guard its silence.
> They wore dark robes ~~with spider threads of silver~~
>   of ragged spider-thread.

This last line employs an image that might well appear in one of the darker fairy tales, one from the Grimm Brothers, that Fred might have read as a lad of twelve years or so. It is unspecific; "they" could be male or female, young or old. He feels that they are elderly but powerful, their strength stemming from sources he can never know.

But if they are agents of a larger power, then they must obey the rules or laws that the power enjoins. They are actually more sinister if they are subservient to something other.

> When a distant bell chimes ~~mournfully~~ softly they turn away
> and do not look back, forsaking him forever.
> disappearing into the grove he had not ~~noticed noted see~~
> ~~disappearing into~~
> entering the grove that enfolded them with ~~shadow~~ silence

So that the fourth line is the preceding stanza must be altered: "They warned eternity to guard its shadow."

Then a possible closing: "He stifles his impulse to follow."

Another: "He steps to follow them and then retreats."

No.

He has recognized that if the fears that have always accompanied him disappear, he will be more lonely than ever. His fears have been for him a solemn, unhappy band, one to which he naturally, preternaturally, belongs. It is grueling for him to live with his fears, but it is likely he cannot live without them and be a whole person.

Now the poem is titled "The Departures."

Chen Chen

The School of Night & Hyphens

The sky tonight, so without aliens. The woods, very lacking
in witches. But the people, as usual, replete

with people. & so you, with your headset, sit
in the home office across the hall, stuck in a hell

of strangers crying, computers dying, the new
father's dropped-in-toilet baby

photos, the old Canadian, her grandson Gregory,
all-grown-up-now Greg, who gave her this phone

but won't call her. You call her
wonderful. You encourage her to tell you what's wrong

with her device. You with your good-at-your-job
good-looking-ness, I bet even over the phone

it's visible. I bet all the Canadian grandmas
want you, but hey, you're with me. Hey, take off

that headset. Steal away from your post. Cross
the hall, you sings-the-chorus-too-soon, you

makes-a-killer-veggie-taco, you
played-tennis-in-college-build, you Jeffrey, you

Jeff-ship full of stars, cauldron full of you,
come teach me a little bit

of nothing, in the dark
abundant hours.

Telling the Truth About Love

What is the role of love poetry in the 21st century? Why write love
poems? There are the abiding, seemingly immutable, reasons: wanting

41

to articulate (or attempt to) the dizziness of falling in love, or to explore being in love, or to sing of the beloved, or to quarrel with the beloved, or to grieve a love lost, or to throw linguistic confetti in jubilation over a bad love's end. But is there some other reason for love poems today? Do we need to write—and read—them differently?

> Disclaimer: I won't be providing any definitive answers, as I don't have those. I do have some thoughts, some wonderings, and as always more questions.

One way to think of love poems today is as inseparable from political poems. Poets before the 21st century have made this connection, but maybe in our time more U.S.-based poets have embraced connecting the love poem and the political; it seems more are insisting on this idea, as more are insisting on the inseparability of art in general and the political. In his essay "Love the Masters," Jericho Brown lays out the love poem/political poem connection in the most memorable sequence of sentences:

> Every poem is a love poem. Every poem is a political poem. So say the masters. Every love poem is political. Every political poem must fall in love.*

I especially love the last sentence here. I'll go ahead and write it out again: "Every political poem must fall in love." I'm in love with this sentence for its emphasis on process and action—a draft of a political poem might not start off with much love, but it needs to find some form of it, if it's going to become a full poem. A true poem. That *every poem* Brown repeats. Is every poem a love poem? It sounds right to me, though I can't verify it with anything resembling empirical evidence. What's more interesting to me than just agreeing with the statement is wondering what its implications are, for writing, for my own writing.

That is, if "[e]very poem is a love poem" is true, how might my writing change? How might I push my writing in a new direction? How could this notion, as a principle or law of writing, push me? One can ask these same questions of the next assertion, "Every poem is a political poem." And the next: "Every love poem is political." If I apply these principles to my own poem-making, what would I make? My political poem might fall in love. I might realize, as a poet, that I need always to engage politically and with love, if I'm going to write a poem that is true, that moves, that lives and lives in a reader's heart.

Yes, *heart.* I never promised not to get cheesy while on the subject of love poems. Every poem is a risking of cheesiness. If *that's* true, I need to examine what I'm leaving out of poems, out of fear of the cheese factor.

---

*Brown, Jericho. "Love the Masters." *The Racial Imaginary: Writers on Race in the Life of the Mind*, Fence Books, 2015, pp. 231–234. Ed. Claudia Rankine, Beth Loffreda, and Max King Cap.

With "The School of Night & Hyphens," I may have succumbed to the cheese. There are tacos in it, after all. And an unabashed, hyphen-filled song for the beloved. The original title, by the way, was "The School of Night & Sewers." Maybe I'll still write a poem with that title, but I'm glad I changed the title for this one, since it became a full-on love poem.

I began this poem in early 2017, when I was living in Lubbock, Texas, and attending Texas Tech University for a PhD in English and Creative Writing. My first book was about to come out. The creative state of mind I found myself in was a state of limbo—between bodies of work. I'd just spent years writing the poems that would go into my first book. I'd put my all into that collection. Now what?

I had written a poem called "The School of Sharpening." I had written a poem called "The School of Morning & Letters." Could there be a companion poem to that, featuring night and ... something else? I'd started writing these "The School of..." poems, trying to figure out if they were my next step, next creative direction. This "School of" thing was in part poking fun at myself for being in school for so long: a BA, then an MFA, and now a PhD (one poem I titled "The School of More School"). At the same, I was serious about wanting to celebrate these sources of learning, and a range of ways to learn, ways to "go to school." To go to the school of night and hyphens—what does one learn there? To go to the school of poetry—is to go to the school of love and politics. "You can't love me," Brown writes, "if you don't love me politically."

Poems about jobs tend to be overtly political, as they have to do with money, class, workplace dynamics, hierarchies, and labor. When I started working on this poem, I knew I wanted to write about my partner's job. He works for AppleCare. He helps dozens of people a day with all sorts of tech issues. He also ends up in the most convoluted conversations where the caller alternates between explaining the tech issue and sharing their life story. I'm fascinated by his job; it seems so different from mine, as a writer and a teacher, but then I see all the overlap. We both have to continually improve our communication skills. We have to guide, offer advice, talk through problems together, explain key concepts, provide constructive criticism, positively reinforce correct actions, and create a welcoming environment in which to learn. We have to, in a word, teach.

So, the first act (so to speak) of the poem focuses on my partner's job. He works from home. He used to work at an Apple store; he gave that up in order to move to Lubbock with me. He still wanted to continue working with Apple and this was the available option. It was difficult at first—he missed his coworkers and felt isolated. We'd just moved across the country for my next opportunity. It made personal sense, then, for the poem to move into cherishing the "you"—I can't write about my partner's job without thinking about how much I appreciate him switching to it so that we could continue living together.

None of that backstory is in the poem, though. It didn't seem like the right place. The transition from the first act (about work) into the second (about love) depends on the bit about the old Canadian and her grandson Gregory. This grandmother is lonely. She's the one carrying the isolation I witnessed in my partner's work situation. She calls because she's run into some trouble using her new phone. She calls because she's feeling alone. She calls, wanting to talk about a tech issue. She calls, wanting to talk.

My partner helps, is so helpful. I imagine how impressed the caller is. That moment leads into the second act, which is more overtly a love poem. This second act sings of the beloved's attractive attributes, his fabulous talents and endearing flaws (or flaw: "you sings-the-chorus-too-soon"), before the intimate ending. I discovered the poem needed to end with a different kind of "teaching." The school of intimacy, the school of two people in love.

Work is political because labor is. Love is political because gender and sexuality are. Learning and teaching are political because knowledge is. Poetry is political because language is. These are just a few of the ways these elements can be interlinked. Another layer: A queer love poem is inherently political because queerness is. Of course, some queer love poems are more overtly political than others, or riskier in the politics they name or embody or enact. I don't think this particular poem of mine is all that politically risky. Still, when I think of when I was in middle school, so scared to come out as anything not-straight I considered killing myself … and now, as a still-alive queer adult, writing about his sexuality and his relationship—I believe yes, I've taken a political risk in this poem, too.

I've fallen in love while living in this world at this point in time. If I'm committed to telling the truth about love as I've experienced and witnessed it, shouldn't I write about jobs? Shouldn't I write about loneliness and isolation? About tacos? Spaceships? Intimacy? My poem fell in love with describing the beloved at his job, how excellent he is at it. My poem fell in love with describing his other lovable qualities. My poem fell in love so feverishly that it needed words to feel closer together, via hyphens. My poem fell in love with hyphens, those little connective lines, little bolts of connection.

I fell into those hyphens; I didn't know when I first started the poem that they were going to show up. I thought sewers were going to show up, thus that earlier title. Every poem is at once an offering to and a blessing from the god Surprise. I don't know if I completely believe any grand statement about poetry, as I want to stay open to a poem doing something else; I want to keep being surprised by what poems can do and be.

Still, I believe in some of these statements enough to write poetry out of trying to practice the stated principles. I certainly couldn't have written this poem without considering it as both a love poem and a political poem. And I've found that when I apply that framework to writing other kinds of poems, say, poems about family, I usually gain a fresh insight; I understand something crucial that the poem needs. An urgency, an aliveness: love is political because being alive—in this world, this history—is.

I'm glad to see more U.S. poets not set the aesthetic apart from the political, the love poem apart from the political poem. I hope more decompartmentalizing occurs, continues to occur—in what ways is a nature poem political? How are elegies political? How are poems about baseball love poems? Can a poem about corporate greed be a love poem? Can a poem about office supplies be a nature poem? Every poem is a hyphen connecting previously unconnected realms. Every poem is a night, impossibly vast and yet right here, on the page.

Marilyn Chin

Bamboo, the Dance

How free and lush the bamboo grows, the bamboo grows and grows
Shoots and morasses, fillies and lassies and shreds and beds and rows
O phloem and pistil, nodes and ovules
    The bamboo grows and grows
Her release, her joy, her oil, her toil, her moxie, her terror, her swirl
Dig deeper into soil, deeper into her soul, what do you find in my girl
Thrash of black hair and silken snare, face in the bottom of the world
Bound by ankles, poor deer, poor sow, O delicate hooves and fascicles
    Dead doe, dead doe, dead doe
Wrists together, searing red tethers, blood draining from her soles
    O choir, O psalm, O soaring fearsome tabernacle
The bamboo grows, the bamboo grows and grows
Through antlers and eyeholes, O sweet soul, O sweet, sweet soul

Thin green tails, purple entrails, the bamboo grows and grows
She flailed and wailed through flimsy veils, through bones and hissing marrow
Nobody to hear her, but wind and chaff, a gasp, then letting go
They loved her, then stoned her, buried her near her ancestors
    My mother, my sister, my soul

Shimmering mesh, a brocade sash, hanging on a distant oracle
Springboks dance on shallow mounds, echoes, echoes, echoes

Poetry of Necessity

"Bamboo, the Dance" was written for the Terezin Music Foundation on the 70th anniversary of the liberation of Nazi concentration camps.

This is one of the most complex forms I've ever attempted. Although it took me several months to refine, I am very proud of this poem. After recently rereading it, I felt that all my creative force and poetic mastery had come together in its composition.

I have loved Bach's fugues all my life. So first I decided to pin Paul Celan's masterwork "Death Fugue" ("Todesfugue") on the wall for intensive study and then to try my own version of a fugue.

46

In music, a fugue is a contrapuntal, polyphonic composition, in which a theme is introduced, followed by rounds of variations. I heard different voices—alto, soprano, tenor, and bass—singing in parts, layer upon layer, creating a complex round, the fugal song.

I hate to pontificate about my own poems, for explication takes away the magic of the process. Who knows how the muse interacts with the poet's intelligence to create a gorgeous monster? However, as for the form, in this poem, "Bamboo, the Dance," the melodic lines offer the theme and variations: The theme is violent death!

Variation 1: We begin with bamboo, lush, growing, growing, thriving, and yet menacing.

Variation 2: A woman dancing is murdered, her black hair ensnared by the bamboo, her body fallen to the earth, seeking the roots of the bamboo.

Variation 3: The dead doe, a theme that comes from the *Shijing,* the book of Odes, the oldest anthology of Chinese poetry, dating back to 1100–600 BC. The dead doe represents the loss of virginity, in this case by rape and murder. She is hunted down, slaughtered, and tied to a bamboo pole for the market.

The poem also implies "shadow" variations: (1) my father's sacrifice of my mother's life, (2) the murders of the women in the maquiladoras, (3) an homage to Paul Celan's haunting poem, and (4) my desire to honor and remember the victims of the Holocaust. I sought to create a polyphony of voices: ancestral singers, ghostly singers, layered in rounds, reiterating the poem's major theme—systematic murder in an unjust world.

The melodic lines:

Recurring images are also bolstered by repetitive sounds and rhymes: the echoing of long Oi- of joy, oil, toil, moil, soil, etc. I also drew on dance, imagining a dance like the Tarantella, the dancer's gown unraveling, with its silks and bamboo sheath; the different variations merging to create a large resounding whole. The woman's murder merges with and evokes the murders of millions of Jews that Paul Celan mourns in "Death Fugue." But this poem is above all personal. All my poems are about my mother, about my feeling that my father and the Confucian family system destroyed her. We watched her unravel in an unsightly bloody dance ... my grief is inconsolable. Personal, political, formal, historical, oracular: I felt physically sick after completing this poem.

No pontification or analysis can properly describe the impact of this poem on me. It may be the best poem I've ever written! The dead spoke through me in a baroque vocal composition, in "echoes, echoes, echoes."

It took me months to finish this poem. I knew that it was special. "Bamboo, the Dance" should be read out loud to be felt in one's heart and vitals. In it lies our devastating, horrific, and shameful histories. It is a poem that transcends the self and cries out into the darkest hours of the universe, a poem that is totally necessary. Yes, this harrowing poem came out of a formal exercise on the fugue, and on an allusion to Paul Celan, the true master of the form. The best way to praise the master is to answer with a masterful poem. But voices of the murdered spoke to me, they sang and danced and spun this poem together. I felt like a vessel for their song. This is the poem in which the poet brings all her training and skill to the task, while stepping out of the muse's way to let the dead speak.

This month, as we learned of the murdered Asian-American women in Atlanta's massage spas, "Bamboo, the Dance" became relevant again. I tried to read it out loud at a solidarity Zoom-reading for the Asian-American Writers Workshop, but I began to sob and couldn't complete the video. I had to replace it with another poem.

Perhaps someday, I will recite it, without sobbing.

Ama Codjoe

Burying Seeds

for Betty Shabazz

Who, when they killed her husband, was carrying
twin girls—not in her arms, but in an armless
sea, with bits of blood as food. She covered

her daughters in the waters of her body.
She covered her daughters in the rooms
her body built, pressed against the wooden

floor of the Audubon Ballroom. She must have
cried, as my mother did, when she stuttered, *Twins?*
into the paper gown of the hospital room.

The body longs for its double. Even twins
stretch long their arms toward other strangers.
The first time I visited a mosque, I was surprised

to be separated from my father and brothers.
I sat, with the women and girls, alone.
From across the aisle, I stared at the men

longingly. As a child, I asked my preschool teacher
why I couldn't play outside, shirtless like
the boys. It was a hot day. Before she could answer,

I relented, wearing my favorite undershirt—the one
with Archie, Betty, and Veronica—chasing
my sun-kissed brothers across the playground.

Lately, when I glimpse my nakedness in the half
mirror above the bathroom sink, I'm looking
at the photograph of Pauline Lumumba baring

her breasts as a sign of mourning. The widow's
breasts and mine hang like four weeping eyes,
without titillation, fertility, or innocence.

I wanted to write a poem for Betty Shabazz
because her high cheekbones and luminous
eyes are like a BaKongo mask breathed

into with life. After her husband's lifeless
body was wrapped in white linen and covered
by the words: *what we place in the ground*

*is no more now a man—but a seed—*she took
one last look at him who *had* smiled at her
and touched, countless times, her unveiled face.

My mother did not wear a veil on her wedding day.
Eighteen years after their divorce, my father
fidgets with the gold band she slid along his finger.

As she made a circle with her thumb and forefinger,
shimmying the ring over my father's knuckle,
which words did her mind circle over: *worse* or *better*

death or *death*? That night, did my mother bunch
the hotel bedsheet in one hand like a nosegay?
Did she allow it—another white dress—to drag,

crumpled, behind her? The vows we promise
one another are veils through which we envision
the future; we enact our dreams using a vision

clouded by tulle and lace. Grief-stricken, Betty Shabazz
said of her husband's assassination, *Well, it finally
happened.* Weeks prior, she had taken to wearing

her husband's hat for comfort and continued to do so
after he died. I want a desire that could be mistaken
for grief to cloud my face, to make me shudder, to twist

my mouth into a cry. Once, I shared a bed with a man
who, as a boy, heard his parents' lovemaking. *I was
confused,* he admitted, *it sounded like they were in pain.*

Grief is the bride of every good thing, Betty Shabazz
reminds me. I'm wearing a veil the shape of a waterfall,
which is also the shape of my mother's dress falling

from her shoulders. Through its fabric, I can see a cloud
turning into a horse and a plane that could be a star—
a star that might be a planet. It's hard to tell from here,

wrapped in the caul of the present, fixed on this plot
of grass, with so many seeds buried underground,
and winter—forged into a circle—threatening never to end.

On Composing "Burying Seeds"

Sunlight granted me a fistful of words. At the end of each day, I carried these lines in a spiral notebook up eight flights of stairs to the small bedroom provided by the residency. Within night's timeless center, another tercet would come. I recorded the lines by hand—often in the dark—not trusting myself to remember come morning. Then, after eating breakfast and filling my thermos with tea, I would descend the eight flights back to my writing studio and type the new lines into a lengthening document on my computer. The poem's length demanded a process that stretched across weeks of composition. Unlike poems drafted in one or two sittings, which often take years to revise, "Burying Seeds" came piece by piece and with a slow precision I didn't fully trust until the poem was complete. In this way, "Burying Seeds" is a gift of a poem, one whose composition can be tracked by a cycle of days and nights.

I composed "Burying Seeds" during a three-month residency in Memphis, Tennessee. During the first half of the residency, I finished a full-length manuscript. Not wanting to squander the remaining time, I decided to experiment with longer poems and documentary poetics and to craft, from those experiments, a stand-alone chapbook—something I'd never attempted. But first, I needed to take a few days off. My break coincided with an independent film festival where two fellow residents screened their films. Also playing was *Betty Davis: They Say I'm Different*, a documentary about the funk musician Betty Davis. Even before seeing the film, I knew I'd write about her. Maybe my chapbook could be about different Bettys, I thought. Other Bettys came to mind: the visual artist, Betye Saar; Betty from the Archie Comics; Betty Okino, the gymnast; and Betty Shabazz, the wife and widow of Malcolm X. I never wrote the Betty Okino poem, and the chapbook *Blood of the Air* dramatically veered from the initial idea, but I did write several "Betty poems." The Betty Shabazz poem became "Burying Seeds."

When researching Betty Shabazz, I learned that at the time of her husband's assassination Shabazz was pregnant with twins. As a twin, I instantly thought of my own mother and the "twinning" and braiding of the poem began. The speaker's body as embryo, the speaker's body in girlhood, and the speaker's body in womanhood became a part of the poem as soon as the speaker's mother's body became a part of the poem. "Burying Seeds," in its first few stanzas, created a map for me to follow. The tercet, with its ongoingness and spilling over quality—not as neat as couplets or quatrains—presented itself immediately. The braid's weaving and three-partedness allowed me to produce echoes and rhymes: Shabazz and Malcolm X, the speaker and her lover, the speaker's parents; pain, pleasure, divorce, death; the widow's veil, the bride's veil, the caul.

Sometimes poets talk about the poem as an independently-minded entity, like when I wrote that the poem "created a map for me to follow." And what can I say? I followed the poem. The composition of "Burying Seeds" was not something I could force, though I did have to create the mental space for it to arrive. After the initial impulse, a desire to write a poem for Betty Shabazz, "Burying Seeds" emerged from what felt like its own volition, in its own time, and with a mind of its own. It was unlike any poem I had written up to that point. When I finished the poem, I knew it would open the chapbook even as I didn't yet know what the chapbook would be.

In order to be written, the poem needed a particular kind of spaciousness. It also required research. During the composition period, I watched interviews, read articles, and studied photographs. I easily recalled the sound of Ossie Davis's voice delivering Malcolm X's eulogy; it is a voice—*Our own black, shining prince*—that already lived inside my head. In addition to direct quotations, I incorporated image systems from Davis's eulogy throughout the poem and in the poem's title. The inclusion of Pauline Lumumba, another widow of a political figure, worked its way into the poem, though research on Myrlie Evers and Coretta Scott King did not. I didn't force any piece *in*—I let my notes be drawn into the poem like magnets. In a similar fashion, I pulled pieces of my own biography, remembered and imagined, into the lengthening draft.

Because I was braiding subjects and themes together, there was always a pile of information to draw from when I felt stuck. Day after day, night after night, I braided the poem. On the last day of composition, I tried to push past its ending. When I deleted the extra tercet and reread the poem, the poem was complete and completed. Though "Burying Seeds" was a gift of a poem, it did not feel easy to write. Each day, all day, I waited for just a few lines—sometimes they fell like crumbs from the table, sometimes they glinted like river-drenched gold. As the poem grew longer and longer, the process felt both mystical and precarious. Each night, I carried a handful of lines upstairs, falling asleep to their music and logic. Then, in the drowsiness of morning, with part of me still dreaming and my eyes adjusting to light, I deciphered my tangled cursive to see what more had come.

Stephen Corey

History of My Present

One could do worse than march toward posterity
sandwiched by *gardens* and *garfish*—
the fate of the only U.S. president
to have a direct descendant
who became a fifth-grade teacher
who had me as one of her students.

This isn't a test, but list three key events
from the Garfield term of office.
Also its length. How about *one* event?
Or maybe the man's first name?
Take as long as you need—
something that he didn't get.

Sexy Miss Garfield, triple-great-grandchild
controlling our daily recess scene,
belting the shit from a softball
kicking the shit from a kickball
nailing the whole class in dodgeball
and always her car top down.

Twentieth president almost by mistake—
drafted to break a Republican stalemate—
James earned the victor's spoils but dumped them
to clear the decks on a rotten ship of state:
Civil Service, thy name is Garfield.
(That's one. You want to switch to Lincoln?)

Marlene she was, blond and twenty-three,
picking up Louie and me—total years, twenty—
in her bright-yellow Ford for a Popsicle run
after school, her hair blowing wild in my face.
What was she thinking, in 1958? What were *we*?
Innocence A, Innocence B and C.

Barton's Red Cross emerged during Garfield's reign,
and Booker T.'s Tuskegee Institute,
but neither through his signature,
though some will say—for instance, *moi*—
he gave his time, however brief, a certain air,
this man who shunned the Credit Mobilier.

I was ten. My pubes were hairless, our town was small.
What did I know of sexual women?
But for thirteen years my life was lived with women
teachers, and only one—Miss Garfield—burns
now when I try to trace the fires back
into the pit still pulsing, bright and dark.

Well, 'twas *Senator* Garfield battled Credit Mobilier
(such a lovely phrase for evil, let's say it twice),
refusing the railroad gang's proffered grease,
so still we've only one grand moment—
but what surprise here when you recollect,
as I asked up front, his length of term in office?

No, she never touched me, and of course,
I never her. It was not like that, though what it was
I could not say. (I mean, I do not know.)
Do senses of power and importance carry down
through families more strongly than otherwise?
Do fears of early death? Was anything James Marlene?

Four years living, three and a half dying.
The plot's too good for truth; this poem must be fiction.
The next year Marlene disappeared, moved on
as the younger ones often did, but I wondered….
Then, I dreamed she could not teach without me
in the room. Now I wonder, was she asked to leave?

The president's killer was unemployed,
denied his purchased inch of public trough,
herded into failure by a test of competence.
Garfield's job became suffering the bullet
lodged against his spine, the draining away
through pain of his one promise: honesty.

I'd like to say I dreamed Miss Garfield
ran off with Charles Guiteau—you know,
John Wilkes Booth, Lee Harvey Oswald—
but I want this story to come around true:
I do not know what happened to Guiteau;
if I dreamed of Marlene, I've forgotten how.

The Star Route scandal had really set James off—
U.S. Mail delivery roads, sold for contractor kickbacks.
He'd see the Civil War brew and begin
from the Ohio Senate, watched it blow up and bleed
as a Union officer, watched it die and fester
from the U.S. House. He'd brook no more division.

March 4th through July 1st, 1881—
those were the president's days on his feet.
Alexander Graham Bell searched for the slug
with a homemade electrical probe. In vain.
July 2nd through September 19th—Garfield's days
for lying-in till death. He was fifty.

I think I scarcely recall her face.
Her hair, its color and fall, I still believe in.
And the shape of her hips under the fitted skirts
she wore while somehow still outrunning us all
on the base paths. The great, slow arcs of her arms
sweeping her notes on the board for emphasis:
Learn this. Learn *this*. Remember.

The History of "History of My Present"

I'll begin with a bit of a cliché, to remind myself not to allow another to enter elsewhere: "Your poem can come from anywhere at any time; the only limitation on any source derives from what you prove able to do with it."

A few of the people/places/events/thoughts/words/theories/beliefs we experience enter our poems—sometimes with immediacy, sometimes after decades—but most of them never do so, at least in any conscious way. Decades went by, and I never forgot Miss Garfield, my fifth-grade teacher and one of the two most memorable classroom leaders from my public-school life. I would think of her now and then, a fact that made her a theoretical candidate for some piece of writing, but my spark to action came from good ole happenstance: I was flipping through the dictionary (as I have to believe all writers do) seeking I recall not what, and my eye fell on the drawing of President James A. Garfield that accompanied his brief factual entry. Recalling again how Miss Garfield had told us she was a descendant of the President, about whom pretty much all I recalled was that he was one of our handful of assassinated national leaders. Moved to look him up in more detail, I was quite captured by his political biography—though in a poetic sense I was initially even more caught by his position in the dictionary, a fact that ended up giving me the opening lines for "History of My Present": "One could do worse than march toward posterity / sandwiched by gardens and garfish."

But, the historical facts provided my broader way into the poem, because they made me feel I could blend intimate personal remembrances with some still-relevant objective information to create a strange (and maybe even unique) portrait that would not surrender my poem either to mirror gazing or to a perhaps irrelevant national past. Fairly quickly, I adopted an intent to alternate passages about James and Marlene, and although I did question myself about this "obvious" approach, I remained convinced it was the one to take: it allowed interactions to blossom that did not occur to me until I reached the next jumping-off place—which is to say, I found "History" achieving a complex organic flow and shape that felt both weird and natural.

The "weird" included the innocence of Miss Garfield's involvements with us, her students—one that would not have been countenanced when I wrote this poem some forty years later, nor would it be now, another twenty years on as I forge this reflection; and *weird* also included my unanticipated finds about President Garfield's assassin, Charles Guiteau, whose name I did not recall previously encountering. Garfield did not get a lot of press in the history books, but his life seemed to deserve at least the brief explanation I give it in the context of my poem.

The "natural" shape ultimately had to include the *intimate* mentioned above, something I had to wrestle with as I worked toward a finished version of the poem. One part of me felt I ought not to include some of what I ended up keeping, but I didn't let go of Miss Garfield's now-inappropriate-seeming behavior because I still believe it was innocent and well-meaning—and because I've learned that if an artist gives greater credence to the mores-of-the-moment than to a gut sense of the artwork's needs, the deepest points of the creative act are compromised and even betrayed. (I know that's a rather blustery claim, but it happens also to be true and ought never to be forgotten.)

So, yes, at the age of ten, on a warm spring day, my buddy and I were literally "picked up" after school for a ride in a hot convertible—color bright yellow, model Ford Fairlane or Ford something—driven by our young teacher.

I don't recall whether we'd had gym that day, though Miss Garfield might have been feeling a bit more bouncy and loose if we had. She took our class outdoors whenever possible, and she participated in every activity—which was most often softball. She was the best hitter and fielder, the best runner (even in her tight 1950s skirts), and the most enthusiastic player.

In any case, she pulled up beside us as we walked along one of the two streets and sidewalks flanking our L-shaped school building, and she invited us for some sweet treat from one of the little neighborhood stores that still dotted our quiet, industrial "metropolis." I don't think we hesitated—or at least Louie wouldn't have, because he was generally "trouble" as fifth graders went in our modest city of 40,000. We cruised (a term I learned somewhat later) to a store—maybe the one on Sampson Street or the one on Chautauqua Avenue,—where we were treated to Popsicles or ice-cream sandwiches, and then were dropped back where Miss Garfield took us in. I don't remember anything we or she said, but I can feel the physical thrill of what was probably my first convertible ride, and I can definitely see Miss Garfield's blond hair flying toward us in the backseat. (Seatbelts were a new thing then—not yet in fashion, a long way from being required, and often not present.)

That spree was never repeated and was never mentioned among us. I don't know what, if anything, I said to my mother about getting home late, but I'm sure it wasn't the truth.

The holes in my memory, and therefore in the story, do not matter; in fact, they almost surely have made the remembered portions even more important, and they were likely the goad to the poem's beginning and, if it has such for readers, the poem's strengths.

All this talk about the content of "History of My Present" needs to give way to more about its making, its "what I was able to do with it." In something like ninety-five percent of my poems, I deploy "open" or "organic" forms rather than "fixed" or "traditional," though not because I lack love and respect for the latter. I believe some of my best poems are ones I framed as sonnets or villanelles—I especially love the difficulty of being successful with the latter—and I still dream of writing a sestina that fulfills its demanding shackles by rendering them invisible.

After making my research discoveries and deciding on the alternation design for the stanzas, I think I soon felt that the clashing-yet-blending contents needed some balance to go with their swirling. I was perhaps too quickly taken by the opening sentence/stanza that came to me, but as things played out, I think my early decision to deploy stanza regularity—six lines each for the first fourteen—helped me to keep the narratives moving, especially as concerns the obscure-but-important-fact-laden parts about the president. As I recall, the adding of a seventh line to the final stanza didn't come to me until I got there (or nearly there), but I can see now—and hope I saw then—how the small contrast provides a vital formal mirror to the concluding expansion of emotion.

The other (and I hope mostly quieter) formality running through the poem has to do with a two-pronged belief I generally hold when writing: the *line* in open-form poems must still be respected *as* a line via various intentional—at least during revision—moves by the poet, moves involving sound, rhythm, repetition, surprise, and more; and the success of these moves is best measured by the degree to which a reader does not notice or think about them *as* moves, but is instead simply touched, emotionally and/or intellectually, by their overall and synthesizing effect.

That said, given how this commentary appears in a book aiming to be read by and of use to practicing writers, I'll point to a few spots where I think I was able to gird "History" with natural-seeming music: (1) In the opening stanza, my intended content let me play off the sounds of *President*, *descendant*, and *students*. (2) In stanza eight, my ear's wish to repeat (from stanza six) the exotic-sounding *Credit Mobilier* needed the word *twice*—which sparked the snarky rhyme with *grease*, which was my favorite sounds-moment in the poem and which got me to the closing word *office*. (3) In stanza three—this was almost too easy, but I decided the naturalness of the game names (*softball*, *kickball*, *dodgeball*) justified the move and thereby reminded me that "too easy" isn't always bad, to say nothing of wrong.

The poem is always out there: in something you can't remember or can't forget; in something perfectly clear or completely inexplicable; in something you've refused to write about or tried unsuccessfully twenty times to write about; in something that, if you got it right, you could not allow anyone to read.

Chad Davidson

Putting In

On an island below Italy, after cocktails,
a lemon tree in a pit by the house
we rented for a week. What lives in recess,
what survives, what can, is bitter.
That house of mortarless stone.
Those gangly roadside caper stems
that left green streaks along our car.
Roads thin enough to keep grief out,
at least sequestered in the port, miles
from our sleep. Our landlord died,
we heard from a neighbor come for lemons.
We capitalized. We were good at that.

When my mother died, the family put in
time sifting through debris. We couldn't
clear it. Or didn't want to. Sewing machines
and tools that cut. Baby shoes, bronzed,
strangely sharp. Dangerously so. Swatches,
frayed remnants of quilting squares, photos
of the year trucks arrived to dig our pool.
Putting in, the workers called it,
though most of it they hauled away.
It took whole crews to carve it out.

The Tricky Business of Elegies

Of all poetic forms, the elegy may be the hardest to pull off. Arriving, as it so often does, already freighted with the gravitas of the great Greek and Latin models, it is hoary and esteemed, haughty and demanding. And if the elegy is then focused on a parent, the dangers increase. To specify one's mother, moreover, might just be the most formidable of elegiac tasks, threatening tonal risks that must be scrupulously managed—lest

59

sentimentality produce the most unsightly kitsch. (Cue the violins, the angels, the clichés about "being in a better place.") On the other hand, the poem cannot sidestep or cordon off emotion. Too much remove gives the impression of coldness, and we thus fail to capture the fullness of loss.

That is why I never intended "Putting In" to function as elegy. Rather it began—as I suppose many poems do—with stray associations and images. We had, as the poem details, rented for a week a rather rustic, stone dwelling on the shores of a wind-swept island south of Sicily, and writing about that experience then seemed an exercise in cataloguing timelessness: the incessant tidal shifts, the wind through the lemon and olive groves, the scent of sage and scrub and solitude. They were resonant details, at least to me. The issue, which I probably did not comprehend at the time, was that those details possessed no sounding board, no emotional surface off of which to resonate. They simply rang.

Later—much later, in fact (that trip took place in 2004, while my mother died in 2011)—those details reached a fuller poetic shape when placed in concert with the magnitude of my mother's death. A sort of reverse-engineered elegy occurred, then, as I overlayed sentiment onto the details, rendering the poem a kind of index of the ways in which loss makes itself known in random moments, and how such grief lies in wait in our daily lives, ready to spring on us and reawaken feelings of sorrow, emptiness, aloneness. Or maybe it was just obsession, that thoughts of my mother haunted my imaginative life.

The two-part structure of the poem offers a clear sign of that pivot inward, that obsession orchestrating the emotions. The single empty space in the poem—dividing the first and second stanzas—might suggest the opening inside which a fact of everyday existence (news of an absent landlord's death, for example) instantly calls to mind the loss that never leaves—that of the mother. Her absence is ever-present in the poem, even in those distant memories. It is dormant (it "lives in recess"), once the initial grief has been processed and the survivors again relive their routines of travel abroad, "cocktails," lemon picking, and the—I sheepishly acknowledge—"capitalizing."

As soon as her absence has been re-invoked, a stream of images returns—all connected to her work on earth—quilting, collecting family heirlooms, preserving photos that record significant moments of family history, such as the "putting in" of a built-in pool. These objects become her stand-ins, reanimating her interests and obsessions as a maker of quilts and of strong familial bonds, resurrecting her impulses to collect and organize instead of discard. The poem, finally, becomes concerned with work: her work, the manual labor of the crew that builds the pool, and—perhaps above all—the work of the writer's grieving, which the text not only suggests but at least attempts to enact.

Denise Duhamel

Recession Commandments

FORECLOSURE
thou shalt not covet thy neighbor's house
thou shalt not covet thy neighbor's corner lot nor thy neighbor's broadband
   connection
      nor granite countertops nor thy neighbor's ease in large groups of
         people
      nor thy neighbor's two-car garage nor pool nor marble tile nor
         screened-in porch
      nor thy neighbor's healthy eating habits nor closet space nor billiard
         room
      nor central air nor salt and pepper shakers nor thy neighbor's direct
         sunlight
thou shalt not covet thy neighbor's wife nor garden nor gardener nor Lexus
      nor thy neighbor's perfect children nor thy neighbor's popularity
      nor clean driving record nor thy neighbor's husband and his sweet job
      nor thy neighbor's credit score nor vacation plans nor thy neighbor's
         wardrobe
      nor washing machine nor friendly hello's nor energy nor energy drinks
      nor hair styling products nor kayak nor spice rack nor thy neighbor's
         Jacuzzi
thou shalt not covet thy neighbor's Merry Maids nor contractors nor
   pedigree dogs
      nor thy neighbor's manicures nor thy neighbor's spa memberships
      nor backscratcher nor matching luggage nor table manners nor
         graceful walk
      nor thy neighbor's passport nor trust fund nor safe full of cash nor
         curtains
      nor down comforter nor leather couch nor thy neighbor's charity work
thou shalt not covet thy neighbor's oxygen bar nor ass nor Assembly of God
   membership
      nor anything else that is thy neighbor's—not tennis rackets nor
         rollerblades
      nor art collection nor wine glasses nor Costco membership nor ice
         cubes

nor commanding presence in a room nor junk mail and catalogues
nor flawless articulation nor perfect posture nor political connections
        nor gutters
nor scrapbook nor table runner nor encyclopedias nor vintage
        postcards
nor brand new hammer nor chopsticks nor straight white teeth nor
        snow globe
nor banister nor microwavable popcorn nor private jokes nor
        flirtatiousness
nor TVs nor sound system nor shoe collection nor recessed lighting
nor magazine subscriptions nor umbrellas nor umbrella stand nor
        sense of humor
nor king size bed nor Sunday afternoon bicycle rides to get fresh air

UNEMPLOYMENT
for six days thou shalt labor and do all thy work
for six days thou shalt post thy resume, hand deliver thy resume, rewrite thy
    resume
        to best suit labor sought, mail thy resume overnight or priority, fudge
            thy resume
for six days thou shalt keep track of all thy efforts to qualify for an extension
    of unemployment benefits
for six days thou shalt feel guilty, cry, wring thy hands, redo thy checkbook,
    pawn thy TV and thy jewelry
for six days thou shalt fill out applications at chain restaurants, hospitals,
    retail stores,
        schools, offices of all types (including temp offices), banks, nail salons,
            hair salons,
        supermarkets, nursing homes, construction sites, topless bars, hotdog
            stands
for six days thou shalt set up an e-bay account to sell thy dishes, and thou
    shalt bring
        thy best clothes to a consignment shop
for six days thou shalt call up favors and let go of thy pride
for six days thou shalt apply for no-interest credit cards
for six days thou shalt fill out applications to become a telemarketer, a customer
        service employee, a tutor, a nanny, a janitor, a maid, a dog-walker,
        a dogcatcher, a cashier, a mail-order bride
for six days thou shalt write letters to government officials when
    unemployment
        extension benefits are denied
for six days thou shalt labor and do all the work thou can find

INFLATION
thou shalt watch *American Idol*, whether on TV or podcast
        thou shalt watch anything that will give thee false hope—that thou
            could compete
        on a show like *America Has Talent* or *I Love Money* to earn a windfall, that

thou could once again afford Heavenly Hash ice cream, Earth shoes,
    or a new Brita water filter
thou though shalt not even dare window shop for a killer purse, adult DVD's,
    sunglasses
    that last year thou would have thought a bargain
thou shalt ignore the news—the Pacific Island nation of Palau threatened
    with disappearance; houses in Shishmaref, Alaska, plunging into the
      sea;
a redrawn map of the United States with Florida (where thou livest)
    chopped off, submerged
thou shalt not relive the hurricanes, especially Katrina, after which thou
    bought gas
    cards and boxed up all the little toiletries, shampoos and soaps, thou
      had taken
    (thou shalt not steal) from hotels to send to New Orleans
    because even people who lost everything might want to smell good
    and rub a little lotion into their arms
thou shalt not buy too much gas, thou shalt not go too far, thou shalt not
    replace
    the stove nor the light bulb nor the shoelaces nor the baking soda in
      the fridge
thou shalt not be nostalgic
thou shalt not bear witness to the sad stories around thee—the abandoned
    hotels,
    once swanky, but now full of crack; the girl squatting in an apartment
    with nothing but a mattress and a webcam; the man living in his car,
    washing in the outdoor showers at the beach before he heads off to
      work
thou shalt not believe it, thou shalt not inflate thine own suffering
    nor the suffering of others
thou shalt not believe it could happen to thee

Lies I Told Myself

In July of 2008, I bought a second apartment with my then-husband, sister, and brother-in-law. We made the purchase so that my parents could be Florida snowbirds and escape the coldest months in Rhode Island where they lived. It was a grand plan that quickly fell apart. My husband left me in September, within days of the Lehman Brothers filing for bankruptcy, and our investment property plummeted in value. My father died in November, and with him died our extended family snowbird dream.

I live in an area that was then drenched with subprime mortgages and witnessed "vertical ghost towns" up and down the beach. From the fall of 2008 until well into the fall of 2009, I saw the number of lit condo windows dwindle. The newly built Trump Tower (four buildings north of me) was reportedly full of mold as unit owners foreclosed and no one bothered to keep the A/C running. My mail carrier told me in March of 2009 that there were only four apartments (out of hundreds) with tenants who received mail in that particular tower. He said the lobby was a dark, dreary place, as if no one could afford to keep on the lights.

I wasn't sure how to write about our country's financial failures. My personal story was mild compared to what was going on around me. Several friends lost their homes completely when one spouse or both were laid off. I took all the Catholic guilt from my upbringing (how could I have been so dumb, etc.) and channeled it into a familiar form—the Decalogue from the Bible. The banking crisis and my own personal crisis of 2008 did have moral components—greed (my country's and my own) and lies (my husband's lies, the banks' lies to mortgage holders, the lies I told myself). The poem wound up being much longer than I originally envisioned. To get a handle on it, I broke it into three parts.

Once I had the 10 Commandments in front of me, I updated them for the first section of the poem, *"FORECLOSURE."* Exodus 20:17 reads:

> Thou shalt not covet thy neighbor's house.
> Thou shall not covet thy neighbor's wife, or his male or female servant, his ox or donkey, or anything that belongs to thy neighbor.

I used that first commandment verbatim and just went for it, expanding the commandment into five more lines as a comment on America's capitalistic materialism, especially in a cultural moment which centered on luxury home-ownership. Writing the poem was for me a cathartic release. I also employed wordplay and more contemporary meanings so that:

> Thou shalt not covet thy neighbor's house....
> nor his ox, nor his ass....

became:

> Thou shalt not covet thy neighbor's house....
> thou shalt not covet thy neighbor's oxygen bar nor ass nor Assembly of God membership

I reimagined "ox" as an "oxygen bar." I let "ass" stay, knowing that the original meaning was a donkey, but today's meaning implied a sculpted bottom, a sign of wealth and a gym membership or possibly even a home gym. Later in the poem, the "female servant" becomes the "Merry Maids."

The second section of the poem *"UNEMPLOYMENT"* relied on a one-line passage, Exodus 34:21, which reads "for six days thou shalt labor and do all thy work." Again, I let that line stand and used the anaphora "for six days," suspending/erasing the last part of the commandment which is, of course, "but on the seventh day thou shalt rest." Americans in financial trouble weren't resting. I combed articles about the newly re-emerging "gig economy," a term first used in 1915, when jazz musicians coined "gig" to refer to performances. There was media spin to make these "gigs" sound fun, giving freedom to workers to make their own freelance hours. But, of course, these workers had no health insurance, no steady paycheck, never mind a union or retirement benefits. Friends of mine, students of mine, were desperate to find jobs in 2008–2009. In December of 2007, the unemployment rate in the U.S. was 5 percent and by October of 2009 it was 10 percent, and this did not reflect those for whom unemployment benefits had run out.

The third section of the poem "*INFLATION*" riffs on the original Ten Commandments most people know from pop culture. The first commandment forbids "idolatry" and, in my poem, this becomes "*American Idol.*" "Killing" becomes a "killer purse." I transcribe "Thou shalt not bear false witness against thy neighbor" to "thou shalt not bear witness to the sad stories around thee...." From there, I take wilder liberties with the commandments, commenting on all the terrifying and disheartening news of those days. I was incensed by the way Americans who took subprime mortgages were told it was their fault for not reading the small print. None of the mortgage lenders or banks were scolded (never mind charged) for their fraudulent practices.

The borrowed form I used for "RECESSION COMMANDMENTS" let me explore all I was observing and feeling, my writing going rogue and then being reined in again. The last two lines of the poem harken to Romans 10:9, "That if *thou shalt* confess with thy mouth the Lord Jesus, and shalt *believe* in thine heart that God hath raised him from the dead...." Though "gaslighting" wasn't as popular a term as it is now, our institutions were telling Americans not to believe the situation was so bad. People impacted by the Great Recession were repeatedly told not to believe it could happen to them.

Camille Dungy

One Night in 1888, as the French steamboat Abd-el-Kader
powered from Marseilles to Algiers,
news reports proclaim *the sky became quite black with swallows*

The channel between
one life and another has always been subject
to sudden explosions. Those swallows
must have been exhausted. *The birds alighted*
in the thousands on the sails, ropes, and yards
of the Abd-el-Kader. I began with birds, thousands.
Some wandered into cabins, ate from passengers'
delighted hands. I will return to the birds, but you
should know the Abd-el-Kader was named for a man
who died five years before they blacked the sky
around the boat that bore his name. If you don't
know how many died, how many more he saved,
in the decades of conflict between France and Algiers
while Abd-el-Kader was emir, maybe you won't know
what a wonder this was to report. I read about it
in *The New York Times*. This must have sounded,
in those days, like the stories we hear now of cranes—
white-napped, red-capped—who nest nowhere securely
but along Korea's demilitarized zone. Those *winged strangers*
remained all night on the vessel, the article claims.
In the morning, fed and rested, they flew off
for coastal islands still controlled by Spain—
which, as you know, once kept as its own our neighbors,
Honduras, El Salvador, Mexico. I've been trying to write
about the Abd-el-Kader swallows for more years
than I am able to count. Yesterday, you apologized
for arriving late for dinner. You'd seen a small, bent
woman walking with heavy bags near the grocery store
and you stopped to ask if she would let you drive her
home. You are the size of black man people here
consider frightening. The woman must have been exhausted.
She settled her body in the cabin and you carried her safely

home. Somedays, especially as I'm reminded of how
we fight the animals we are—who need to migrate
as much as we need to settle, to stay—how we'll tear
apart and strand and starve and slaughter that part of us
who takes flight from one place to some other—
I try to recreate this. *A rather curious episode
in natural history occurred the other day*, the story
I love so much begins.

One Night in 1888

The poem, "One Night in 1888, as the French steamboat Abd-el-Kader powered from Marseilles to Algiers, news reports proclaim *the sky became quite black with swallows*," took me eighteen years, six days, and four hours to write. It required that I live in three states and five different houses. I had to grow familiar with risk and rupture. Perhaps all poems arrive in such a complicated fashion, but I can track the development of this one more easily than most.

In my last spring living in Virginia, while I was conducting research for my second book, *Suck on the Marrow,* a collection set in the mid–19th century, I came across an archived article from a June 5, 1888, issue of *The New York Times*: "Swallows Take to a Ship—Paris Dispatch to the London Daily Telegraph." I can't tell you why I was so taken by the story, but I was completely drawn in and made a copy to keep on my computer.

Do you know how hard it is to keep a computer file active for nearly twenty years? I've lost old drafts of unpublished poems because the files in which they were saved are too old to be recovered without special technical prowess. But this article about the swallows remained accessible. I must have opened it nearly every year, reading and re-reading the facsimile by the glow of my laptop.

I love the report's wide-ranging tonal openness. I love its language and its attention: "The little winged strangers remained all night on the vessel, and in the morning at 7 o'clock the head lookout bird no doubt sighted the Balearic Isles, for the whole flock made for land, after having spent a comfortable and refreshing night on board ship." I love the sense of place the story gives me. I understand this is a story from over a century ago, on the channel between the African continent and Europe, but I can see it all unfolding as if it were happening here and now. I wanted to recreate that sense of presence and urgency in my own poems. The story put me in mind of human experiences of war and displacement, welcome and ruin. Despite its being nearly 200 words long, again and again I worked to cram the whole dispatch into some collage poem or another. I suffered disappointment upon disappointment "for more years/ than I am able to count," but I never completely gave up.

In June of the 18th year—coincidentally right around the anniversary of the time I left Virginia to move to my beloved California, and in the same month that the 1888 dispatch was originally published—I traveled with my family to Bemidji, Minnesota, where I taught a week-long generative workshop at the Minnesota Northwoods Writers Conference. I asked my students to bring two poems they felt were close to completion but were confounding them somehow. I also asked them to bring along two hopeless drafts they hadn't yet completely forsaken. For six days, we tried various approaches to giving these drafts the boosts they needed. Without being in the company of others who were so diligently accepting new possibilities, I would not have been able to complete my poem in what, without context, seemed like four hours.

One assignment I gave to my class, and to this poem as well: Write down some everyday things that happen in your life, like doing the dishes, going grocery shopping, finishing homework, sending an email to a supervisor, wiping crumbs off the counter, calling your mother, sweeping the floor. Don't write these things as if they are extraordinary. Describe these actions as they really are. Be open to the mundane in your life and be open to where the mundane may lead. "Yesterday," I wrote in my poem, "you apologized/ for arriving late for dinner. You'd seen a small, bent/ woman walking with heavy bags near the grocery store…" and from that came the moments of vulnerability and grace that would personalize my attachment to the story of the swallows. Writing into my daily life, I was able to make a connection that swung wide a door that had been closed before.

Another assignment I gave to the class: Take the draft that makes you feel most hopeless and cut it up, literally, with scissors. This finally allowed me to break up the 200-word text block. I could focus on the lines that sang to me, separating ideas from the language locked into my facsimile.

One more assignment: circle words in your draft to look up. We think we know our language, and we grow lazy in that knowledge but, often, time with a quality dictionary will reveal possibilities for deeper meanings we were closed off from in our certainty. I spent time researching Marseilles, Algiers, the Balearic Isles, the word *channel*, the word *swallow*, and Abd-el-Kader. Why had I never done this before? I had charged myself with writing a poem about an incident that moved me, but I hadn't done the work to understand what it might reveal. Looking up definitions, I learned about the language's histories, contexts, possibilities, and sources of power. Without that research, I could not have gotten to these lines: "In the morning, fed and rested, they flew off/for coastal islands still controlled by Spain—/ which, as you know, once kept as its own our neighbors,/ Honduras, El Salvador, Mexico." I would have missed the connection between this 1888 story of human kindness toward lives deemed so different and stories of welcome, and welcome's opposite, from our present time. The lack of this clear connection, I realized, is why my previous attempts to handle the dispatch had failed.

In addition to scissors, I gave the students in Bemidji some glue sticks and tape. And, importantly, I gave them time. Once they took everything apart, I asked them to put things back together. I suggested they write into the gaps they had made. That, too, came to me during the four hours I sat at my own desk working on this poem. Despite the fact that we'd just returned from a week that was billed as a family vacation but during which I mostly worked at showing people who weren't in my family some pathways into poetry, the people in my house let me disappear into my study for one entire morning. This might not sound like it has anything to do with how to craft a poem, but I believe it has everything to do with crafting poetry: you should surround yourself with people who understand and value the life of the word. I needed to immediately draft off the energy I carried from Bemidji, and I needed the time to focus on the words in front of me. I realize how blessed I am to live with a family who encourages me to write, and I make sure to express my gratitude to them in numerous ways. This paragraph, acknowledging my family's support of my practice, is one of the ways I show gratitude while also being honest about how my poems are made.

The original version in my notebook begins: "Those swallows must have been tired." I shifted to "exhausted," a much more specific word, and as the draft developed, I added the title and the current first lines to both tighten and broaden the context of that initial first line. I wrestled with the words in the dispatch until I figured out which lines could be directly quoted and which I would paraphrase. I realized I was thinking outside of a linear chronology, and so I added language that would signal that indirect mode of narration: "I will return to the birds, but you/ should know the Abd-el-Kader was named for a man/ who died five years before they blacked the sky/ around the boat that bore his name." Because I detached the poem from linear chronology, and because I was figuratively cutting and pasting parts of several stories together in the places where they most suited the poem, I was able to give deeper context to the story of the ship and the swallows, to the story of the emir Abd-el-Kader, and also to the story of my own life: "You are the size of black man people here/ consider frightening." I purposely invited the reader into my own mind and home— into the body of my love—when I used the second person in a poem that might otherwise seem to have nothing to do with them.

Cutting and pasting, taking things out of one context and placing them inside new ones, and opening up the resonances and histories inside everyday language became—over eighteen years, six days, and four hours—the key projects of drafting this poem.

Stephen Dunn

Elementary

1

There was death.
And there was the occasional touching
which reminded the body
it was alone.
And there was the weeping.
And the laughter which understood death.
And the laughter we couldn't bear.

2

There was the house or the apartment.
And there was the office
or the factory or the field.
And there was sleep.
And there was the in between.
If work was satisfying
love was possible.
If we loved power there was
an emptiness that never stopped
needing to be filled.

3

There were fire, water, air,
and machines that made them ours.
There were wild things
and things on shelves.
And there was boredom when the rain fell,
boredom on the most beautiful days.
After the pleasures came
we wanted them to return.
And got sad.

4

There was play, our bodies in motion
forgetting they would die.
And the sudden remembering

after the sweat dried.
And there were the questions,
the old ones, over and over.
And the hard work in the yard,
the routine erasures,
the cleansing of hands.

5

There was language.
And what had to be written
because it couldn't be said.
And there were the translations
from other languages.
And the daily translations
of our own.
And each thing in the world
had a name,
and was waiting for a name.
And there was silence
with its history of bad timing,
coming our way again.

Resuscitating the "Elementary" Poem

I can't remember much about the genesis of the poem, since I wrote it in 1980. It was the last poem in my 1981 book *Work and Love* (long out of print), and for some neglectful reason, I never included it in my *Selected Poems*. It came to my attention because a young man from San Francisco wrote me a fan letter, in which he said it was his favorite poem of mine. He didn't specify where or in what he had read it. This was a temporary problem for me because I didn't remember writing it, nor where it had appeared.

My literary executor B.J. Ward (who knows my work, I think, better than I do) found it for me, and I was astounded by how good it seemed. In the book, it was titled "Elementary Poem," and the only change I made was to eliminate the superfluity of "Poem." Everything else seemed to hold up. I'll let the reader decide on its worthiness. Looking back, it may have been the best poem in the book.

When I was putting together *Work and Love*, a book that was traversing those twin themes, "Elementary" didn't seem to fit the thematic structure. Yet, I placed it as the last poem in the book, a place I usually try to reserve for a very strong poem. So how to figure? All I can say is I'm grateful to the young man who wrote to me and for his good taste that has urged me to resuscitate a poem that has a chance now to be a little less lost than most poems written over a lifetime.

Cornelius Eady

Baldwin

"The story of the blacks in America
Is the American story" says Baldwin,
Or words to that effect—and as I watch
This doc on him, I take this to mean
The baton the cop rises in Selma
Falls on the skull of the protestor
In Ferguson, how the foul devil's breath
Of tear gas drifts between those streets,

Like that special effect
In movies to tell the viewer we're about
To take a little trip through time;
The sight of the black man, Baldwin, alone
Surrounded in the white lecture hall, and the thought
Of Phyllis Wheatley, alone, in the white lecture hall
With only their words to persuade, that wall, that
Argument.

Writing "Baldwin"

First off, a disclaimer: I believe that, up to a point, the more one can see or read about the process of writing a poem, the better. I even have poets Skype into my poetry classes these days; my students receive a semester's worth of no agreement as to what makes a poem fly, but instead, a weekly live encounter with the various ways poets regard craft. Listening to what the poet of the afternoon thinks they're up to, hopefully, allows my students to try out their own ideas without feeling they aren't allowed to have their drafts crash and burn—like many of the guest poets' examples tell them.

But I also feel that too much information can get dangerously close to what happens when you try to break down a joke. Part of the process has to be surprise—good craft, I think, prepares one for surprise, at least if one believes Frost's famous essay on the topic.

So, instead of writing about a published poem and working backwards to how it got written, I instead submit this draft, which may or may not have gone as far as it needs to—time is also a factor in writing for me. This one was written on Sunday, June 7, 2020, in the mid- to late afternoon.

I am writing this in my office in the house that my wife and I have on Long Island, in the small town of Center Moriches. We share the place with my mother-in-law. My wife is in the garden, and I'm tending to this.

It may sound like an idyllic moment, but don't be fooled; the world happens to be on fire. Over a week ago, a black man, George Floyd, was murdered by a cop on a city street, in broad daylight. The cop put and kept his knee on George Floyd's neck. It took over eight minutes to kill him. While he was dying, he said what Eric Garner, another black man about six years earlier, said as the cops were choking him: "I can't breathe." Mr. Floyd, however, had time to cry for his dead mother and to ask one of the crowd who was also pleading with the cops to let him up, if not let him go, to get word to his kids that he loved them. He knew at that point he was going to die, like a deer, whose neck is vised between the jaws of a large predator. That's how they do it in the animal kingdom: the big cat crushing the windpipe, the pack, making sure there's no mistake, that the prey won't kick loose. The last three of those eight minutes George Floyd was out cold, but still the cop refused to remove his knee.

What I didn't know was how old that knee tactic was, until I saw it done, more than once, in old film clips of police taking down protestors—mainly black—in the 1960s. The knee on the black person's neck. The black person telling the officer he can't breathe.

This was part of the documentary on James Baldwin, *I Am Not Your Negro,* which we had watched the evening before. Among other points, the filmmakers, to me at least, seemed to be saying how porous history is: fires on the streets of Detroit in the 1960s; fires on the streets of Ferguson, Missouri in the early 2000s; fires on the streets of New York; and Washington, D.C., right now—the difference being?

Sometimes, poems begin as uninvited guests, when writers don't actually believe they are thinking "poetically." In the doc, I watched the clip of Baldwin addressing a white lecture hall in Oxford in the 1960s and had the fleeting thought of the poet Phillis Wheatley, when she read her poems at Cambridge, Massachusetts, in the 1700s. Black face, white crowd. Black face, all by themselves, trying with words to convince—to prove—to that white world that they, Negros, actually have a brain, can process complex thoughts, are actually, fully human.

This was quickly thought of and then let go as I watched, I thought, but actually, it appears it decided to hang around overnight.

I've been writing a small cycle of poems on Wheatley, on what a complicated "mercy" it was for this slave to be taught the language of her captors, and I suppose this, plus the images, plus the line from Baldwin (which I'm sure is not a direct quote but am leaving at the moment for just the tone) became the trigger of the first draft. The Baldwin line simply popped into my head, and I could hear two or three lines that would follow after, so I just sat down to see what it wanted to say. The tear gas image allows the turn to the larger idea: the difference being?

And this is where I leave it for now. It is two stanzas; there may be more. There are a few things available on that page that I may or may not use. It may become another poem in my Wheatley cycle. It may never have another life, beyond this project—the surprise for my writing may have been the essay this triggered. There is rage in the streets, which my poem can't contain. Yet. There are calls for justice, but I am a poet who understands, given the right mix of events, he could easily end up on the pavement, kneed. My draft can't shout out that lyric dread. Yet. Maybe I just wanted to say, "Hey, Jimmy, I am working on it." It's a first draft.

Martín Espada

Letter to My Father

October 2017

You once said: *My reward for this life will be a thousand pounds of dirt
shoveled in my face.* You were wrong. You are seven pounds of ashes
in a box, a Puerto Rican flag wrapped around you, next to a red brick
from the house in Utuado where you were born, all crammed together
on my bookshelf. You taught me there is no God, no life after this life,
so I know you are not watching me type this letter over my shoulder.

When I was a boy, you were God. I watched from the seventh floor
of the projects as you walked down into the street to stop a public
execution. A big man caught a small man stealing his car, and everyone
in Brooklyn heard the car alarm wail of the condemned: *He's killing me.*
At a word from you, the executioner's hand slipped from the hair
of the thief. *The kid was high*, was all you said when you came back to us.

When I was a boy, and you were God, we flew to Puerto Rico. You said:
My grandfather was the mayor of Utuado. His name was Buenaventura.
That means good fortune. I believed in your grandfather's name.
I heard the tree frogs chanting to each other all night. I saw banana
leaf and elephant palm sprouting from the mountain's belly. I gnawed
the mango's pit, and the sweet yellow hair stuck between my teeth.
I said to you: *You came from another planet. How did you do it?*
You said: *Every morning, just before I woke up, I saw the mountains.*

Every morning, I see the mountains. In Utuado, three sisters,
all in their seventies, all bedridden, all Pentecostales who only left
the house for church, lay sleeping on mattresses spread across the floor
when the hurricane gutted the mountain the way a butcher slices open
a dangled pig, and a rolling wall of mud buried them, leaving the fourth
sister to stagger into the street, screaming like an unheeded prophet
about the end of the world. In Utuado, a man who cultivated a garden
of aguacate and carambola, feeding the avocado and star fruit to his
nieces from New York, saw the trees in his garden beheaded all at once
like the soldiers of a beaten army, and so hanged himself. In Utuado,
a welder and a handyman rigged a pulley with a shopping cart to ferry

75

rice and beans across the river where the bridge collapsed, witnessed
the cart swaying above so many hands, then raised a sign that told
the helicopters: *Campamento los Olvidados: Camp of the Forgotten.*

Los olvidados wait seven hours in line for a government meal of Skittles
and Vienna sausage, or a tarp to cover the bones of a house with no roof,
as the fungus grows on their skin from sleeping on mattresses drenched
with the spit of the hurricane. They drink the brown water, waiting
for microscopic monsters in their bellies to visit plagues upon them.
A nurse says: *These people are going to have an epidemic. These people
are going to die.* The president flips rolls of paper towels to a crowd
at a church in Guaynabo, Zeus lobbing thunderbolts on the locked ward
of his delusions. Down the block, cousin Ricardo, Bernice's boy, says
that somebody stole his can of diesel. I heard somebody ask you once
what Puerto Rico needed to be free. And you said: *Tres pulgadas
de sangre en la calle: Three inches of blood in the street.* Now, three
inches of mud flow through the streets of Utuado, and troops patrol
the town, as if guarding the vein of copper in the ground, as if a shovel
digging graves in the back yard might strike the ore below, as if la brigada
swinging machetes to clear the road might remember the last uprising.

I know you are not God. I have the proof: seven pounds of ashes in a box
on my bookshelf. Gods do not die, and yet I want you to be God again.
Stride from the crowd to seize the president's arm before another roll
of paper towels sails away. Thunder Spanish obscenities in his face.
Banish him to a roofless rainstorm in Utuado, so he unravels, one soaked
sheet after another, till there is nothing left but his cardboard heart.

I promised myself I would stop talking to you, white box of grey grit.
You were deaf even before you died. Hear my promise now: I will take you
to the mountains, where houses lost like ships at sea rise blue and yellow
from the mud. I will open my hands. I will scatter your ashes in Utuado.

Notes on "Letter to My Father"

"Letter to My Father," my poem in this book, speaks of the catastrophe in Puerto Rico after Hurricane María, with a focus on Utuado, a mountain town in the Cordillera Central. My father, Francisco Luis (Frank) Espada, was born in Utuado. My grandmother, Luisa Roig, was born in Utuado. My great-grandfather, Buenaventura Roig, was the mayor of Utuado. My cousin, Gisela Conn, says that Utuado is "la cuña"—the cradle—of the family.

Jon Lee Anderson, writing in *The New Yorker* (October 10, 2017) said: "The municipality of Utuado … has become a byword for the island's devastation, an equivalent to New Orleans's Lower Ninth Ward after Hurricane Katrina."

I wrote "Letter to My Father" in October 2017. My father died in February 2014.

The poem evolved from the practice of talking to my father's remains, the ashes that sit in a box on my bookshelf. Said Gisela: "I loved your father, but I'm glad he's dead. If he were alive, this would kill him."

My words to my father in the poem—and his words back to me, words he actually said in life, lyrical or bitter—perpetuate the illusion that he is still alive, as long as I can keep up the conversation. I write to him as if he is still here—and yet I report the devastation of his birthplace as if he has no way to know what happens in the land of the living, in Puerto Rico, an island he loved with such ferocity that he kissed the ground when he returned after many years' absence.

This is how the dead speak: not from heaven or hell, not through a spirit medium on the boardwalk, but through lost letters found folded into books, or delicately pressed into those pages like dried petals of paper and words. Yet, this is not my father's letter to me, from the dead to the living, but my letter to him, flying in the wrong direction, from the living to the dead.

This letter is for him, but not for him. This is an open letter, a public declaration full of the intimate details, shared experience, and hard-earned confessions characteristic of private correspondence. I read the poem at *#PoetsforPuertoRico: A Reading for Hurricane Relief* in New York City on November 4, 2017. The gathering at the Poets House raised funds for Comedores Sociales de Puerto Rico, a grassroots community kitchen providing desperately needed meals on the island.

The official government death toll as a result of Hurricane María stood at 64 by the end of 2017, while independent investigations would eventually place the actual death toll at well over four thousand. (In August 2018, following a George Washington University Study, Governor Ricardo Rosselló revised the official death toll due to the hurricane from 64 to 2,975.) The failure to count the bodies piling up in morgues across the island served a propagandistic purpose, conveying the impression that the situation was well in hand, that the crisis had been averted, that President Trump, FEMA (the Federal Emergency Management Agency), and the governor of Puerto Rico rose up to slay the hurricane. The failure to count the bodies—as if the dead were enemies in wartime—had ominous implications: the slackening of public attention, a plunge in funding and material aid for Puerto Rico.

The island faded from the headlines, slipping like Atlantis beneath the waves of public consciousness as if it never existed. The poem is a letter folded into a book, a poet's dissent from the official story, a reminder that the humanitarian crisis is not over, a testimony to those "who have been waiting in line for centuries to get into history," as Eduardo Galeano put it.

Demagogues have their own poetry. They act out metaphors. President Trump tossed paper towels to a crowd of hurricane survivors in Guaynabo—where, as the poem notes, my cousin Ricardo lives—in a gesture of megalomania and contempt for the subjects of empire. The poem imagines him as a roll of paper towels, soaking in a rainstorm, exposing the hollow cardboard core at the center. Some may read this image as magical realism. This is not magical realism. We are real.

The former president was born in 1946. A New Yorker of his generation grew up with the stereotypes of Puerto Ricans endemic to that city in the twenty-five years of migration following World War II. A decade separates us. I grew up with the same stereotypes, at the same time and in the same city, the difference being that Trump internalized those racist caricatures, and I saw those caricatures refuted everywhere, especially in my activist household. My father was an organizer in the East New York section of Brooklyn, a leader of the Puerto Rican community, a photographer who created the Puerto Rican Diaspora Documentary Project.

When Trump tweeted that Puerto Ricans "want everything to be done for them," he was invoking the hoary myth of Puerto Ricans on welfare, lazily shunning labor. After the hurricane, this myth, lacking only the sombrero and cactus of its drowsing Mexican counterpart, formed the foundation of criminally negligent social policy. Thousands of Puerto Ricans, well aware of Trump's sneering, organized themselves into "brigadas," work brigades armed with shovels and machetes to clear away the wreckage, opening the roads to Utuado and much more.

The reference to these brigades in the poem also indicates an awareness of "the last uprising." There was a Nationalist rebellion in October 1950, called the "Grito de Utuado" or "Battle Cry of Utuado," demanding independence from the United States. U.S. warplanes bombed Utuado. The authorities marched Nationalist prisoners to the town police station and shot five of them dead.

María was not Puerto Rico's first hurricane. Colonialism is itself a hurricane. After Hurricane María, a sign rose in Utuado, as it rises in the poem: *Campamento los Olvivados: Camp of the Forgotten.* The sign articulates an ethical imperative not to forget, to bear witness, to tell whatever we know with urgency.

No essay on the poem would be complete without citation and acknowledgment of sources. The quotation in stanza five, "These people are going to have an epidemic. These people are going to die," comes from nurse Alicia Schwartz, cited in "These Volunteer Nurses in Puerto Rico Fear FEMA is Failing" by Jennifer Bendery, in the *Huffington Post*, October 16, 2017. Stanzas four and five rely in part on several background sources, including "In One Puerto Rico Mountain Town, a Wall of Mud

Came Crashing Down" by Molly Hennessey Fiske, in the *Los Angeles Times,* September 24, 2017; "Stranded by Hurricane María, Puerto Ricans Get Creative to Survive" by Caitlin Dickerson in *The New York Times,* October 16, 2017; "The 'Forgotten Ones': 37 Days After Hurricane María, Puerto Rico Neighborhood Still Stranded" by Kyra Gurney, in the *Miami Herald,* October 29, 2017; and an interview with Rosa Clemente by Amy Goodman on *Democracy Now!,* October 18, 2017.

My cousin Gisela was an essential emotional and informational resource.

Of course, the greatest influence on "Letter to My Father" is my father, gone but present in every word of the poem.

Beth Ann Fennelly

What I Think About When Someone Uses "Pussy" as a Synonym for "Weak"

At the deepest part of the deepest part, I rocked shut like a stone. I'd climbed as far inside me as I could. Everything else had fallen away. Midwife, husband, bedroom, world: quaint concepts. My eyes were clamshells. My ears were clapped shut by the palms of the dead. My throat was stoppered with bees. I was the fox caught in the trap, and I was the trap. Chewing off a leg would have been easier than what I now required of myself. I understood I was alone in it. I understood I would come back from there with the baby, or I wouldn't come back at all. I was beyond the ministrations of loved ones. I was beyond the grasp of men. Even their prayers couldn't penetrate me. The pain was such that I made peace with that. I did not fear death. Fear was an emotion, and pain had scalded away all emotions. I chose. In order to come back with the baby, I had to tear it out at the root. Understand, I did this without the aid of my hands.

Out of the Quarrel with Others

A few years back, I was in the audience at a reading series in a hipster bar when a young man stepped to the microphone to introduce the next writer. The writer had apparently been a mentor to the young man, who spoke about the writer's work and influence, becoming emotional. All this seemed to me rather charming, but not to the young man: "I can't believe I'm up here crying like a pussy," he said.

In the days that followed, I kept thinking about and around that sentence. What troubled me? Not that he'd sworn—I can swear like a truck driver—just ask the witnesses of my IKEA baby crib assembly. No, my rejection of his statement is not because "pussy" is vulgar but because it's a bad metaphor—how did that strong part of a woman's strong body become co-opted as a symbol for weakness? This could not be. I picked up my pen.

I'll mention that this piece is in my book, *Heating & Cooling: 52 Micro-Memoirs*. I came up with the term "micro-memoirs" to indicate I was writing small, true stories. I didn't want to use the term "poetry" because I'd grown wary of my "speaker," my mask; I wanted to claim my experiences as my own. Further, I didn't call the pieces "prose poems" because most of them weren't. The piece above is an exception, composed with a poet's sensibility, including the rhythms of poetry—its repetitions and syntax—as well as composition through metaphorical leaps.

Let me think through the differences between the line versus the sentence, a distinction that would seem twee to those who aren't obsessed with words, who assume lines are chopped-up sentences. But those of us who *are* obsessed with words know the distinction changes not only how, but what we write. After all, if lines were merely chopped-up sentences, and line breaks merely visual, we could delete them with no change to the material. But when losing the line break, we lose the white space that shapes the way we process meaning. Line breaks provide a rest, so the words on either side of the rest can require more effort in the processing of lyricism, tropes, syntax, and sound. These resting places—like stair landings in a walk-up—interrupt the exertion with a breather (literally), and so give us the strength to keep climbing. Without them, too much is demanded of us, so our absorption is hindered.

The poetic line also affects the reader because it highlights the artfulness and artifice of the experience of reading, as opposed to the sentence, which distracts us from it. The line, followed by its white space, metes out comprehension, followed by its disruption. The power play of the line break is that of withholding. We're never unaware that our experience is being modulated by another as we follow the choreographer's orders to leap and rest, leap and rest. This is fundamentally different than how prose pours itself into the vase of the page. *Here*, says the line, *Now we are here. Now we are here.* But *everywhere*, says the sentence. *You are everywhere and nowhere.* The sentence is always pointing outside of itself. I believe this is what Cole Swenson means when she writes, "Prose exists somewhere other than the page."

William Butler Yeats wrote, "Out of the quarrel with others we make rhetoric; out of the quarrel with ourselves we make poetry." I disagree with Yeats on this one; my poem was prodded by a quarrel with another that I wasn't able to have at the time. If I'd had it, maybe I wouldn't have written the poem. Life rewards the quick of tongue who have the comeback at the ready. Poetry rewards those who want some space to deepen their reflection and, hopefully, nudge it toward art.

Annie Finch

A Root

What happened when he grabbed me at the root?
I stopped. It all stopped; spirals fought to win
My spiral life (from an unspiraled root—

From thick cigar stubbed in my young tongue's root—
(Heart beating uncle lifetimes through my skin!)).
What happened, when he grabbed me—at the root

Where women learn to starve—our open root?
One broken body—(one more!)—broken in?
One spiral life from an unspiraled root-

Lorn pomegranate? (in the basement; root-
Torn hell of seed—as if seed might have been
What happened.) When he grabbed me at the root,

Did ancestors throw chains down through our root
To rot and winnow, with their pain and sin,
My spiral life? From an unspiraled root?

Oh sisters, keen our sisters / Till the root
Of loving! turns! (and not! from! twisted kin!)
WHAT happened (when) (he) (grabbed) me at the root?
Our spiral life! From an unspiraled root;

The Roots of "A Root"

My belief that poems are gifts is probably a major reason that my plan, in the winter of 2006, to get up early on a regular schedule and write poems before anyone else woke up lasted only for three mornings. We were living in Maine. So tiny was my writing studio that there was literally room for nothing in it but a huge desk that had been my grandfather's and my father's. It had heavy wooden cubbyholes and a hidden ivory-colored buzzer for calling your assistant.

When the alarm rang, those three mornings, I'd turn it off instantly, grab my winter night writing outfit off the hall floor, and tiptoe into the studio while my husband and children still slept. By the light of one window barely gleaming in the dark dawn, I'd suit up: thick wool knitted hat, sheepskin-lined boots, and, during especially cold weeks like that one, a purple full-body goose down zip-up ski suit from the thrift shop. I was a mother of two with a full-time job, a huge roster of writing and editing projects, and a temperament that gets miserable if I don't write poetry. I was desperate for time to write. Theoretically, it made sense that I would take time each dawn to create a new poem. But in practice, it felt strange and cynical to start to write with no idea what it would be about.

The Muse to me is a Goddess. I trust that if She wants me to write about something, ever, She will let me know. And She does! Sitting by a stream or a window; washing dishes or sweeping a floor; falling asleep or waking up; watching a candle or waves, a parade or stars, a play or a dance, a party or an argument; opening a book, lying in the dentist chair, receiving a massage, nursing a baby; kissing or fucking or making love, drinking wine or water or tea: even when I am not prepared for the Muse, I am open to Her pulsing voices, whispering or shouting lines, phrases, or entire poems into the darkness of my brain, throwing out the tips of their rhythmical tentacles like spider silk, forcing me to seek paper napkins at a party or coasters in a bar, to commandeer the flyleaves or inside covers of books, the blank spaces in advertisements in theater programs, or the margins and backs of student manuscripts, to scrounge scratch paper from waiters, clerks, and librarians, to stash tiny notebooks in the waistbands of skirts with no pockets, to hoard index cards in hidden spots in cars or in plastic bags in kayaks, and to harbor legal pads and flashlights under the bed for scribbling my lyric poems in the dark. And I have an outer Muse as well. She's the one who prompts me to promise poems for Valentine's Day, a baby naming, a library dedication, a crisis like 9–11, a feminist rally, or a witch-circle to the people I feel accountable to as a poet—and who incites me to create narrative poetry, like my epic on abortion, or dramatic poetry, like my plays. Poems written for both my inner and outer Muses feel necessary and useful, connected and alive. I never throw out a poem that the Muse has gifted to me. I honor them all, saving them to revisit and revise even when they seem to be leading nowhere, and then I coax and dance with them until the truth they carry, the way a fruit carries a seed, finally sprouts, then blooms with my help to reveal itself, just as I'd trusted in Her that it would.

While earning my MA in creative writing at the University of Houston in the mid–1980s, though, I learned about a completely different approach to writing poems: "getting a poem out of it," to use the words of one of my teachers there, Cynthia MacDonald. This way involves sitting down to write a poem about anything or nothing, not because of the call of the Muse or your tribe or community, but simply because you have decided it's time to write a poem and you figure you'll hit on some stimulating topic. "That was an awful thing that happened," I'd hear Cynthia say, "but at least you can get a poem out of it." The phrase made me wince, as if the fount of Helicon were natural gas being fracked for profit regardless of the destruction of ecosystems. Of course, sometimes it may be necessary to force a lyric poem, if there's a deadline or assignment to meet and the Muse remains silent. But to my mind those moments are exceptions that prove the rule. To accept "getting a poem out of it" as an *ars poetica* felt dangerous, as if it could cause muddiness in the creative waters and lead to confusing true inspiration with ego. It felt disrespectful, like spending precious poetic energy on a whim or an exercise—or worse, a lie. It felt depressing—calculating, cynical, lonely, and no fun.

So, after only three days and three poems that Maine winter, I returned to warmer, lazier mornings and my normal writing process of scribbling on napkins at the Muse's beck and call. But a new deed had been done, during my three-day flirtation with ego as Muse. Yes, two of the poems were just as I'd feared, distracting and forced—empty, useless exercises. It still drains my poetic energy to recall them. But the poem I'd written on the second day was alive. It was called "A," which was maybe a nod to *The Scarlet Letter*, and it was about a subject I'd written about cryptically and indirectly for thirty-eight years but had not addressed directly before, barely even in my diary. And yes, there may be a reason for this: I had recently started Rolfing, a process of very deep bodywork. The second session had suddenly and dramatically awakened the memory of being molested by my uncle at age twelve, and I had ended up sobbing in a fetal position on the floor of the bodyworker's studio....

"A" told that story of that early wounding, with a beginning, a middle, and an end. Though it was only six lines of iambic pentameter, it felt like a poem—not just a piece of a poem. It also felt unrelenting and hollow. Inscrutable. Closed. When I tried to revise it, it sat there unbudging, like the little shiny trick boxes that sometimes used to appear in my childhood Christmas stocking. The trick boxes were impossible to open unless you knew how to slide back a hidden panel and reveal the spring that would pop up the lid. Was there a hidden spring that would let me open the poem, let more air in, invite in breath and contrast, energy and movement, discovery and change?

I put "A" into a book manuscript. In my poetic world, this is not necessarily a mark of completion. You'd think that gathering together forty-five or fifty finished poems, many of which have already appeared in magazines, would yield a finished book. But instead, as I've leafed through the manuscript pages of each of my poetry collections, preparing to send it to a publisher and imagining it all in print, I notice poem after supposedly finished poem starting to thrash around in vulnerable and embarrassing ways, screaming with new assurance, now that they are gathered close to their siblings, the truth that they're nowhere close to finished after all (interestingly, the only collection of mine for which this didn't happen was *Spells: New and Selected Poems*, whose poems remained calm and finished while being collected. I take this as a sign that the revision process before publication in their original volumes had been completed).

So I entered a new revision phase, moving through the manuscript and spiraling through layers on layers of interlocking revisions, uploading the changes to all the poems and to the manuscript's order and organization, and printing it out over and over. If there are many months between successive drafts of a manuscript, I welcome the time because it allows me to reenter the poetic labyrinth with a fresh eye. I'm so attuned to this method by now that the instant I turn the title page and begin to read the title, the dedication, and the Table of Contents, I can feel my heartbeat slow. By the time I begin reading the first poem, my consciousness has become so still that each syllable moves like the circling ripples caused by a slight wind on the surface of water. It's a combination of listening and feeling, as much as it is reading or seeing. My attention to the universe of the manuscript is so entire that it blocks out any noise around me. But if anyone addresses me directly, the spell is broken. Crashingly. It takes up to an hour for my body to calm down and recover, and then I need to start all over from the beginning to regather the momentum in which the trajectory of the manuscript will reveal itself.

Moving through the manuscript poem by poem, I hear the words, or feel them, resounding through my body so thoroughly that anything that's off scratches me in a physically painful way. It's not a matter of thinking. At the height of the process, I become a spider spinning all the threads of the manuscript out of my belly anew, all of me disappearing except the part—at once will, mind, body, heart, and spirit—that is combining and intercutting poems, reworking and rearranging poems, reordering and resectioning and retitling poems, listening the unfinished poems deeper and deeper still. The process continues until each poem is either more itself than it was when it lived alone, or has "clicked shut like a box" (as Yeats described it), or else has revealed itself as what I would call "dead" to the current revision process and is removed.

But "A" was different. This poem stayed in the manuscript for years, un-revisable, apparently neither finished nor dead, yet refusing to open a way into the deeper layers where real revision takes place. The secret panel would not reveal itself, and the secret lock would not budge. Around it, other poems changed, arrived, changed again, left. Only "A" remained, impervious, stubborn, locked, but impossible to kick out—because it would not die.

I did more bodywork. Found more memories resurfacing. Started writing a prose memoir about the wound. Got stronger in my public life. Went deeper into therapy. Completed a twenty-year dream of co-editing an anthology of villanelles. Journeyed with a Norse shaman. Got an agent and spent a year writing a lengthy proposal for a memoir about my life. Spent many years in a powerful women's circle. And kept trying to work on the poem. In 2011, the year I got the agent, I renamed it "Silence":

SILENCE

A wedge of posture driven in to death.
A weight of shoulders forced in like old stairs.
A heartbeat thick as rain that finds no root;
A wealth of burning rawness dropped like fruit.
A skin seared into mine. A foreign skin.
A silence where there could have been a bird.

The next year, I renamed it "Assault" and broke it into couplets:

ASSAULT

A wedge of posture driven in to death.
A weight of shoulders forced in like old stairs.

A heartbeat thick as rain that finds no root;
A wealth of burning rawness dropped like fruit.

A skin seared into mine. A foreign skin.
A silence where there could have been a bird.

But still nothing much changed. The poem sat there, tight in its coiled sourness. There was no invitation, no crack of light, no frayed edge. Like the impermeable tightness of the deep muscles that still held the secrets of my repressed pain, it appeared calm and self-contained, as if it needed nothing. There wasn't anything else I could do but let it be, holding its spot in my manuscript. At least it deserved that much.

And then the next year I was in Maine again, alone in a small cabin on a rainy summer night. A full moon loomed outside and the hard wind rattled loose panes that needed caulking. I sat crisscross in layers of sweaters on an olive-green futon couch, piles of papers on my knees and around me, working by the light of three kerosene lamps and five candles, moving through the manuscript I'd been working on for years, cutting some poems out and revising others… And then it happened. Something frayed. Suddenly I noticed the rhyme in lines 3–4, which I had read a hundred times, differently. "Root" and "fruit." In a flash, the line "A heartbeat thick as rain that finds no root" became the repetend in a villanelle, and I could hear the line "A skin seared into mine. A foreign skin" as the central line of a villanelle stanza. I had found the poem's hidden spring, hiding in plain sight; it showed me that the insistent grip of the traumatic moment on my memory was a perfect theme for the relentless, circling, healing dance of my new favorite poetic form.

I don't know exactly which words I scrawled in my excitement, in green ink I'm pretty sure, across the backs of several pages of the manuscript; I don't even know if the book at that point was called *The Witch in the Moon, Invocations to the Five Directions, Amulet,* or another title, because the version I was revising that night is in my archive at the Beinecke Library and hasn't been catalogued yet. I do know that my scrawls tell the story of the changes that happened within me on that full-moon night. And I remember that at the climax of my excitement I spurted my triumphant joy and relief all over two or three pages in huge words with multiple exclamation marks: VILLANELLE!!!!!!!!!! BINGO!!!! THAT'S IT!!!!!! AT LAST!!!!!!!!!!!!!! THANK YOU GODDESS!!!!!!! I also remember that I turned over that poem and the backs of the poems around it, keeping them clipped together in the corner so that only about half of each page was available for writing, and composed the first draft of the villanelle version on the backs of those same manuscript pages.

"A" would not be finished for a while. But for the first time in its six-year life it was accessible, open to revision. For the following five years or so I revised it as a villanelle, switching and rearranging stanzas and refrains as well as words and lines. Here's a 2015 version that still does not yet follow the villanelle form exactly, including the unrhymed words "death" and "bird," and longer than a classic villanelle by two stanzas:

TWELVE

A wedge of posture driven in to death.
A weight of shoulders forced in like old stairs.
A childhood stricken like a blasted root.

A family story coming back to root.
A sad strange love with no new way to spill
A wealth of burning rawness dropped like fruit.

A pomegranate in a basement. Fruit
As red and angry as it could have been.
A childhood stricken like a blasted root,

A heartbeat thick as rain that finds no root,
A kiss so hard that love was twisted in,
A wealth of burning rawness dropped like fruit.

A family tree with anger at the root.
A skin. Seared into mine. A foreign skin,

A childhood, stricken like a blasted root.

A taste—cigars—deep in my sweet tongue's root.
A huge hand—harsh—against my smoothest skin.
A wealth of burning rawness dropped like fruit,

A mother-loss, an orphan come to root,
A body broken, one more, broken in,
A childhood stricken like a blasted root,

A root of terror, root of fright, oh root
Of tortured body, decades deep as sin,
Oh heartbeat, thick as rain, oh find no root—
Oh, silence—where there could have been a bird.

Over the next three years of revision, the poem grew tighter and more complex as I entered it more deeply and began to claim the right fully to express my experience of the molestation and its aftermath: the rage and agony, the generational nature of the trauma, my fierce insistence on transformative healing not only for myself but for all who have suffered in this way. Parentheses were added (a poetic strategy I inherited from my mother Maggie Finch and used many times in my book *Calendars*). A slash was added, in homage to the style of my beloved teacher and mentor Ntozake Shange, who had held space for my healing as no-one else ever had. Also, as I revised the book (now called *Spiral*) further and associated a punctuation mark with each of its five sections, semicolons were added—the punctuation mark that goes, according to my system, with iambic meter and the mind. Spirals were added into the imagery, as I developed this symbol into a central motif in my cosmology. And ultimately, the two repetends would end with the same word—something I'd never done or seen before, but which seemed to have arisen directly from the unrelenting nature of the wound.

By the time I finished "A Root," it had been twelve years since the wounding that, in just a few minutes of January 1969, had shocked me apart from the first twelve years of my life. By the time it appeared in *Poetry* in March 2019, I was living in Washington, D.C., and only a few lines remained from the original version I'd written on a freezing morning in Maine. I didn't mean for the poem to take twelve years to complete, but the fact that it did seems inevitable now: a year of revising to a year of healing. A year of childhood, a year of post-menopause. Twelve years of perfecting a poem, twelve years of reclaiming a self.

Greg Fraser

The Good News

Hurtled down in buckets
    swelled the sewers
        doused the drains
    made lakes of all the lawns.

We threw on clownish costumes
    (floppy hats and slickers
        oversized galoshes)
    and sloshed about like children

dizzy with the thought of children
    bound to be ours at last. Right
        to left the good
    news swept in torrents

like the Book of Daniel
    in Hebrew script. I hoisted
        sail and veered out in the surge—
    my one hand clutched the rudder

the other gripped my wife
    our twins packed deep in her hold.
        All day and half the night we tossed:
    Achaeans boldly scudding past

Charybdis. Next morning
    aground again
        under a cloudless sky
    we found the news in puddles

on the walk. Peering into glossy pools
    how joyful we appeared
        how free of fear
    drenched in that early light.

Delivering "The Good News"

It's 2014, and my third collection of poems, *Designed for Flight,* has come out earlier in the year from Northwestern University Press. I wrote much of the book in 2009, while my wife Milada was pregnant. I had been granted a sabbatical by my university, and I knew that I had to write fiercely—every day for at least a few hours—before our twins arrived. I knew that, as a tenured professor with a relatively flexible schedule, I would soon become the primary caregiver of the children, since my wife works long hours at a hospital. I knew that I was forty-seven years old, that these were my first kids, and that I had no clue whatsoever how to be a good father. I knew that my time to work on poems would decrease. What I could not calculate, however, was the possession of parenting—the power of it, the mutuality of it, the scope.

It manifested first in the form of terror. The kids came out shrieking. I was sitting right there in the delivery room. It sounded like the harrowing of hell. In double surround sound. They seemed terrified. I most certainly was. Terrified in a baby-blue hospital gown, with matching surgical mask and head cover like a puffed-up shower cap. All I remember from the first several months are my dreams. I saw the babies suffocating in their blankets, choking on their pacifiers, stealing each other's bottled formula, which would suddenly transform into blood (omega-3 fortified, of course). My nights were Dantean. Kafkaesque. Even my daydreams—dawn to noon to dusk—unfolded like the triptychs of Hieronymus Bosch.

I was spent and dopey. I was nervous about my sanity (not really), my marriage (yes, a little), and my future as a writer (most assuredly). My time to work on poems had not dwindled, as I had earlier feared. It had disappeared. I began to think—quite seriously—that I would never write again. Gradually, though, I found my bearings. The kids stayed healthy and grew, we settled into a family rhythm, and in 2015, I was fortunate enough to be awarded a grant in poetry that provided a year off from teaching. That year, I was able to revitalize my poetic life while continuing to work hard as a husband and father.

"The Good News"—which appears in my fourth collection, *Little Armageddon,* also from Northwestern—centers on a couple's discovery that they will soon become parents. Other poems in the book make clear that they have already lost a child by miscarriage, so their joy is heightened in relation to the previous loss.

And that's precisely what makes such a poem dangerous to write, with lots of pitfalls to avoid—easy emotion, slippery slide into cliché, the treading on well-trodden ground such as the elation of welcoming children into the world. "Welcoming into the world": even there, a cliché enters. Even in the best of news, the bad news of shopworn sentiment—the enemy of poetry—can intrude.

If it works at all, then "The Good News" does so not by outright celebration and ecstasy—although those sentiments remain present in the poem, perhaps most noticeably through formal strategies such as the off-balanced lineation and the sonic callbacks (pairings such as "galoshes" and "sloshed," for example, or the description of the expecting couple's behavior as "like children / dizzy with the thought of children"). More so, though, the poem seems to complicate such excitement with imagery pulled from the most unlikely sources: biblical apocalypse and Homeric myth. The good news of the pregnancy assumes the magnitude of mythological flood, out into which the poet and his wife first tread "in floppy hats and slickers" and then later, as the waters rise, "hoist / sail and veer out into the surge." It recalls the travels and travails of Odysseus. And the mashup, it would seem, revels not just in the news brought by doctors but perhaps more so in the energy extracted from the unexpected pairing of beginning times and end times—the marriage of good news with its more apocryphal insinuations.

Alice Friman

Under a Blind Eye
Seville, Spain

Despite bad dreams, I've come back to find
    the glass case where I stood forty-six years ago
        when that man leaned to me and whispered—

Look, the crucifix of Hernando Cortez. Now
    I'm wandering the recesses of this cathedral,
        this Stygian colossus of no air, marble,

and stolen gold, when a cloud of nuns in white
    float across the stone floor and I want to confess,
        but how would they believe me—an old woman—

for *didn't your mother tell you?* here in this
    dim echo chamber where even Mary is in the dark,
        Mary, Mother of Remedies, when there was none,

and my own mother, *didn't she tell you not to get into?*
    albeit a clean one, a new one driven by a smiling man
        with kind eyes who took me where I don't know,

somewhere in the country out beyond the city limits
    then shoved me out of the car into a ditch
        only to fish me out later with his voice that went

singsong up and down so I knew he was not quite right,
    but *didn't your mother tell you?* yes, of course, yes, but
        that was about candy or lifts to lessons not

under a vaulted ceiling whose oculus is God's eye
    where I've come back to find the crucifix of Cortez
        where that man hooked me with the promise

of Come, *but your mother, your mother,* but he said
    Come I'll show you the real Spain, real flamenco—
        the crucifix my witness—only to be told it's not

on display anymore, being so heavy-precious, that gold
    icon before which each night Cortez blessed himself,
        so pumped up on his own swagger as was this man

backed by the triumph of nailed-up flesh and lions
    lapping at the feet of saints, and yes my mother told me
        but that night, that night of the twisted arm

when he pushed me out of the car into a ditch and drove off
    crazy only to turn around with squealing brakes
        and a cooing voice—Did you really think I would hurt you?—

and I got in that car again even though mother told me
    never to, never to but what could I do in the middle
        of nowhere without a deliverer in sight?

Confession: On "Under a Blind Eye"

To relate how this poem was written entails returning to the circumstances it was written about in the first place, and that is painful. Everything about this poem is painful, but, indeed, life is painful, so let's begin.
Thirty-nine years ago—perhaps if I looked through the travel journals, it
was thirty-nine years to the day, for it was summer and I was in Spain. I
had gotten a grant from the school where I taught, the University of Indianapolis, to travel. After my divorce from my first husband, I began traveling whenever I could. I had been to Greece twice, England, and Italy, and I
think I imagined myself an experienced, savvy traveler. Little did I know.
I traveled alone, a duffel over my shoulder. I was in my mid-forties and figured if I wanted to see the world, which I did, I had little time to wait for
a suitable "companion." Besides, I liked being alone, experiencing things
straight on and not having to share them, or, worse, having them filtered
through a tour guide who would tell me what to see and how to see it.

As I said, I was in Spain, which in 1981, wasn't what it is now. In
Madrid, swastikas were spray-painted on the sides of buildings, and I saw
too many men, ex-soldiers I imagine, on crutches, without limbs. The people seemed thin-lipped, taciturn, and unfriendly. I had difficulty being
waited on in restaurants because I was a woman alone. One could feel the
influence of Franco, who hadn't been dead that long. This certainly wasn't
Italy or warm and friendly Greece. This was different. I was there for six
weeks, and no one talked to me, no one. Perhaps that's an excuse for what
happened.

But let's get to the story. I was in Seville, rattling around in the cathedral, that gigantic barn of a place, standing in front of a display case when
this pleasant voice introduced himself, said he was a medical student
and had spent time in the States. He proceeded to point out which one of
the many glittering crucifixes before me was the famous one, the crucifix that belonged to Hernando Cortez (the one he took with him to Mexico and prayed before on his knees every night in the midst of his bloody

campaign against the Aztecs). The young man was friendly and funny, and it was a relief to have someone to talk to, if only for an hour. We went out for a drink, and he said how he would love to show me, not what tourists see, but the *real* Spain, the neighborhood festivals, where everyday people dance the flamenco in the streets. So, I got in the car with him. The rest is in the poem. What's left out is uglier, and, perhaps, someday I'll write it.

I left Seville the next day at dawn, terrified, running to the car in the half light, the duffel banging against my side as I looked over my shoulder, expecting to be waylaid, beaten up, or worse. I drove like a maniac from Seville in the south to Santander in the north in one day. And I vowed never to go back.

Two summers ago in 2018, my husband was invited to deliver a paper at a conference in Spain—Seville to be exact. It was an important conference for him, and he wanted me to go. How could I not? This conference meant a great deal to him, and we could go to other cities too, like Madrid where there's the Goya to see, and Velazquez. Besides, I thought, surely after thirty-six years, Spain must have changed. But I tell you, I did not want to go. He would be conferencing for days, and I would be on my own, back there in that beautiful city which I ran from, which to me was a place of violence I wanted to forget. My solution? My only solution for the past fifty years of my life: to write about what happened. But how could I do that when I dreaded not only writing about it but even thinking about it? Besides, what could I say? And how would I say it? And worse, where to begin?

It was a very hot morning, with my husband off already to the first session of his conference, and I off to the cathedral armed with pen and paper. Perhaps if I start where I started from thirty-nine years ago, I could pick up a first line, or a rhythm. Those of you who write poetry know what I mean. I told myself if I could only find the display case where the Cortez crucifix was, I could begin. I could stand there and call up that man's voice beside me and tell the story. The trouble was, what story? What simply happened? His intentions or my complicity? Or, was it stupidity? Or the airless cathedral filled with stolen gold and silver, that dim cathedral that loomed around and over me, filled with its dark Spanish history of crucifixes, blood, and swastikas? The only light, if you could call it light, filtered through the cathedral's oculus, that small round window at the apex of the dome through which, like an eye, God supposedly watches. It was stuffy and hot, and I, a little dizzy. So, I found a bench and told myself what I always told my students: *Write what you see. The poem will find its own way. Just write what you see.* It was then that I glanced up and saw, floating across the cathedral floor, a troop of nuns dressed head to foot in flowing robes of white—they reminded me of birds, sea birds perhaps.

So, I wrote it down, got up from the bench and wandered for hours, jotting down images, telling myself I was looking for the crucifix of Cortez which, by the way, I never found, it being locked away—too precious, the guard said.

So, the poem's pieces were written. How they all fell together I'm not sure I can tell you. But I know this: a poem, if it is to be, will find its way, its own way to be born.

Ángel García

Barely
after Ted Kooser

These days, the climb out of bed
is hard. But not impossible—not

yet. The soft pulse beneath your
eye is just enough a reminder you

cannot stay in bed one more hour.
Somehow, you wrangle into what

clean clothes lay nearby—if any.
Maybe you tie your shoes, or not.

It doesn't matter. Finally, when
you turn the ignition and drive

down a two-lane highway with
nowhere to go, what matters is

how you reconcile the distance,
each mile you can mark between

you and a room you've remained
in most your life, aching for one

sound reason that makes your life
worth living. Still, outside your

breeze-filled window, how easily
the shadows crawl through fields

of corn. How seamlessly the sky
crops itself from purple to black.

How slowly the song on the radio
fuzzes before the fade out, you

barely notice, miles later, how long
you've been listening to the static.

The Man Inside the Poem

It's almost always difficult to write about origins—my own, my family's, the origin of a particular poem—because, most often, the work of determining where something begins or from where something or someone arises necessitates an excavation of memory. The truth is, for most of my life, memory has been an elusive phenomenon. Suspect. Unreliable. A thing not to be trusted.

More than memory, or the act of remembrance, I've come to rely on sensation, on what I felt or feel at a particular time in a given place. More than memory, what I feel, is truth. Or conversely, the truest moments in my life have been when I feel most strongly. And so, where this poem began for me, began not in the idea or the making, but rather the first time I chose solitude over the company of others, absorbed by the silence of being, willingly or unwillingly, alone with the darkest of my emotions.

Depression is a difficult condition to describe. Only that over the years, from my youth through my adulthood, it is something I have felt on a Sunday, at three in the morning, at a friend's birthday party, while driving along a highway, or seated in a bar. And despite the work I've done in my life: the therapy, the anger management, the self-medication and prescribed medication, the open-chested conversations I'd learned to have with those I love and trust most, depression lingered always. Lingers still. So, in March of 2020, I became afraid. I understood that with the pandemic, with quarantine, I would have to face what I feared most: being alone in a room.

What brought me to poetry, and what continues to feed my obsession with it, is that poems often rely on truth, not facts. I won't delve into what I mean by truth (I'm no philosopher) but suffice it to say that what stops me from being carried off by most distractions in the world and what centers me are truth and beauty. Or rather, the objects or occasions or circumstances in life that one cannot look away from, such as an emotional truth or truths reflected in a work of art. Or in this case, an honest poem. A vulnerably, honest poem.

In many of the Ted Kooser poems I've read (and the many more I'll read in the future, I'm certain) I've always been fascinated by the seemingly mundane moments—a gesture across a dinner table, the movement of afternoon light through a kitchen window, the ash from a cigarette drifting past—that Kooser makes profound. It is through these moments of detail, in the lingering reverberations after the poem, that we, the readers, are left to reconcile what collectively we might understand but can only personally feel: a larger emotional truth, the frailty of love, the everlasting nature of grief, the brevity of moments in our lives, so on and so forth.

During the pandemic I came across Kooser's poem "The Sigh," originally published in *Poetry* in 1983. In the nine lines, the fifty-four words—a short poem to say the least—I was struck by the sharp turns the poem takes, the forceful use of the second person "you," and struck most of all by the emotional truth of the poem: the inescapability from of one's sadness, one's sorrow. Most importantly, and necessarily more selfish during the pandemic, the poem reflected so much of what I had had to contend with while living several years in Nebraska, alone. That loneliness was then amplified by the quarantine.

Assumedly, like the speaker in the poem lying on a noisy spring mattress, I too had begun to spend most of my hours in bed, in a cradle position or sprawled across the mattress, wrong-side-up, or napping and sleeping, or awake at all hours of the night and morning. The few occasions I left my bed, I left only to forage for food in the kitchen or use the bathroom, always knowing that despite where I had to go or the responsibilities I needed to fulfill, I would return to the mattress.

"Barely" began as an imitation poem (and in many ways still exists as an imitation poem), thus the obligatory "after" in the epigraph. As the quarantine has been an especially difficult time for me to write, imitation poems have been and continue to be a useful way to get started, warmed up, and moving the pen across the page.

The first few drafts, if memory serves me correctly (and it rarely does) came easily enough. I inclined the poem would be about depression. I imagined it would be on the "shorter" side as I wanted to avoid the complexity of describing the condition. But more than all else, I knew that I wanted to make the idea of movement and non-movement more complex. Movement is an important concept because so often my depression manifests as non-movement, while the physicality of movement is what has kept me alive over the years. But as the title of my poem suggests, "barely."

The initial draft began as a prose poem, the most comfortable form to get started. Consecutive drafts shifted into one long stanza, tercets, then couplets. I then ordered and reordered the couplets to create what I thought to be a cohesive narrative.

What was once a pair of jeans, became in a later draft, non-specific items of clean clothing. Initially, the character in the poem was a smoker, but in a later draft there was no room for the cigarette and the cigarette smoke, and so he became a non-smoker. Twists and minor tweaks to arrive at what would seem an accomplished draft. But never could I stray far from the line in the Kooser poem that had seemed to contradict everything I had been told, at one time or another, about my depression.

It would seem that the people who had offered easy prescriptions such as, "just get over it," "go do something," "try to smile," "step outside," and "get some sun," had never experienced depression. And, had I had a copy of "The Sigh" in my back pocket, perhaps I would have offered them the chance to read it, asking them to pay special attention to these three lines:

"mocking your sadness. It's hard—
not the mattress, but life.
Life is hard."

I'm uncertain whether "Barely" is finished or not. There are lines with which I am still dissatisfied. There is a certain level of depth, emotionally or in terms of vulnerability, I feel the poem has not quite reached. But I trust in the path. And so, in the final lines of the poem, a reader might understand the speaker as the man inside the poem, or as depression itself, personified. Either way, the truth, I hope, remains, that our suffering, no matter how we attempt to heal from it, lingers always. Maybe it never ends, so that we might survive, should we be so lucky.

As for this poem and the many others I've written, as well as for my own depression, I would suggest that perhaps because there is no end, that itself is what makes poetry and one's apogee so hard, yet worthwhile.

Margaret Gibson

Exchange
a letter to David

Now that you've entered the great silence
I search out your scribbled notes and drafts

the remains of your work-in-progress
Each word I say aloud, drawing each one

into my body as if body were a vault
for *treasure*—a word you used to say with

a long *a. Treasure, pleasure, measure*—
I echo your odd torque of the vowel

Had your luck been otherwise, those words
would have been forged by you into memoir

and genealogy, your life a well-made
volume of breath. And so I gather

the scraps, piece by piece; I try to finish
your sentences, I forage through files

and boxes, I nose about for treasure
as do the midwinter deer outside in a year

the oaks put out few acorns. I'd eat
the bark off a pine if I thought I'd find

beneath its tight inscrutable cover
a trace of your voice. I want to get through

winter, too—I'm simply an animal who
feeds on words, finding yours spilling into margins

balanced steeply on underlinings
many more crossed out in your rough-hewn drafts

I savor the words, listening for your voice
in a continuous, if tenuous, exchange.

I see it everywhere, exchange—nothing's finished
I breathe out carbon dioxide, the summer oaks

take it in along with the sun, the leaves
power up, unfurl more leaves, give out oxygen

those doubled molecules I breathe in and in
without thinking much about it, but for

an occasional burst of gratitude
the sheer luck of being alive. *Sheer....*

A word so transparent, it might house spirit
the spirit I'd say, if I could make out

what it is. Up late, we'd often talk for hours
about a single word, a spirited exchange—

who knew where it would take us? And words
kept us close. But *sheer's* partner is

stark, and together they make and unmake
treasure, pleasure, measure. What stays?

Firewood is a moment of *being time*, ash
also. Being time, we are like the shavings

that curled from the oak you planed into planks
to frame this house and lay the floors

Being time, we are whatever it is in us arises
meets, and merges into everything else....

Over the phone last night, your daughter
read me a letter you'd written her, found

tucked away in an old cardboard box
in the basement. Its subject: *How many*

can we invite to the wedding? A question
of some urgency back then. A time of *treasure*

pleasure, measure. Hungrily, I listened
to your words in her voice. Gentle words, and

wise, as you traced in an eloquent narrative
your passage in time through hardship to an

exchange of love no numbers can tally. That was
a moment. That was a meeting....

Perhaps a life's work is just this moment
just this much, breath shaped and released

given freely into the clear light.... *How many*
can we invite to the wedding? All of it

is wedding—an exchange of words and sunlight
a moment of bud and blossom begun

in a rustle of leaves, a never-before-now
utterance suspended in sheer daring

the words shining, briefly held by who knows
what, before being swept once more

syllable by syllable, vowel by vowel
beyond the passion to endure, beyond

the passion not to be lonely, beyond
beyond, into the full and everlasting furl of silence

On Writing "Exchange"

Essentially an elegy, the poem that came to be entitled "Exchange" began a year after the death of my husband, David McKain, a poet and writer of creative non-fiction, who, after eleven years of Alzheimer's disease, died on our wedding anniversary in late December 2017. My poem is in part an elegy for the prose book he had failed to finish, as well as for the absence of his physical voice, the voice I'd heard daily in conversation, its various tones and timbres, his particular way of saying certain words. I had already lost David; I was beginning to lose the sound of his voice in my head.

The conditions out of which this poem arose influenced both the voice and the structure that gradually evolved. I had been going through David's drafts and notes, preparing to send his papers to a library archive. After a close reading of his narrative prose, I slipped easily into a narrative cadence of my own. Wanting to recall his voice, I remembered certain words he pronounced in a singular manner—*treasure, pleasure, measure.* Gradually, these words seemed like thematic clues as well as idiosyncratic pronunciation. One evening, our daughter called on the phone and read me a letter he had written to her while we were in the midst of planning her wedding many years earlier. Listening to his words in her voice made me want even more to listen to his voice in the words of my poem.

I have long been a writer of elegies for loved ones, more recently of elegies for the earth during climate crisis. Traditionally, an elegy moves from grieving to acceptance, then to celebration or affirmation. I knew I was grieving as I went through those boxes of manuscripts. I had no idea that the poem would define "a life's work" as "just this moment / *just this much*, breath shaped and released / given freely into the clear light." Nor did I realize that the image of light would lead to language that celebrates life and to the furl of silence from which life emerges and back into which it sinks. I didn't have a shred of affirmation in me early on, when the speaker of the poems says, "I'd eat the bark off a pine if I thought I'd find / beneath its tight inscrutable cover / a trace of your voice." But, amazingly, all the elements of elegy emerged in the first draft. I only needed to recognize and develop them.

A poem weaves a spell of identity out of the speaker's voice. Finding the right word is as crucial to that enterprise as losing words is tragic for that human being who suffers verbal memory loss and, therefore, a diminished sense of self. In writing "Exchange," therefore, I was engaging in a double venture: while I mourned the mortal loss of David's voice and identity, simultaneously I created a voice for the poem that would remember David's voice and values, at times using words he'd used.

In the early drafts, I tried not to impede that flow of words by making "decisions" about structure. The poem was originally a long spill down the page, no stanza breaks, but as early as version four, I was breaking the lines into couplets. I honestly don't know why I made that choice, but I stayed with the two-line stanzas perhaps because of the growing number of dualities in the poem's use of image and idea: life/death, husband/wife, words/silence and so on. Form and content echo each other. I also decided to write the couplets so that no end punctuation in a sentence would fall at the end of the line. I wanted the lines of the poem to be ongoing—much as a loving relationship continues for the one who is left despite the absence of the loved one.

When I wrote the poem, it was January, a cold winter with heavy snow cover. I live in the woods in a house David loved and rebuilt. These are facts, and behind them is also a fact of nature—we human beings are defined by and inseparable from the environment which surrounds us. The identity of the speaker in a poem is no different: what surrounds the speaker inhabits and defines voice and identity.

During this time of global climate crisis, I am looking to write poems that show how living beings interrelate and reciprocate, how our lives are interwoven in the ecological systems that sustain us. The passages that detail the exchange of oxygen and carbon dioxide are in the poem for this reason. Those that lines gave birth to the lyric burst of bud and blossom at the close of the poem surprised me initially. The lines came in an onrush, like a river after rain. In the midst of composing a poem, onrush may seem unbidden—hello, Muse—but in most instances it is a sudden recognition of the implications of earlier images, a completion of what they promise.

Because the first draft of the poem ended with my reference to the letter David had written to our daughter before she married, I took "Letter to David" as the title to the second draft. Draft #4, newly titled "Exchange," begins: "Now that you've entered the great silence / I search out your scribbled notes and drafts / the remains of your work in progress." I was now, in part, "answering" his earlier letter to my daughter: I was talking to him, not so much about him. Once I saw that this private exchange of letters was just one exchange in the poem, the title was secured.

Title provides focus. The heart of any poem is the metaphor that connects all the parts. The title of the poem, in this case, signals the crucial metaphor. Exchange, and change in a variety of forms, are what the speaker observes and contemplates, and the forms of exchange are many: epistolary, marital, monetary, material, biological, spiritual.

Altogether, I wrote nineteen drafts of the poem. The major ideas came early, some of them hazy. There are some phrases that come forth in the early drafts and remain pretty much unchanged. That's not rare, but more common is the labor to simplify expression so that complex ideas and themes achieve clarity. The passage about firewood and ash, that change of form in time, is based on koan-like statements by Zen Master Dogen. The firewood and ash entered the poem as part of a passage that celebrated David's carpentry and home-building. Most of the stuff about the house got cut; the lines about firewood and ash remained and, eventually, after periods of silent meditation, I solved the koan and could move toward finding language that might approach that realization.

Silence and meditation are integral to the writing process. In this process, the initially awkward language of early drafts is taken as both a gift and a challenge: *Think this through. Hear it. Go deeper. Go deeper still.* The writer's job is to write coherently; it's also to listen patiently through the incoherent passages and, by listening, savor, distill, and give shape to the voice and life's work that's emerging, "just this moment, *just this much.*"

And the process ends, as it must, when there is nothing left to say, or no better way one can find to say it.

Nikki Giovanni

Knoxville, Tennessee

I always like summer
best
you can eat fresh corn
from daddy's garden
and okra
and greens
and cabbage
and lots of
barbecue
and buttermilk
and homemade ice-cream
at the church picnic
and listen to
gospel music
outside
at the church
homecoming
and go to the mountains with
your grandmother
and go barefooted
and be warm
all the time
not only when you go to bed
and sleep

It's Your Decision When You Want to Share

I am sharing "Knoxville, Tennessee" which is not only one of my favorite poems but a rather clear one. I was the first person in the Giovanni family to be born in a hospital: Knoxville General Hospital. I was, of course, born during the age of segregation, so Knoxville General could just have easily been named Knoxville Colored. I had an older sister who was born at home. Home would have been my grandmother's home. Grandmother, and I'm sure a friend, or someone who was a nurse, helped bring my sister into the world. We forgot the naval cord had to be cut and mother had to be sewn. We also forgot how many women died in childbirth though there is no record at all of how many men created those pregnancies. Mommy was well taken care of and ultimately had her second daughter: me. I am three years younger than my sister.

During the age of segregation, jobs were scarce. Though both my parents were graduates of Knoxville College, finding a job paying enough to take care of the family was not easy. My father had a friend in Cincinnati who told him about a job opening at Glenview School, which was a home for boys. They waited until my birth in June, then moved to Cincinnati that September. I have a photograph of my sister and me standing on the steps of Glenview School. And there is a sort of memory of it, but I'm not sure that I remember it or if I just heard about it. My parents had difficulties, mostly, I would imagine, financially, and we moved to Woodlawn, which was a village just outside, but now inside, Cincinnati.

What I remember about Woodlawn was the outhouse. Most people don't know outhouses now, but ours was brown wood. I think I liked something about it because I felt safe there. My parents argued a lot, but I could not hear the back-and-forth while sitting in the outhouse. There were flowers there, and I remember a clean smell. And I seem to have always seen a rabbit, or maybe that was a dream.

After a while, we moved to Wyoming, which is also a village, now a part of Cincinnati. We lived across from Aunt Lil and Uncle Rich, which is where I had my first job. I would wash their breakfast dishes for a quarter a week. I don't know why Aunt Lil asked me to do that, but she did. They only had coffee cups and glasses of orange juice. My sister, who didn't really like to play with me, would always come around on Saturday, when I got paid, to help me spend. I was old before I realized maybe that wasn't the right thing for her to do.

Then, we bought a house in Lincoln Heights where my sister and I shared a room. I liked to dust, and I still do, so that was my Monday job. Gary Ann was talented, so she practiced her piano lessons, her dance lessons, and her singing. I just liked to dust.

Our parents still argued, and it went to fighting. It became more than I could understand. It was always comforting to know summer was coming, and Grandmother would send the Rev. Abrums to the train station to pick us up.

I wrote the poem "Nikki-Roasa" because I knew I needed to make decisions about my life. I said I was happy because I recognized happiness is a decision. It was my first important poem. But "Knoxville, Tennessee" is always special to my heart because I had Grandmother to keep me warm.

I don't know why people write what they do or how they remember things. I just know it's your decision when you want to share and when you are not ready. It's your life. And you can't let anyone take it away from you.

Beth Gylys

My Father's Nightmare

His daughter's a poet. (Lord, save us!)
And he's sitting at some big reading event,
held in some big city. She's reciting
a long narrative poem about an abortion,
and she keeps saying the word fuck.
Fuck, in fact, seems to occur three or four times
in every sentence she reads.
He can't stand the thought of her doing that.
Why does she need to say it in front of everyone?
He happens to be the honored guest.
She keeps telling jokes about him.
She talks about his martinis,
and how he falls asleep on the sofa,
newspaper covering his chest.
He smiles wanly. She reads another fuck poem.
She reads a poem about kissing a woman.
It's clear she must have done this.
She describes the tenderness of lips,
the special hue of skin, the curves
and the moistness all so vividly.
He wonders, *Why can't she write poems about nature,*
something along the lines of Robert Frost?
He can't believe that's his daughter.
She winks at him. Now she gyrates her hips,
moving, he notes grimly, like a dog.
Why didn't she become a lawyer like her brother?
Or even a waitress—they make decent money.
He thinks, *Maybe I should go to the bathroom*
and sneak out the back door,
wonders, *Why did I fund all those years*
of college English? He's reading his menu,
holding it up, so it blocks out her face.
She recites a poem about a married lover.
He thinks he's going to puke.
She says the word fuck twice really loud,

and he's had enough. He gets up, turns,
knocks into someone's arm,
but it's only my mother shaking him awake.
"Honey, are you coming to bed?"
kitchen light behind her like a halo.
Life couldn't be better really,
house by the shore, endless martinis,
children gainfully employed.
Sure, his daughter's a little strange
with her poetry, her divorce,
but she works hard, never asks
to borrow money. *She seems*
all right, he tells himself,
as he climbs the stairs to go to bed.
She's always been a pretty good girl.

My Father's Daughter: Sex, Lies, and Telling It Slant

After he first read "My Father's Nightmare," my father called me and asked, "Beth Ann (he and my mom have always addressed me by my first and middle name), thank you for including my review of your work in your book." It was his indirect way of saying, *I'm all right with this poetry thing. We're good.* I didn't honestly know how he would react when he read the poem or the book. I was … beyond nervous when I mailed my parents a signed copy of *Bodies that Hum,* the book—my first—in which it appeared. It took them weeks to acknowledge the receipt of the package, a period during which I half-worried that they had disowned me. His comment was pretty much the only thing my father ever said of the collection. My mother, on the other hand, kept calling people and reading "My Father's Nightmare" to them, or buying and sending them copies of the book, making sure to tell them to read it. I think she was both amused by the poem and relieved that it wasn't about her.

I wrote "My Father's Nightmare" in graduate school during one of the most emotionally fraught but productive writing periods of my life. The poem is a "true" poem in that it speaks to the subject matter I was exploring in my work (obsessively, almost feverishly) at the time, namely sexuality and sexual relationships, and also to the unvoiced expectations I had about how my parents would or might respond to that subject matter. Many of the details in the poem are indeed true. My parents lived in a beautiful house on the Shrewsbury River in New Jersey at the time of the poem's creation. My father often would have a couple of drinks at night (Manhattans, not martinis) and fall asleep watching television or catching up on the news of the day. The poem—in one of those miraculous moments when the writing is effortless—emerged almost whole in a rush of feeling, my fingers typing feverishly.

I gave a reading in New York City with Denise Duhamel around that time, too. I think the reading happened before the poem, but I can't say for sure. In some ways they seemed to happen simultaneously or for the poem (though I know it's impossible) to have manifested the event. Maybe the reading had been scheduled and the poem was my paranoid, imagined, worst-case-scenario of the forthcoming event since I knew my parents planned to attend.

The weekend of the reading, I convinced two of my graduate school friends to make the road trip from Cincinnati with me. We stayed the weekend in the apartment of my uncle's brother Bill, a musician and composer who owns a flat in Spanish Harlem. I recall his apartment as a magical, open, artistic space, a grand piano—where he practiced and taught students—the focal point of his large living/dining room. That trip remains a highlight of my graduate school career. My two friends and I caught an Off Broadway production of Oscar Wilde's "An Ideal Husband." We ate pizza from a street vendor and had drinks at the Plaza. We bought funky sunglasses and dipped into record shops in the Village. The night of the reading, my parents and two of my brothers drove into town from New Jersey, and we all stuffed ourselves on pasta afterwards at a cozy Italian restaurant nearby.

Who was I reading when I wrote the poem? It's hard to say. So many voices haunted my psyche at the time. I was studying for my Ph.D. comprehensive exams and consuming an enormous array of poetry and fiction. One of my areas of study included twentieth-century poets in translation. Awash in the language of Neruda, Rilke, Lorca, Drummond de Andrade … their playfulness, their passion, their rich sonics (even translated!), who knows how I might have been shaped by that work or by the twentieth-century American and British poets I checked off my list: Elizabeth Bishop, Philip Larkin, T.S. Eliot, Yeats…? My attic apartment was strewn with books and notecards. It was a mess, and I was a mess.

In the middle of a divorce, and hopelessly in love with a married man who had young children and who was never going to leave his wife. I didn't know who I was. I had poetry and poetry had me—it was the one steady presence in my life, helping me to voice and make sense of the confusion, the pain, and the excitement that was a part and parcel of my existence through the course of my Ph.D. studies.

I'd married at age twenty-five, somehow securing a full-time teaching gig in western Massachusetts with only a master's degree, but after several years, the funding for my job got cut, and my husband (who taught high school science) and I made the decision to apply to Ph.D. programs (in psychology and poetry, respectively). When we received acceptances with funding to programs in Ohio (but three hours apart from one another), we were thrilled.

A month after we'd begun our programs and were living separately, I fell in love with a fellow graduate student. Several months later, having confessed to my husband, started couples counseling, and broken things off with the fiction writer, I fell in love (again!) and began a years-long affair with the married man whose presence can be felt through the whole of *Bodies That Hum,* and who definitely figures importantly in the emotional tenor of "My Father's Nightmare."

How can a young, untethered woman, whose relationship with her parents has been loving but distant, explain her multiple affairs to them? We'd never talked sex in my family. Ever. The extent of my Mom's sex ed talk with me happened during a car ride when I was in sixth grade, and she asked, *I understand you've been learning about sex in school, do you have any questions?* I mumbled a faint *no,* practically crawling out of my skin with embarrassment. She clearly didn't want to talk about sex with me either.

The poem is over-the-top and suggests a speaker/woman/daughter who is totally comfortable with an in-your-face sexual persona. She is almost the opposite of who *I* had been through most of my life. Raised Catholic, until I was a junior in college, I thought I'd "save myself" for marriage. Then (being both naïve and having an unhealthy relationship with my body) my first sexual experiences were unpleasant at best—horrifying at worst. Julius, my first husband, patiently coaxed me through what I now know amounted to trauma therapy after I'd been both inappropriately groped and kissed by multiple men when I was a girl and then date raped as an adult.

Graduate school and meeting so many like-minded, creative people opened me up to the possibility of an intense, mutual, emotional-sexual encounter. And poetry helped me work through the trauma and the anger and the loss I was processing—to heal in a certain kind of way. Poetry at its best enables us to get at the truth beyond the truth: to access parts of our psyche that we don't fully understand, sometimes not until well after a poem's creation. "My Father's Nightmare" represented my coming to a place of acceptance of the dualistic sides of myself: the Catholic-raised naïve and damaged girl I had been, and the (more) fully realized sexually vibrant 30-year-old woman I was becoming. The poem also bridges the space between my family of origin—the conservative/conformist world in which I grew up—and my chosen profession/peers who were liberal and liberal-minded and gravitated toward complexity. My father and mother had wanted me to become a scientist or mathematician. They were confused by my creativity—they thought of writing and reading more as hobbies than as a through-line for a successful professional career. Still, there I was (gasp!), a poet: publishing, giving readings, becoming a known writer. I was probably as surprised as my father. "My Father's Nightmare," I hope, pokes fun at and teases out these complicating family and psycho-social dynamics.

I'll mention in closing that I showed the drafted poem to Ellen Bryant Voigt soon after I wrote it. That version ended before the last scene with the mother entering the poem. Ellen told me that the poem wasn't finished. I balked when she said it, but later, I knew she was right—she almost always is. I worked on the end and finally, that last segment emerged. The father of the poem needed to come to a place of acceptance, as did I. Those final words, "She's always been a pretty good girl," are indeed his and mine. I will always be a pleaser, and (mostly) a do-gooder, and even if I am a poet, I will always be my father's daughter.

Janice N. Harrington

Layered Pigments

White pines, deer,
three crows in flight, and in a craze
of pastel strokes—a waterfall.

Holding his canvas, I listen to the water's slip, the beat
of hooves against matted duff, the cawing crows.
I see his labor and the flames that burnt it all: the drawing
that hung once on our basement wall, a phantom image
in my mind, inside a frame he built himself.

Sadness, why do you mutter? Why are you here?
A black man drew and sorted light.
He made *Waterfall with Deer.* He left us.
He left me—his imagining, proof that I too
might imagine, see beyond or despite or take
for mine this chaotic light and open black wings
in flight. Yet how poorly he layered and blended,
the colors plied in quick, shallow strokes—hardly an artist.
Have I misjudged or judged too quickly?

The boy who sold tickets to the peanut gallery,
to the colored seats, who would never
let his children wear red or colors too loud, surely
he knew the shadows, the lines, the things erased,
the contours given to all things black.

Ghost, you brought me *Waterfall with Deer,*
or *In My Father's Eye* or *What the Fire Took*
to hang, by whatever name, between my ribs.

It hangs there still. In the night, I hear the scrape
of a colored pencil, quick strokes,
someone imagining, choosing.

The Layered Pigments of Elegy and Racial History

"Layered Pigments" had other titles: "Waterfall with Deer," "Meditation on a Colored Folk Artist," "To Use Shallow Strokes," and several more. It moved from a modest nineteen lines into a multi-part, poetic sequence and back again to one poetic unit. It changed rhythm (stanzas, couplets, and tercets) and visual shape. Once it started with the following line: *The fad for adult coloring books ended by late 2017,* and another time with the words *Without throat or tongue or tethers of flesh / my father sends this sign,* and another time with *Unbidden, startling / as a pheasant's cry / from the swaying bluestem.* All to say, I struggled with this poem. At one time (before I came to my senses), the poem featured my father, and a Jewish electrical engineer from Chicago, and Adolf Hitler.

> Hitler too kept colored pencils at his desk
> and used them to study maps of the war,
> the encroaching lines of Allied Troops. Imagine
> if he were forced to make a hash mark
> for every death, or wound, or prayer;

My goal to reach beyond the personal led to strain and forced connections. But eventually my writing on and meditation over the work of folk artist Horace H. Pippin, in a book of poems called *Primitive: The Art and Life of Horace H. Pippin,* led me to re-imagine my father as a self-aware artist (not just a hobbyist). I asked *why* he drew pictures and what a palette of colors might have meant to someone who grew up during the Jim Crow Era. The poem merged the elegiac with race and racial history. I expanded it by delving into areas suggested by my father's life in a small rural town in Alabama where his life intersected with the color line. Gradually, the poem came to offer a broader definition of grief as not mere sorrowing but as the resurrection of uncertainty and unanswerable questions: what does a Black father leave his abandoned daughter? How should we judge a Black artist? What signs do the dead send to us?

It takes strata of color to shape a vibrant colored-pencil drawing. But a poem layered with words and lovely lyrical description can grow heavy and slow, drained of urgency. I decided to pare away the word-weight and begin with a brief description of my father's drawing, a drawing that triggered my own questions. Why did a drawing long ago destroyed in a house fire return to memory when my father died? What did his forestscape reveal? Why did I remember this one drawing but not others? I wanted to place an unexplained image in the minds of readers so that they too might wonder why and what and who.

The poem goes beyond visual description, however, and presents the *sound* of water, hooves, and crows, immersing the reader in the drawing's imagined world, a world that a Black man has made and has shaped boundaries for. Afterward, the poem moves into an explicit question: sadness, why are you here? Implicitly, it questions: what did I learn from my father's art? And then the poem questions its own understanding: maybe I didn't know him. In earlier versions, after the opening I tried to "paint" a stronger image of the artist.

> Self-taught, he knew nothing of layering and blending,
> of minute circles and color plied in shallow strokes—again,
> again, again—till glacially it built its bright architectures.

or—

> Haunted, I hear his pencil's wander. I hear the hooves of deer,
> and water spilling in long ladders. I hear flames nothing
> will ever extinguish now. Does he say, Mr. Samuel C.,
> that I have lost nothing and nothing can be taken from me?
> Does he say that art is now the only language we can share?
> Does he say my moments will be more than this: a frenzy
> of quick impressions, erasures, cross-outs, skewed perspectives?

or—

> he returns to a world his flesh has set aside
> to find me. His pencil moves back and forth, back
> and forth, making its music. Perhaps he wants me
> to follow him, or to enter the picture,
> *Waterfall and Forest with Deer,* or to follow
> the pencil (erasures, cross outs,
> the lead pushed inward or breaking beneath
> a heavy stroke), or to listen to the worry
> and frenzy of a pencil slide again, again
> across a cardboard canvas.

But again, the wordiness, even though striving for lyricism, drained away the poem's energy. I deleted lines and stanzas. I tried to allow the poem to ask its questions and to plumb the speaker's grief. *Why* such sadness?

The poem moves from the personal to the historical, and then toward its resolution. A West African proverb explains that no one is dead until they are forgotten. I am haunted by my father's colored-pencil drawing, an image that has grown into a bond and almost my only communication with a lost father. As the proverb implies, my father is not forgotten, and so he lives. The fact that he lives in memory meant that I couldn't end the poem with lines such as *Def, he would have said, not death, the softening useful. / Sometimes a lack of clarity makes the best precision,* or close it with *Forest, waterfall, deer, and three crows—/ black v's, in the farthest corner of his canvas—in a sky / they can never enter and never fly beyond,* or with any of my other flawed attempts that sounded too abstract and did not connect to the poem's main questions, or that didn't address the father that I could still hear or feel. The final revision suggests instead that both the heart and the poem are spaces where the dead continue to act, that making art is a way of grieving and of keeping lost ones alive. We wrestle with the images left to us, how to understand them, restore them, preserve them, and merge them into our living.

Terrance Hayes

A Poem by You

I cannot say where a successful poem comes from or goes, honestly, but I know what it feels like to have an unsuccessful poem stay with me. More common than the feeling of a poem worth talking about, is the feeling when a poem is stalled. I carry flawed passages and revisions everywhere. "A Poem by You" is my attempt to sidestep a conversation about a poem while moving in the direction of actual practice. I believe first and foremost in a poetics of practice. At the root of "practice" is *praxis*, which is Greek for "doing." "Practice" as in exercise, application, as in "practice what you preach." "Practice" as in "to do or perform often, customarily, or habitually." In law or medical or middle-school basketball practice, practice is where you exercise your craft. Practice is where you experiment and take risk, where you can "fail," but where failure isn't really possible. Practice is where failure means try again.

To "grasp" literature, I think you have to practice it. Giambattisa Vico, the eighteenth-century Italian philosopher came up with the theory of "Maker's Knowledge." His principle, which states that truth is verified through creation or invention, is in contrast to Rene Descartes' much more well-known notion of truth verified through analysis. *Cogito ergo Sum.* "I think, therefore I am." Vico offers an alternative, or adjacent view of how knowledge is gained. Not *I think therefore I am* as the beginning of inquiry, but *I make therefore I grasp.* According to Vico, "the criterion and rule of the true is to have made it." You gotta hold it (insert love/truth/understanding) to know it. For Vico, we can only know what we make: computers, cars, systems of government, but not what we do not make: the universe, the mind, the soul. Only making a poem reveals what a poem is made of. In discussing a poem, my aim is very much akin to the "give a reader a fish versus teach a reader to fish" mentality. I think anyone trying to understand a poem, should write a poem.

A POEM BY YOU

A poem by you is so translucent at birth
you can almost read your fortune drifting
beneath its skin like the letters in alphabet soup.
It eats as much as it poops and pukes, and wallows

and wails to be cleaned. To woo it into being,
recall a favorite refrain. If you softly sing
the refrain no matter how awful or muffled
or muffed, the poem will adore you.

There can be no right or wrong with what you make
If the poem fattens on the ink in your vessels and veins.
The poem is born with fangs. Because it is a creature
easily entertained by your attention, be decadent

with your care. Though it will quickly outgrow its outfits
continue dressing it in refined designs, lavish tones,

and elaborate patterns. Teach it to prize mystery
over generalization. Let it wander. Don't explain.

> QUOTE A LINE OR REFRAIN FROM A SONG OR
> POEM YOU ARE MOVED BY.

Consider any misstatement, misunderstanding
or misgiving an opportunity to improvise.
Consider any misstep a moment to dance. How free
are you when grief, euphoria and uncertainty arise?

What shape is your head on the inside? Would you see
through dots, circles, glasses, walls, or windows
if you drew a self-portrait of yourself? Be surprised.
The hour is momentous because you are alive.

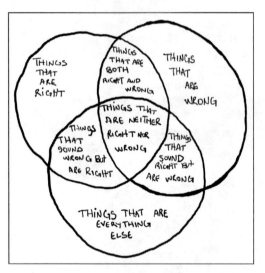

Fill your sentences with nonsense, senses and scents
such as the smell of a name written in beach sand
with the business end of a matchstick or lipstick
on the lips or on the mouth of a bottle of water.

Measure residual and residential resonances
such as the syntax of your father's snores and sores,
the traces of fur and smoke in your hair and pockets,
the advanced sensations of your unprecedented witness.

What would you say is your mother's favorite
color in the poem? It's okay if she'd say otherwise.
My mother's bathroom towels, bathmats and curtains
were a surreal, cerulean, baby boy blue, for example.

The walls were cornflower with a satin finish.
But her favorite color may be leopard print or paisley
or floral pastel or maybe the pearly polyester
of a wedding dress bought on sale at a second-hand store.

IMAGES/OBJECTS/ THINGS YOUR FAVORITE COLOR
1.
2.
3.

She sent me pictures wearing the thing.
Her cheeks were hastily rosied, her joy was dazzling.
The poem makes you aware of the people around you:
The people before you and the people behind you,

the people who come after you and the people
behind you. It will venture wherever you will it.
Have you gone to knock at your window to find
a transparent countenance awaiting release?

Did you open and enter both carefully and carefree,
with a look peppered in swing and discernment,
deliberate, demented and slightly dramatized?
Did you then sit and watch the night begin to glow

as you noted the enchantments? One hopes so.
You may conjure fire roaming the edge of sunset
like an adolescent looking for dinner
if you cannot recall the aroma of evening's arrival.

> FINISH THIS:
>
> I AM AS _____   AS A _____
>
> FULL OF_____.

Because I cannot remember myself, I conjure
my son shipwrecked in his bedroom with the name
of his girlfriend burning like starlight in his head
though he may have simply been waiting to be fed.

Or I conjure the cloistered water burnishing the edge
of morning when my daughter studies her shimmer
humming in the bathroom mirror.
If you have no children, what can it hurt to conjure

nicknames for the twins you raise in a dream.
Are they frank or merry? Do they fuss or cuddle
watching movies? Do they whisper together
in each of their mother's ears? Details are up to you.

> DESCRIBE A FAVORITE CHILDHOOD TOY

The poem is like the old black woman smoking
a few rows back on the train purring to someone nearby,
"Would you like one of my cigarettes, Honey?"
Followed by a sort of barked chirp, the sound of a swan

> BRIEFLY EXPLAIN HOW YOU GOT A SCAR SOMEWHERE
> ON YOUR BODY.

snarl, a little sawtooth lilt snappy as two bony black
batwings on a Rottweiler, the bite of a beguiler
when she snapped, "Then why you all
up in my goddamn mouth?" The poem is like that.
Try to overhear the things. The poem can grasp
the sounds in Saginaw and Akhmatova,
It has a sense of the weather all over,
it demands forest walks and swims in forbidden lakes.
Give the poem a piece of your mind when it's mean
Or careless, its dirty socks and underwear everywhere.
Discipline it with vision. Assign it permanent watch:
Birds-eye, bullseye, stink eye, but permit blindnesses.

> OFFER AN IMAGINARY DEFINITION OF YOUR LAST
> NAME.

One wild bean can transform into a capricious beast
when cared for expressively. Any day you take note

is noteworthy. Try to mine the sort of magic required
to stay alive, mine the plots and lowlands filled with folk

making holes in God's dominion, mine the way rain
unbuckles and bursts by like a bustler down the block,
gone in a pound of minutes. Measure the music
in everything. Let the poem have it.

HOW DID YOU COME BY YOUR FIRST NAME?

It will help to tell yourself the poem is in your grasp
Though it may be shaky as a matchstick bearing
the will of a flame. The poem prizes the freedom
of mouths above all other power, freedom of teeth,

Freedom of glossolalia, freedom of shouting
and shushing and sharing syllabic babble and turns
of phrase, consonants curling in the jaw, the tongue
adorning vowels, flocks of plosives, the sometimes counter-

intuitive calculations of counterculture, counter space
and counterparts. Canoodle the intangible where possible.
When harnessed, the inscrutable can flower,
the mouth becomes more than a trapdoor,

the phantoms shake free of their shackles.
Try to overhear the things you say to yourself.
The poem is able to travel the time and relative
dimensions in space between your ears and eyes.

WHAT'S YOUR FAVORITE THREE-WORD SENTENCE?

Who can say better than you the way you dream?
The poem is the bestowal of your selfishness,
The currency of your current thinking and feeling
between heaven and earth. You can swallow the sky.

FINISH THIS:
I AM NOT AS_____ AS THE SMELL
OF _____.

The poem is a private pirate time traveling creation,
yes, but it is important you share it with someone.
Otherwise, everything disappears. You must vow
to share it with someone before I see you again.

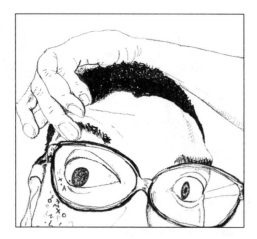

That could be anytime, that could be anywhere.
You must vow to read it aloud. Practice is suggested.
It's right because you made it. Are you brave enough now
to see what someone else makes of what you've made?

Construct a poem using only the most charged parts
   of another participant's responses to at least three
   prompts.
Repeat their favorite three-word sentence at least twice.
   Use the subjective first-person "I" (eye). Return to
   author.

Edward Hirsch

For the Sleepwalkers

Tonight I want to say something wonderful
for the sleepwalkers who have so much faith
in their legs, so much faith in the invisible

arrow carved into the carpet, the worn path
that leads to the stairs instead of the window,
the gaping doorway instead of the seamless mirror.

I love the way that sleepwalkers are willing
to step out of their bodies into the night,
to raise their arms and welcome the darkness,

palming the blank spaces, touching everything.
Always they return home safely, like blind men
who know it is morning by feeling shadows.

And always they wake up as themselves again.
That's why I want to say something astonishing
like: *Our hearts are leaving our bodies.*

Our hearts are thirsty black handkerchiefs
flying through the trees at night, soaking up
the darkest beams of moonlight, the music

of owls, the motion of wind-torn branches.
And now our hearts are thick black fists
flying back to the glove of our chests.

We have to learn to trust our hearts like that.
We have to learn the desperate faith of sleepwalkers who rise out of their calm beds

and walk through the skin of another life.
We have to drink the stupefying cup of darkness
and wake up to ourselves, nourished and surprised.

Something Wonderful

Detroit, 1979. I used to write in a fast-food joint just off the corner
of Woodward Avenue and Nine Mile Road. It was shockingly unpoetic, a

neighborhood called Ferndale, but I liked the light in the booth by the corner window, and people mostly drifted in and out without paying attention. The staff left me alone. It was a couple of miles from our house on the other side of Eight Mile Road, the rougher side. I'd walk up the street with the cars whizzing by and get myself into some sort of semi-altered psychological state, some drift of reverie or semi-trance. I'd say things over and over again to myself, lines and phrases, or recite poems by poets I liked—at the time, I was memorizing the French surrealists, Paul Éluard and Robert Desnos, who could block out the racket and put themselves into full-fledged trances. I suppose I was trying to carry my overnight mind into daylight working hours.

The first line that came to me was *"Our hearts are thirsty black handkerchiefs."* I had no idea what it meant, or what our hearts were trying to drink or salve. There was something inside of me that was trying to get out. I imagined our hearts flying around: "Our hearts are trying to get out of our bodies." No, "Our hearts are getting out of our bodies." No, *"Our hearts are leaving our bodies"*—that was it. I could see the empty Fair Grounds across the street. There was a place called "The Last Chance Bar." I wanted to throw down something rich and strange.

It was a four-coffee day. I was still working in the late afternoon. Large cups of insomnia. The opening of the poem came to me as a sort of challenge: "Tonight I want to say something wonderful…." That was my premise. I repeated it to myself a couple of times and scrawled the title at the top of a page of lined paper, "Something Wonderful." I felt as if I was waving my arms around as I was walking home down Woodward Avenue. I was not—my hands were at my sides. But I was excited—I had found my project. My job was to figure out what something wonderful was going to be.

Night after night I returned to the poem, day after day. I was a serious insomniac in those days, and I was writing a group of intermittent poems chronicling my experience. I liked the set-up of insomnia in a poem, the lone individual who is still awake at night, the sole consciousness, the spot of lamplight in the dark. I thought I might extend the range of those poems and turn to something different. I had been a sleepwalker as a child. My family had a lot of stories about my nocturnal escapades. I seemed to have a penchant for trying to leave the house at night, even in the dead of winter. Once, I woke up just as I was stepping outside into the freezing cold. The cold air blasted me awake. Sometimes my parents guided me back to bed, sometimes I returned on my own. I had strange dreams—I felt I had been walking somewhere, but I couldn't quite remember where. By the time I wrote this poem I was no longer a sleepwalker. I was still a fitful sleeper, but I no longer needed to walk it off. That personal history is the backdrop. I'm not sure why, but it never occurred to me to write a poem about my own sleepwalking; for some reason, I wanted to write a poem for all the sleepwalkers, those who are walking off by themselves in the night. A community of solitaries. The individual incommunicado turned into a citizenry.

I love the poets of comic holiness—Christopher Smart, William Blake—and I wanted to capture a sort of desperate joyousness. That's how I heard the beat of the lines. It started—"Tonight I want to say something wonderful." That was very grand. My idea was to lift off and then take it down a notch: "Tonight I want to say something wonderful / for the sleepwalkers." That seemed nicely targeted. I'd extend the line: "Tonight I want to say something wonderful / for the sleepwalkers who have so much faith…." That seemed grand and quasi-religious to me. I thought I'd take it down a notch again: "Tonight I want to say something wonderful / for the sleepwalkers who have so much faith / in their legs…." That seemed comically deflating. I thought I'd lift it again: "Tonight I want to say something wonderful / for the sleepwalkers who have so much faith / in their legs, so much faith in the invisible…." I was veering wildly between the deflationary and the sacred. I thought to blood the image, work out the implications, dramatize the story:

> Tonight I want to say something wonderful
> for the sleepwalkers who have so much faith
> in their legs, so much faith in the invisible
>
> arrow carved into the carpet, the worn path
> that leads to the stairs instead of the window,
> the gaping doorway instead of the seamless mirror.

This seemed to hit the note I wanted, something funny and miraculous.

That's the operant mode of the poem. I was following a line of thought and working out a dream logic. There is a framing device operating throughout, a speaker who is very much present, even a little intrusive, making claims, establishing a poetic: "Tonight I want to say…"; "I love the way…"; "That's why I want to say…"; "We have to learn…." This speaker is connecting the dots, trying to make sense out of dream life, an imagery that keeps going off the rails, heading out into the inexplicable night realms.

The surrealist images, which are hopefully welled up from the unconscious, are placed in some sort of context and consciousness. This highlights the tension in the poem between form and formlessness, the shapely three-line stanza and the wild imagery that keeps breaking loose, the incantatory buildups. I was challenging myself throughout, continually upping the ante: "That's why I want to say something astonishing…." You make a statement like that and have to come up with something that seems

astonishing. Much of the poem is a search for the right simile or metaphor, some figuration that will capture the strangeness of our hearts flying
around, our unleashed thoughts and feelings. And I was consciously trying to make meaning out of the images, the experiences, my hymn to the
unconscious.

"For the Sleepwalkers" is a poem that tries to make sense out of something that is both very ordinary and very strange. There is something daily
and reckless in the simple experience of going to sleep at night, something
I have never quite been able to figure out—the nocturnal life, some stupefying nightly oblivion. For a while, we're allowed to go to sleep and wake
up again to the world, nourished and surprised. We find a way to return to
the quotidian life. It seems so simple, but it takes a sort of desperate faith.

Jane Hirshfield

Today, When I Could Do Nothing

Today, when I could do nothing,
I saved an ant.

It must have come in with the morning paper,
still being delivered
to those who shelter in place.

A morning paper is still an essential service.

I am not an essential service.

I have coffee and books,
time,
a garden,
silence enough to fill cisterns.

It must have first walked
the morning paper, as if loosened ink
taking the shape of an ant.

Then across the laptop computer—warm—
then onto the back of a cushion.

Small black ant, alone,
crossing a navy cushion,
moving steadily because that is what it could do.

Set outside in the sun,
it could not have found again its nest.
What then did I save?

It did not look as if it was frightened,
even while walking my hand,
which moved it through swiftness and air.

Ant, alone, without companions,
whose ant-heart I could not fathom—
how is your life, I wanted to ask.

I lifted it, took it outside.

This first day when I could do nothing,
contribute nothing
beyond staying distant from my own kind,
I did this.

On Writing "Today, When I Could Do Nothing"

Poems, like climbing peas, have their lattices, the circumstances and conditions that allow feeling and thought to take hold, deepen, climb. This poem was written on March 17, 2020, the first morning of shelter-in-place protocols in the nine San Francisco Bay Area counties, the first in the country. A new book, *Ledger,* had come out from Knopf on March 10. I'd read in New York, Chicago, Seattle. After that, everything cancelled. Now, others' lives and plans had also stopped. All around, as if under a sudden deep snow, was stillness. One line in the book seemed, oddly presciently, to describe it: "You go to sleep in one world and wake in another."

Silence is the strangest of crisis-manifestations. I sat on the front room window seat, laptop open, thinking I'd work on one of the still-doable book-launch tasks, a written conversation with Mark Doty, for *Guernica.* Instead, I listened, I looked. I saw an ant, where there wouldn't ordinarily be one. After a while, I took it outside, came back in, and heard the words: "Today, when I could do nothing, I saved an ant." A sentence plain enough, yet recognizably the start of a poem. Its sound and tone are *formal*—by which I mean that it isn't quite natural speech and also that these are words aware of themselves as the music of making, the formation of meaning. The fly-fisherman's cast is in them, the spinning sound of unspooling search.

The world-going-on-as-it-does is sufficient unto itself. It doesn't need a poem to be complete. Yet a person, well, a person sometimes does; especially if they carry certain hungers, curiosities, perplexities, restlessnesses, dissatisfactions. If they carry the wish for an increase of heft, or the wish to murmur confusion into changed comprehension.

A poem isn't an action, not exactly. Yet it carries the keyrings of agency and change. "Idea" is also too narrow a word for what a poem holds. Poems shape a lintel of language, tone, time, and music: they fill, but also hold open, a space for passage.

The request of this book was to describe how some particular poem came to be written. But I do think it worth noting that the moment before the poem arrives is the most important. The hunger for something still-unknown, but searchable out by words, is poetry's gravity. As still unexplained as the gravity of physics is, it constellates stars, planets, ants' nests, stories, stanzas, verb forms, the m-dash, the white space. The first thing needed to write a poem is *need.*

And then, to be a person not only speaking, but listening. Listening backward in time, to all you bring with you into that moment. Listening forward in time, for something that does not yet exist. Listening also to this very moment and for what else of the world and of words may want to enter. Listening to hear the words that come, and then to hear the question you may not know you had but have already started answering, the question that will shape to itself the poem's arrival and revising.

That is how it was for this poem: it began with a listening met by its opening sentence, then the listening for what might follow from that premise. What came into it first were thoughts close to the ones I'd already been having: wondering how the ant had come in; noticing that the paper had been allowed to be delivered. The poem's thinking, though, like its opening sentence, was different in quality: it is under tension. Poetic voice is made by diction, selection, distillation, invention, direction of looking, reticence and revelation, but also by certain choices of arc and shape. This poem is centripetal. It orbits its precipitating shock, the abrupt erasure of ordinary life.

Poems search by moving, by exploring, as the ant did, searching its own continuance and future. This poem describes, speculates, ponders. It also recalibrates. The thought "I am not an essential service" struck me as both a little funny and also medicinal—as the accurate perception of one's place in the world generally is.

I remember the happiness of finding "silence enough to fill cisterns," the happiness of describing the ant as a bit of self-detached ink, a newspaper's punctuation mark suddenly walking. Such small by-gifts of imagination restore resilience. They hold the promise that expanded seeing, change, imaginative freedom itself, are still possible. But they were not yet alterations of the day's understanding—not yet a completed poem. And so, the writing returns to observation and description. To find any way forward, simply to continue to write, is one way to allow to slip in the undertow question, the self-knowledge of subject a poem hasn't yet found.

This poem found its own necessity when its explicit question arrived: "What then did I save?" Had I done any good? As it turns out, I may have. An editor from the *San Francisco Chronicle* phoned a few hours after the first draft was finished, to see if I might have something they could run that spoke to the moment; the poem, published two days later, circulated widely. An entomologist soon emailed to say that the pheromone-tracking ability of ants is strong: if it had been set down anywhere near its colony, it would have made its way back.

For the poem, though, the doubt is the point. Its center is the powerlessness felt by a person who has no resources to bring to a crisis's direct repair or rescue. This helplessness of witness was tuned not only to the 2020 pandemic. The crisis of virus joined the crises of environment, inequality, social justice, hunger and wars; multiple political crises; decades of watching my own species' too frequent failures, of kindness, of kinship-connection with all existence.

A poem is both an emergency and an emergence. It requires an ending, however provisional—some "momentary stay against confusion," in Frost's invaluable phrase. And so, more informed of its own directions of doubt and disturbance, this one turned back again to the doorway of description. What slipped into that invitation first was tenderness, intimacy. "How is your life?" echoes a haiku written by Basho, when, deep in his final illness, the poet suddenly wondered how his neighbor down the road might be doing. The change of looking felt, again, like a shift into a larger sanity. One's own life and separate well-being aren't all that matters.

This still, though, wasn't an ending, though ending felt rhythmically, musically, near. When you can't find a poem's close, one thing to try is going back to some premise already present. "I lifted it, took it outside." The poem repeats its opening gesture, to see what has changed. And something has. "This first day, when I could do nothing" holds an enlarged seeing: if this day is the "first," others will follow. To use the language of film, the camera has pulled back, into a long shot. "When I could contribute nothing, beyond staying distant from my own kind" admits powerlessness, but also recognizes inaction as action, a contribution the ensuing months—I write this piece in mid–October of 2020—have proven out. Staying separate in a pandemic is consequential. And then, the last line: "I did this." The pronoun points both to moving the ant and to writing the poem it closes. A line of three equal beats, musically sure, conceptually, grammatically, and emotionally ambiguous. The sum felt right. Had I done nothing? Yes. Had I done something? Yes. Had I done nothing? Yes.

Christine Kitano

Dumb Luck

Such luck, I think—driving to work, wheels skidding
      to a hard stop when a chipmunk darts in front of my car,

pauses, then scurries back into the browning shrubs.
      Motionless in that moment, the possibility of one

outcome gives way to another. Then breath, then the voices
      on the radio, then they're saying my name—no, the name

of Dr. Christine Blasey Ford, who has entered the Senate Chamber,
      taken a seat. I look around at the empty street, press the pedal.

In exaggerated whispers, the reporters blithely describe her, surprised
      she's not a "surfer girl," as a woman "under a lot of pressure."

I'm late for work, unusual for me, but earlier this morning
      had heard from a friend about another friend, that her husband

has left her, just months after their marriage and announced pregnancy.
      What terrible luck, I said, then wanted to take back, not sure if "luck"

was the right word. This news, and the news on the radio, skirt
      each other in my mind, strike sparks when they get close.

Then this: in college, I waitressed at a Korean-owned sushi restaurant
      in an unassuming strip mall where I would arrive straight

from class, apply lipstick and eyeliner using a simmering pot
      of miso soup as a mirror next to the chefs knifing clean the fish,

sloughed scales sharp and translucent like chips of glass.
      It was luck that had gotten me the job, or so I believed—

over eighteen and authentically Japanese (half, anyway)
      and enough comprehension of Korean (the other half) to get by

in the kitchen. Korean enough to not question tossing salt
      on the front stoop to chase away bad luck,

like that night a man walked into the restaurant,
      lifted his hoodie just enough to reveal the triangle butt

of a gun tucked into the waistband of his jeans,
      then walked out with our fishbowl of dollar tips.

My boss's mother, the cook, ran from the kitchen hurling
        fistfuls of salt, cursing the gods, her son, and me.
I admit I was distracted by the greasy swastika inked
        across the man's throat, can still see the wound's wet.
Then, not so much bad luck but still rude, one time an *ahjumma*
        from my boss's *gye* group tossed a crumpled napkin at me,
which hit my chest before landing on a tray I was carrying.
        And many customers would, at some point as we ferried
platters of raw fish to their tables ask us
        where we were from, where we learned to speak
English. Once, a table of white men asks to make me
        a deal: they'll bring me a pie if I say, "Me love you long time."
They're older than me, but not by much; they wear trucker-style caps
        backwards, the mesh pressing into their pale, fleshy foreheads.
I remember then the sound of their laughter, then their faces reddening,
        then the odor of sweat and hormones and stale beer, and the words
spilling out my mouth before I had full comprehension:
        "What kind of pie?" It was a joke, I thought, or think I thought,
but their howls sent a phantom finger down my spine.
        After my shift, my boss handed me a wad of cash,
said the group had "tipped big," to buy myself a hamburger
        on the drive home. I counted the bills in my car, under a streetlamp
in the parking lot, all those soy sauce-stained one-dollar bills.
        I think of myself then, nineteen years old, alone in a dark parking lot,
money fanned across my lap. Nothing but unearned luck has kept me
        safe and alive these thirty-three years, a dumb, gift-luck
whose mouth I pry open every morning for inspection.
        But not this morning. Through the radio speakers
I hear a woman shivering. I think of my friend, newly pregnant,
        also on her way to work, how she'll twist a ring off her swollen finger.
I think of the tattooed man's eyes—what I thought was desperation
        but maybe was not, was maybe hate, or power, or fear, or even
hunger—how I couldn't hold his gaze, my eyes unable to resist
        the twisted omen he'd chosen to stab into his flesh.

                                        *

When I was nineteen, alone in that dark parking lot, dollar bills spread
        on my lap, thinking (of all things) about a hamburger, I failed to notice
the white pickup truck that will pull out after me, follow me down
        each side street, the red laughter of the men in my rearview mirror,
and for a breathless moment I recognize how this scene is narrowing
        to that one outcome, how it feels inevitable, like the easing on
of a mask for a role I had been destined to play. But no. But what luck.
        I lost them, made it to the anonymity of the freeway where I maneuvered

through five lanes of easy traffic, the chorus of identical brake lights
    a radiant red shield. Despite the betrayal of my own mouth, through
no good choices of my own, I survived. But is there no other word
    for it than luck, or as my mother would later say, *bok*, fortune—
in her eyes, something you're either born with,
                    or not. Such *luck* to get home safe
when so many do not; is there really no other word?

What Is the Ethnicity of the Speaker?

I first began drafting this version of "Dumb Luck" in September 2018, and the movements of the poem mirror the drafting process. I was driving to work and listening to Dr. Christine Blasey Ford testify in front of the Senate about how Brett Kavanaugh had sexually assaulted her when they were in high school. When the reporters on NPR announced her name, for an instant I thought they were calling my name, "Dr. Christine." The moment sent a surge of adrenaline through me, and I found myself holding my breath as she began to speak.

I try to write daily for thirty minutes, and much of what happens when I sit down to write is "doodling." I'll describe what I see outside the window, the day's weather, anything notable that happened on the drive to the office. Most of these doodles never progress beyond the pages of my notebook, but sometimes I'll strike an image or memory that becomes the kernel for a poem. On the day of the Blasey Ford hearing, I got to my office and sat down to doodle. I described listening to her name called by the reporters and lingered over that feeling when I thought they were saying my name. Why did I feel such a punch in the gut when I heard this? What might I be called to testify for? It was also around that time, during the widespread coverage of the #MeToo movement, that a friend had asked me if I had ever been sexually assaulted. I answered "no," and in that moment marveled at how lucky I was to be able to answer in this way. I felt lucky, blessed, fortunate … but all these words seemed somehow wrong. This memory came to mind, and I knew there was more I wanted to explore about this confluence of experiences.

I often find that the present moment feels neutral and un-noteworthy; it's only in hindsight that urgency and significance reveal themselves. Therefore, a large part of writing a poem is working with memory, discovering the past through the lens of the present. For the past several years I've been teaching a first-year seminar for college students, where we spend dedicated time talking about how to transition to college life—academically, socially, and otherwise. Teaching this course has allowed me to reflect on my own college years, from which I now have greater objective distance. Though it seemed utterly mundane at the time, it now seems remarkable that I waitressed at a sushi restaurant in a strip mall in Riverside, California, as an undergraduate. I was twenty, and not even legally allowed to open a bottle of wine in front of a customer. And though scary things happened (all true as documented in the poem), at the time, they didn't feel notable, certainly not anything I'd put in a poem.

But years later, talking with my undergraduate students, I note how much time has passed since I was their age. How young they seem, and the realization of how young I was, and how vulnerable. The next realization, of course, is how vulnerable I still am. And it was this realization that propelled the first draft of this poem. It began with thinking about Dr. Christine Blasey Ford, then my own luck, but then my own vulnerabilities. I began remembering more about my time as a waitress, and how all those indignities were symptoms of larger systemic issues that put women—and in my case, women of Asian descent—in a constant state of fear, so embedded in my life that it's almost invisible to me except in retrospect.

I wrote a draft, then another. I am a slow drafter and reviser, so the fact that it took me three years to publish the poem isn't necessarily indicative of anything other than my usual writing process, though I did feel a particular impulse to be patient with this poem. Some poems can't be rushed. I shared several early drafts at readings, but knew the poem wasn't yet ready for publication. I was primarily concerned with portraying the speaker as a full, present person as I didn't want her to come across as a one-note victim. I continued to flesh out her story and to try to dramatize the tension between the present and past.

Then, in early 2020, I saw a call for submissions for *#We Too: A Reader*, a special issue of the *Journal of Asian American Studies*. The editors were looking for submissions of critical and creative work about sexual violence against Asian Americans. One of the questions posed in the call was, "What does sexual violence look like in the lives of those hailed as 'model minority'?" I submitted a draft of the poem and received fantastic feedback from the editors, erin [*sic*] Khuê Ninh and Shireen Roshanravan. Among the questions they asked about the poem was one I had never been asked before: What is the ethnicity of the speaker? This question, among others, helped me to recognize more of the invisible, unsaid contexts surrounding the poem, things I had taken for granted, things I believed my audience wouldn't care about. It was through this revision process that I also recognized a psychological hurdle that was holding me back: I thought the poem wasn't worth writing because the speaker is ultimately safe and unhurt. Recognizing the various ways this idea—that my story was not worth writing about—had been conditioned into me, and then working past this, learning in a sense to allow myself and my real experience to be the center of my own poem, was a revelation.

A poem is never a complete story. But this poem is an accurate record of how I wanted to tell the story at the time of its writing. For poets, this may be the most we can hope for our work.

Yusef Komunyakaa

My Good Hand Plays God

My thumb & index finger
    frame a zero, then an 8

sleeping on its side, & I say,
    Leonardo, show me how

the miraculous scapula
    moves like a torn wing

half-fused, barely unstuck,
    & a life dares to lift off.

Floating rib, boomerang flat—
    if it comes back or not,

I don't have the stomach
    for doubt & vivisection,

reshaping flesh, muscle,
    & tone into a portrait,

or mock-up of a machine
    glimpsed on the edge

of destiny, a daydreaming
    five hundred years early.

What if, born out of wedlock,
    a silky caul over his face,

Leonardo brushed light under
    skin of oils, science & art.

I could stand like man-X
    moving toward night-

time, feet parted, ready to do
    some one-handed magic,

singing Judas's old plea.
    My left hand holds up

a sketch, showing a way—
    good hand & bad hand,

circle half-broken, let there be
a truce, embrace the fall.

The whole contraption of
gore & math, just here,

as I go over the blueprint,
hand raising the brain

to higher order, working
in the dark, step for step,

hovel to temple, & I draw
a cross down my chest.

The Hands

I have long believed that the human hand has bearing on the evolution of the modern brain. Think, given the hand's propensity for almost unbelievable dexterity, it would have naturally influenced the journey of humankind, who we are. I have always written my poems first in longhand; and then I type them, before revising them with pencil or pen. And then I'd retype the poem into what I could finally trust—let it linger for a while. Indeed, writing is process, and each poem is shaped, made. Seldom, if ever, a poem leaps out of one's head onto the page.

On January 7, 2018, I suffered a stroke. The right side of my body was impaired; my dominant right hand was paralyzed. After spending over a month in bed at the hospital and rehab, I typed the title of a poem (which remains unfinished): "At the Top of the Staircase." I had spoken a ream of lines into my cellphone not yet transcribed. Of course, after my stroke, I sat, wondering about a swarm of things. How did I survive that morning on the staircase? Would my health continue to improve? Had I been lucky, blessed?

Thinking such thoughts, naturally, I knew I would attempt to address the stroke through writing. I had a dialogue with myself. Should I write essays? Or, maybe I'll write a one-man play? I was in bed, unable to move my body, scared. I had already spoken hundreds—no, thousands of lines into my cellphone. I was happy that I could speak. I could hear in rehab the opposite of that reality: the urgency of certain sounds that erupted from the mouths of a few patients disarmed me almost as much as it frightened them.

Then I said, "My Good Hand Plays God." The line arrived through an impulse of language and music residing in me. I knew it was the title of a poem. Sometimes a single phrase tells the poet where to venture, what's important, and how to capture feeling. I knew the line suggested to me that the cranium is a temple, but perhaps no one else would have readily understood this.

Why did the first four couplets have to open as a question to Leonardo da Vinci? Perhaps the speaker responds to the fact that this master crafts-man learned how to produce an alive image of the human body in an ate-lier of death.

I first visited Italy in May of 1988. I traveled there on behalf of the Poetry Society of America with William Matthews, Stanley Plumly, Heather McHugh, and Deborah Digges. One early afternoon, after visiting the Ideal City, we went to an open market where I bought a copy of Leon-ardo's *Notebooks*. Upon returning to Bloomington, Indiana, while reading the *Notebooks*, I became taken by how this artist's mind worked. In fact, he was more than a so-called Renaissance man. Years later, at an exhibit in Florence, I was amazed by his drawings of horses, how he captured a mus-cularity of motion in time and space. It was as if he began in their core, and had drawn his way out, motivated by mind and feeling. The poem's speaker addresses Leonardo directly, as if both are in a theater of autopsy where many of the classical artists were tutored on the natural designs of and within the human body, as if they had to know the interior to capture the exterior—especially the radiance of skin in classical art.

First, I wrote the forty lines of "My Good Hand Plays God" with-out stanza breaks; but after reading it through several times, I realized I wished to slow the poem down, and to let the reader take in the images, jest, etc. I thought triadic. Then, I felt the poem had to be rendered in cou-plets—bridges of constructed, regulated silences—light and sound as movement. Yes, a poem has to breathe. Not as something to be resolved lyrically or metaphorically, but as a near-physical reckoning. I tried to imagine how Leonardo must have stood before those subjects of death, and how they had allowed him to see inside the body and map the inter-nal and external contours of human flesh. Were such moments of tutelage truly methodical enquiry or at times merely intrigue, and could my cou-plets hint at living lines of calibrated feelings on a journey? Could they convey the two-handedness of the brain?

In the fifth to ninth couplets, the speaker queries himself through what he knows of the master artist Leonardo. But this self-interlocutor arrives at a juncture where he does not wish to encounter anything that takes him out of this world.

A couplet can contain wholeness, movement, or it can be a release that creates a turn in the narrative. I shall not point to where such may exist. The eyes and ears of each reader do that work, and in this sense, reading—especially poetry—is not passive. In fact, it is often an action. The reader or listener is fully in the poem, because a single word can shape a metaphor or vary meaning in language. I want the poem to grow slower, as if within a paced meditation.

Then in the tenth couplet, the speaker shares a conceit regarding Leonardo's linage. In a sense, this moment creates a different bridge, perhaps rendering him more an ordinary man. But does birthright have anything to with this artist's individual spirit and tenaciousness? Perhaps it became the foundation of this artist. Did he live his life as a dare, pitted against his inherited birthright, and does this fact have anything to do with the innate determination of this unique person? For the artist, most likely the human body was first dissected on a sheet of paper—diagrams and measurements, etc. Here is the moment when sentiment and abstraction are exchanged for one's knowledge of tools and actual knowhow. Did he have something to prove to the world, something that would embrace his existence, his state of being? Did he think of the human body as a complex, living, natural prime mover? And was the wounded to him merely a doppelgänger?

Of course, innuendo exists in the body of this poem. The tenth couplet is an example, but as the poem expands and the sentence unfolds, the eleventh couplet becomes a positive force. Leonardo grew into himself, regardless of birthright and societal rules. Because of the force of his talent, genius, and works of individualized perfection, he becomes a symbol of the modern man, perhaps even the power of religion: "science & art" and "man-X" could be now. Matter-of-fact, man-X is a symbol on a T-shirt I brought in Florence. And it seems a rather progressive symbol when placed beside some of our recent branding.

Throughout "My Good Hand Plays God," the speaker is rather informal, even in life and death matters. I wanted each couplet to be self-contained, and yet an internal part of the overall imagistic terrain.

Sometimes, I recite a word or short phrase that changes the tonal arc of a poem, and that happened when I wrote "contraption" in the seventeenth couplet. I erased the word. But I said the phrase five or six times, thought about the meaning, the music on my tongue, and then I reinserted the word: "The whole contraption of/gore & math, just here…." I had returned to a fertile moment when I first read Leonardo's *Notebooks* and saw how he had designed objects, gadgets, and instruments—some functioned and others seemed to merely exist for their shapes and mystery casted. In this sense, I do not wish to comment on the science of art. But Leonardo was definitely an observer. Not only did he see how something was made, he seemed to have had the capacity to see into things—corporality and the ethereal.

The last couplet surprised me. It was one of those moments when a poem ends and one feels that there's no other place it can continue. If I feel a poem has traveled slightly beyond where I know and feel it should end, I revise from the bottom, which usually means cutting words, phrases, and even stanzas. I have a philosophy that each reader or listener can reside as a co-creator of meaning, and there's a little door left ajar. In the last couplet of "My Good Hand Plays God," the speaker becomes an artist. Or, perhaps the speaker is only a dreamer when he draws a diagram, which links him to the living and the dead, as well as the past, present, and future, even if it happens in a world of dreams. The act of creating art and truth can be transformative, and one may come to see the small moments of existence differently. Recently, I placed my right hand lightly on a table and my body rose to a straight standing position. And this, I felt, was a feat, a moment of active grace.

Ted Kooser

An Entrance

She appears at the edge of our vision
wearing an ankle-length red winter coat
and a trailing white muffler, looped once
then draped loosely, as she quickly steps out
of the side balcony's velvety shadow
and into the house lights, her coppery
shoulder-length hair phosphorescent, afire
at the edge of the auditorium's murmur:
the orchestra tuning, the strings having
their own conversation, that brief quarrel
resolving. We watch her locate her row,
excuse herself to those there, and step in
with the wave-like, side-to-side motion
of something afloat, her back turned to us
as she bobs over the low crests of knees
pulled back to one side or the other
and, nodding, excusing, she approaches
the one empty seat, two-thirds of the way
out across all that brief irritation,
as the house lights dim once, and then
once again, and she faces the rest of us,
looking us over, then carefully drapes
her coat and her muffler over the back
of her seat, turns away and sits down,
tossing her hair, an explosion of flame
as the house lights go out and the curtains
begin to squeal open, and now the director
pinches his reed-like baton and a fanfare
blares out of the end of it, welcoming her.

Poems of Gesture

In recent years, I've found myself trying to describe people in motion, being a poet who likes to describe things, and I've written poems about watching a man leave a day-old baked goods store with a plastic bag of bread in each outstretched hand, about a child sliding through one of those colorful plastic tubes on a play-set, about a woman in jeans with rhinestones leaning into a truck to talk to the driver, about seeing a man flicking an ash from a cigarette at a glance as I drove past, and so on— poems of what? Well, let's say they are poems of *gesture*. In these I try to stay out of the way and let the description do all the work. I don't need to be in those poems, and I wouldn't like being there if I were, calling attention to myself, mentioning what I was wearing at the concert, whether I liked the music on the program. Please! No opinion!

Instead, I just want my reader to see what I've seen, without having to suffer my opinion or feelings about what we're seeing together. I want to be the spy in a chair in the hotel lobby, peering at someone over the top of a newspaper I'm pretending to read. My job is to see and record.

All I ask from a writer is an account of what he or she has seen while out and around in the world. If she returns to the mouth of the cave where our community is clustered and waiting for her and tells us about a red and green dragon who chased her through the forest, that's all I need, all I want. Just the account. I don't want to learn that she stubbed her big toe on a stone and that it's now swollen and throbbing, and do we have any aloe in our first-aid kit? I want to see that dragon galloping toward her, breathing fire.

I woke up the other morning with the image of the woman I describe in "An Entrance" in mind. We've all seen this woman, arriving late, arriving right at the opening curtain, stepping on everyone's best shoes as she makes her grand entrance. Could I describe that motion, that sideways, step-to-step, scissoring movement down a narrow row of auditorium seats, over the knees, over the feet pulled back out of her way, as if seen from a few rows back?

The main problem in writing description is in doing so in a manner that enables the reader to see what we want them to see. That requires a measure of specificity. If, as a poet, I say there are chickens on the highway, the reader sees what he or she wants to see: five chickens or forty chickens, and white Leghorns or yellow Buff Orpingtons, or ... if I want to control their imagining, want them to see the same chickens I see, I need to offer some guidance, to say "a dozen white chickens are out on the highway." If your poem is entitled "Midsummer in Kansas" and you mention a tree, you don't need to say that the tree has green leaves. We readers expect green leaves in midsummer in Kansas. Mentioning leaves is enough. We supply the color. In "An Entrance," I want the reader to see that red coat, that white scarf, that coppery hair standing in contrast to the absence of description of the colors in the auditorium. Had I neglected to mention the color and style of the coat, the reader would have to supply a winter coat of their imagining. But again, one doesn't want *too much* description, too many modifiers. The challenge is in being judicious, in offering detail, but not too much.

One might ask, is it *enough* for a poem to describe a person doing something like this? A critic once wrote a review in the Sunday *New York Times* that my poems were "good, but not good enough." Perhaps a poem like "An Entrance" doesn't do it for you, but for me it's enough. For me, it's plenty. It's not a grand, profound poem like "The Wreck of the Deutschland," but it is what it is. It's a "slice of life." A slice of life's enough for me.

Elizabeth Bishop was once asked what kind of a poet she was, and she said that she was a "descriptive poet." And while my "An Entrance" is nothing so fine as Bishop's "The Fish" or "The Moose," it's something, as we'd say in my family, "along the same lines."

Dorianne Laux

Facts About the Moon

The moon is backing away from us
an inch and a half each year. That means
if you're like me and were born
around fifty years ago the moon
was a full six feet closer to the earth.
What's a person supposed to do?
I feel the gray cloud of consternation
travel across my face. I begin thinking
about the moon-lit past, how if you go back
far enough you can imagine the breathtaking
hugeness of the moon, prehistoric
solar eclipses when the moon covered the sun
so completely there was no corona, only
a darkness we had no word for.
And future eclipses will look like this: the moon
a small black pupil in the eye of the sun.
But these are bald facts.
What bothers me most is that someday
the moon will spiral right out of orbit
and all land-based life will die.
The moon keeps the oceans from swallowing
the shores, keeps the electromagnetic fields
in check at the polar ends of the earth.
And please don't tell me
what I already know, that it won't happen
for a long time. I don't care. I'm afraid
of what will happen to the moon.
Forget us. We don't deserve the moon.
Maybe we once did but not now
after all we've done. These nights
I harbor a secret pity for the moon, rolling
around alone in space without
her milky planet, her only child, a mother
who's lost a child, a bad child,

a greedy child or maybe a grown boy
who's murdered and raped, a mother
can't help it, she loves that boy
anyway, and in spite of herself
she misses him, and if you sit beside her
on the padded hospital bench
outside the door to his room you can't not
take her hand, listen to her while she
weeps, telling you how sweet he was,
how blue his eyes, and you know she's only
romanticizing, that she's conveniently
forgotten the bruises and booze,
the stolen car, the day he ripped
the phones from the walls, and you want
to slap her back to sanity, remind her
of the truth: he was a leech, a fuckup,
a little shit, and you almost do
until she lifts her pale puffy face, her eyes
two craters and then you can't help it
either, you know love when you see it,
you can feel its lunar strength, its brutal pull.

Love in Spite of the Facts

> Science is how we solve problems.
> Art is how we cope with them.
> —David Zinn, chalk artist

"Facts About the Moon" began in the summer of 2004 at dinner with friends in Eugene, Oregon—poet Maxine Scates; her husband, Bill Cadbury; and my husband, Joseph Millar. We were sitting on a deck overlooking the Willamette River with a full moon out in all its mid-summer glory when one of us asked how the solar or lunar system works.

Bill began to tell us. He was doing fine up until it came to how the earth, sun, and moon rotate in tandem. We used the candle as the sun and the sugar bowl as the moon. The Sweet'N Low ramekin was the earth. For planets, we stole salt and pepper shakers from neighboring tables. No matter how we twisted and turned them, we couldn't quite figure out how they rotated. Hardly anything stumps Bill, and so over the next few weeks, it became a game of looking something up and then explaining it to the others, but we were not getting very far and no one could really visualize how these things rotated.

Sometime later I was watching an amazing special about the moon on *The Discovery Channel.* Among the many facts, one stuck out—since the expansion of the universe, the moon has been steadily and significantly backing away from the earth, which meant the moon once appeared much larger in the past and would only appear smaller in the future. I couldn't get over it. I went to bed trying to imagine this then woke up thinking about it. I was obsessed. I even re-watched the movie *Joe and the Volcano* with Tom Hanks because there's this scene where he's left everything behind, his job, his country, his life, and he's floating in a makeshift raft on the ocean when he wakes to the moon rising over the water. He struggles to stand and face the moon, then he is dwarfed by it: "Dear God, whose name I do not know, thank you for my life. I forgot how big…. Thank you for my life." I read everything I could get my hands on about the moon. That fascination has been long-lived as I'm still reading about the universe and I'm just now finishing up Timothy Ferris' *Coming of Age in the Milky Way*.

The second aspect of the poem is that my extended family was going through a life-crisis, not an uncommon state of affairs for them. While that was in the back of my mind, I was in the process of working to pull away from them. Maybe I became obsessed with the moon as a way to curb my obsession with the latest family crisis, but the tug of the family is tremendous. Even a crazy family can seem better than no family. "Facts About the Moon" is two obsessions in collision.

I was inspired by the moon at first, then by the facts, then by human affairs in relation to the facts, then love vs. the facts. The sweat and tears occurred while figuring out how the lunar system worked, imagining how the sky looked to people eons ago, wondering what it was like to be made so small by the moon, how bright it must have been at night, and how dark the night sky will be in the future. This was a fun, curious, childlike kind of thinking—not too much sweat and few tears, except for thinking about the suffering of my family, and the moon. I had thought about it abstractly in my head for months so when the poem finally arrived, it came out fairly close to being finished.

Listing the facts in the poem was in some way my only concern. The form is open and easy, just a voice speaking in a fairly regular broken line. The leap from the planetary to the personal might have been a technique had I thought of it consciously, but I didn't. It happened naturally, organically, without my being aware of it until the poem was finished. I thought the poem was about the moon and these two people I had made up—the woman and her boy, strangers to me, but then I realized they were my mother and my sister, or my sister and my niece, in disguise. There's the violence of the situation, too; the adolescence-out-of-control; the mother alone; the fuck up, little shit; the family-in-crisis; the Philip Levine-ish forget us; the guilt and shame and what have we done; and the in-the-final-hour love of it.

This poem is more of an example of how facts are negotiated. There are scientific facts recited one by one, and then the fact of human love set against those facts. Human love, especially family love, is complicated, scary, irrational, and messy. The moon's historically romantic symbolism is also set against this more complicated aspect of human ruin, and love: unjustified love, harmful love, a kind of unconditional love, or love in spite of the facts. The narrative appears halfway through the poem and so the lyric is set against the wall of science. My hope is that the human narrative gives life to the facts or that the facts give life to the narrative.

Around the time I wrote "Facts About the Moon," I was reading James Wright's *Above the River*. He's famous for making leaps, so he was probably an influence. Philip Levine's uncompromising vision and voice was influential as well. I showed the poem to my husband when he got home from work and he made some suggestions, then to my writing friends who made a few more. I called Bill Cadbury right after I wrote the poem as it felt like the culmination of all our failed research. He said, "I think you've got a winner there." It felt good. In that sense, the poem was written for Bill who was a linguistics professor for thirty years at the University of Oregon, and our little group of moon-gazing poets. Clearly, I write for him and them, too.

Science is new, but the human side of things—that's my ultimate interest. Who are we in relation to the world around us? What, here on earth, is the meaning of our lives?

I like my poems to be understood by anyone walking down the street, waiting at a bus stop, driving a cab, waiting tables, or even a mother sitting in a hospital room with a kid who has OD'd. Unfortunately, those people read very little poetry. Even so, I write for them.

Sandra Lim

A Tab of Iron on the Tongue

Each time you see a full moon rising,
you imagine it will express
what your life cannot otherwise express,
that it's a figure of speech.

This really means watching yourself
turn something unknown into
something manageable.

As human tendencies go, this one is not
so terrible, and possibly winsome, besides.
Say *November*, and you name
the death working itself out in you,
season after season.

Call the bed you lie down into each night
a *raft* or an *island*, depending on
whether it's love or work you're running from.

Every moon has so much to say
about the unsolvable losses.
When it disappears behind a cloud,
filled with its own shining intentions,
it's an important translation.

When Schoenberg pointed out
the eraser on his pencil he said, "This end
is more important than the other."

The Lunacy of Lyric Poetry

When I sat down to write "A Tab of Iron on the Tongue" one night in late fall, I mainly remember that I had a feeling about the cold weather that I wanted to get down on the page. I don't think there was a full moon outside my window, and even if there had been, I imagine in that case I might have been slightly self-conscious about addressing that most *de rigueur* of all lyric subjects. But the chill in the air probably raised the idea of the moon in my mind. At any rate, if not the moon, I had before me at least: a freighted image; a weight in my mouth brought on by the cold air; a stirring sense of pointless beauty; and maybe even an acoustic and visual hint of the *o's* that will pop up here and there throughout the poem. I also had the Schoenberg quote that I liked (originally cited by John Cage), copied down at two different instances in my notebook, but the impulse to use that came in much later.

I've come to think of writing poetry more and more as the outcome of a blocked understanding between the conscious and subconscious mind. In my poem, my conscious mind was busy with an idea about the moon as a formal link to the invisible forces around us and within us. This notion is neither particularly inventive nor grievous. The conscious mind goes on to consider some things figured by speech, naming objects and concepts in the third and fourth stanzas, as it tries to figure out what the urge to signify the moon means or avails. There's a bed, the month of November, love and work and the drama of the seasons. I recognize my conscious preoccupations in these topics, but my use of italics, in retrospect, alerts me to another instinct: I wanted to highlight the words, for a moment, as pure signifiers with those italics. That is to say, I wanted that gesture in typeface to make the words themselves at once stress meaning and shoot past their metaphorical objectives.

As I now reread this poem, I see where my subconscious was at work in the last two stanzas, or rather, where the conscious mind intensified its engagement with things going on beyond its reach. Its awareness of its own frustrations are there in the summoning of disappearance, translation, and erasure; it really can't *see* around its own preconceptions about paraphrase, ineffability, etc. But while the conscious mind is busy thinking, the call back to the elusive nature of the moon in the penultimate stanza animates the notion of the subconscious doing its work in a poem. I believe that the subconscious wants nothing less than alchemy in a lyric; that's the deep thrill of commission, for a poet, to act on the world, even if acting on the world in this case results in the shape of relinquishment. The deliberate non-sequitur of the final stanza returns us to the physical properties of the poem: it reminds us that writing and erasing might be hard to tell apart. In the end, the moon is not a figure for ineffability itself. Rather, it is a figure of the unconscious, which is intimately and sensuously known, even by the mind. Ultimately, I wanted the image of the moon—as whatever the bullying superego can't touch or articulate or moderate—to open out inside the reader's fine and private night of imagination.

The coldness of the moon intimidates and allures. Its conviction leaves no room to moralize or project psychotherapeutic language on it (despite my repeated attempts). Or so goes my story of this lunar beauty; it provides a kind of sensibility, which is why I think so many poets go to it. The moon is both serious and terrified of being sentimental. The hang of the moon has something of the artist's disinterestedness, as well as the serene movement of truly free consciousness. These are all further projections still, yet I trust that my subconscious mind knew I was most interested in this seductive unfathomability and eerie dispassion. Even the light of the moon itself is light reflected from the sun; it neither claims nor pretends to possess the world.

Some of that pleasing inscrutability and aristocratic remove is in the Schoenberg quotation. I liked the tone of grave certitude applied to a humble call to expunge. It is also sort of playful. Moreover, the image of conjectural, hovering white space seemed to expand the ending, rather than sum things up and close things off. I think this is why I ended the poem with this quotation rather than began with it. Maybe, too, I wanted the quote simply for the alternative taste of white in the image of erasure, after the metallic black in the title. So the moon becomes a poem becomes an eraser becomes an absence becomes a sensation that cannot be put into words—and slyly, almost punctiliously so. The poems that I favor explore what goes on within us without formulating it as a statable, reducible concept. Like the moon, they have a saving complexity.

What compels the imagination starts in that confusion of life and art: a crispness in the late autumn air is mistaken for momentousness, or a feeling of helpless yearning is sensed as a bitter taste in the mouth. In a state of solitude and abstraction, I came to the fact of aging (*November*) and the lonely bed, doleful things both. I can despair over the outcome of all our existential homework (death, it's never quite "manageable"!), and over a love affair that will come to reveal itself as somewhat minor in the scheme of my life: so emotion means both a lot and nothing. The poem knows this, down to its nerve endings, and some of its lunacy lies in the fact that it wants to develop and extend this knowledge that the mind can just barely intuit.

Adrian Matejka

Gymnopédies No. 2

In NYC, we stalked fishes
      in filets of sounds: delivery
      engines & ashy doors

clapping shut, venders
knuckling their fin & silhouette-

      shaped words into salty
expectations. My daughter

& I walked down a couple
      of slim-bricked blocks
      that smelled like snapper

& afro sheen with no afros
in sight. On snaggletoothed

streets, we double-took the wet
alleys where things jumped

off the hook like smart seafood
      before lunch. We parted

the perfect & abundantly wintered

streets. My daughter said,
I know these parts, like a tired
      pianist resting on her bench.

What Really Happened

One of the great gifts of poetry is that it is portable and transportable. Like the memories that often inspire it, a poem can be carried in a notebook or glove compartment, shirt or pants pocket, without interrupting our usual folds and creases.

The same applies for the act of writing poetry. Poems can be written by anyone with a desire for self-expression. Poems don't require a lot of materials or a dedicated room to be brought into the world. They can be written on a bench at lunch, in a field surrounded by wildflowers, on church pews and desks, or on a plane while somebody snores next to you.

Because of this, poetry is a great enabler of voices—the art empowers many people like me who were previously disenfranchised, silenced, or otherwise ignored in the larger public discourse. Poetry has the power to amplify the natural voice in protest or praise. It gives us the opportunity to make the inner world audible for others.

I'm thinking about all of the possibilities poetry offers for expression because my favorite poets find a balance between the interior and exterior. Their work is simultaneously public and intimate. A poem like Lucille Clifton's "[cruelty. don't talk to me about cruelty]" speaks to personal experience while also being a critique of class, war, racism, and economic inequity—"when i wanted the roaches dead i wanted them dead" her speaker says, "and i killed them. i took a broom to their country / and smashed and sliced without warning." The moment remains personal and exact even as the metaphor becomes more public and more violent.

The whole poem is a revelation, but the public metaphor is what confounds me the most. How is it possible to take something as personal as trying to clean the kitchen and write about it so broadly? How does a poet use autobiography to activate emotions in others? I'm not a particularly open poet in that I'm not as comfortable sharing my personal experience as "autobiography" in poems for fear of saying too much.

Emotional autobiography, sure, but I'm less inclined to include specific episodes because it's so easy for me to get caught up in what really happened rather than exploring the surprise of what might have happened. How many times has *what really happened* been used to excuse mediocrity in a poem? This gets even more complicated as it relates to dear friends and family. How can we write about or for those closest to us with any real clarity? How can we make metaphors out of the people we love?

I'm asking a lot of questions here because these are the same questions I was struggling with when I wrote "Gymnopédies No. 2." I have mostly avoided writing about my daughter for years even though I wanted to catalogue every trip to the park and all of our minor adventures the way most proud parents do. I simply couldn't figure out how to craft something that would do her or those experiences justice.

I couldn't figure out a form or framework for something that would need to be complex, yet still legible enough to embody my love for my daughter, my perspective in those moments, and also her autonomous movements in the world. Robert Hayden did it in "Those Winter Sundays" even as he captured the most essential part of divide between people: "What did I know? What did I know / of love's austere and lonely offices?"

Sometimes the truest moments of the poems are those in which the poet is lost or doesn't know and finds the way later. Hayden is looking back on his father's morning ritual with remove and a mature-enough perspective to evaluate everything. He is able to see clearly—just as Lucille Clifton does—the ambiguity of experience that gets clarified with distance. It's impossible to know anything in the middle of the action. It's only with reflection that most realizations happen.

"Gymnopédies No. 2" is a simple reflection, an urban pastoral inspired by Eric Satie's composition of the same name. The moment of the poem is modest enough: a father and daughter are walking down Mott Street in New York City for the first time. The soundtrack of the city follows them as they try to find their directions, the distance between where they started and how to get back there.

Distance and geography in poetry has always been a mathematic equation for me. Lucille Clifton talks about taking "a broom to their country" while Hayden takes a similar approach with "the chronic angers of that house." In poetry, knowing where the action happens is as important for me as the octave of the lyricism or the brightness of the simile. Distance matters in verse the same way it does in the world.

For most of my daughter's seventh year, I worked in a different city from where she and her mother were living. I only saw her on the weekends when I made the five-hour drive between the town of labor and the town where my daughter was. Love is physical, and in those days, the physicality of it became overwhelming. I missed my daughter so much I would wake up crying after useless dreams. The pictures of the two of us I had up in my rented basement studio didn't cut it. Video calls after school and before bed just made it worse somehow. I finally decided that I needed to write about this absence, the deep sadness I felt every day despite all of the questions I've posed here about the efficacy of writing.

In this poem the form and elevated white space are meant to reflect both the distance I felt from the experience and the refraction of the sounds around the father and daughter in the poem. That's what poets and parents do. We build little, movable worlds so that those receiving them might commiserate. It's all we can do. It's the best we can do. All of this reflection might seem adjacent to craft, but it isn't: at its finest poetry transposes those things we can't articulate through our sobs or through our fist-shaking anger. It can, when given the right frame, distance, and geography, gift someone else with the insight of the ancestors.

Airea D. Matthews

If my late grandmother were Gertrude Stein

I. Southern Migration
Leech. Broke speech. Leaf ain't pruning pot. Lay. Lye. Lie. Hair straight off. Arrowed branch and horse joint. Elbow ash. Row fish. Row dog. Slow-milk pig. Blue-water sister. Hogs like willow. Weep crow. Weep cow. Sow bug. Soul narrow. Inchway. Inches away. Over the bridge. Back that way. Fur. Fir needles in coal. Black hole. Black out. Black feet. Blame. Long way   still.
        Not there.   There. Here.   Same.

II. Feed the Saw
Old Crow. Liquor. Drink. Drunk. Girdle. Grits. Grit. Tea. Grit tea. Tea git. Get shaved. Shook. Shucked. Shit. Flour. Flower. Lard and swallow. Hardedge chew. Chipped tooth bite. Tool chip. Bite. Bloat. Bloat. Bloat. Blight seat. Blight sit tea. Be light city. Down town dim. Slight dark. Old Arc. New Arc. New Ark. New work. Newark. Lark-fed. Corned bread. Bedfeather back. Sunday-shack church fat. Greased gloved. Dust-rubbed. Love cheap-heeled shoes. Window seat. Mirror eye. Window. I. Window. Window. When though. When though. Wind blow. November.
December. No cinder. No slumber. No summer. Branch. Branched. Blanched. Fried. Freed. Fly. Want. What.   Want. What. Graves want.

III. Miscegenation
Good. Smooth. Curly-haired baby. Baby rock-a-bye. My baby. Mama rock-a-bye that baby. Wrestle the earth, baby. No dirt. No. Dirt-shine. Shine. Shine-neck. Porcelain. Tin. Tarnish. Powder milk. Pout her. Milk. Powder-silk inheritance. Front the washtub. Top the bed. Bin. Leaky numbers run in. Run in. Run on. Red fevers hold your palm. Sweat it out. Hot. Hot. Heat the rest. Pretty melt that wax. Wide flower. Ellis-Island daddy. O, Daddy's bar. Banned. Mongrel hum. Come. Come now.
Little bones bend. Old crack. Creak. Crank. Crick. Curly-Q. Fuck. Them. Then fuck them. You hear me. Walk through good-haired baby. Half of you.   Belong.

IV. Gertrude Stein
Who. Bills mount. Picasso. Who. Matisse. Who. Mortgage. No currency canvass. Pay brushes. Stroke. Stroke. Bridge. Brittle. Blend. 10 miles daybreak. 10 miles they break. They broke. No brick. Widgets in the envelope. No railroad green. Agriculture. Pea snap. Earth under nails. Spine and stilt woman. Roach-kill heel woman. Roaches in the crawl. Woman, creep. Keep 5th grade. Every where. Wear every where. We're every. Where. Any. How. We sacrifice and hammer. They sacrifice the hammer. Never. Ax and hatchet make callous. Hard hand. Prison-pen privilege. Prison. Privilege pinned. Bar-thorn pinned. Pine cross. Crown. Weight. Weight. Wait. Iron is harder. Chicken fat can is full of spark. Spark kill. Ore. Sparkle. Or. Spark cull. Spark.   Cull. Hoe. Heave. Heave-holy. Heavy. Heavy. Heavy lights genius. That is that Gertrude.   Who.

If Ain't Is

I didn't like Gertrude Stein's work for a very long time. When I had to re-read *Tender Buttons* for a grad school course, I doubled down on that dislike. In fact, I was so angered with the way she bucked convention, largely because she could, that I took to Facebook and wrote a status message that intended to parody Stein's writing through the voice of my late grandmother. Two or three days later I took the stat down because I wanted to more deeply interrogate what exactly it was about Stein that got under my skin. Why was I feeling so viscerally oppositional to her writing and style, and why was I triggered? My contemplation and cobbled-together reasons led me to excavate my relationship to aesthetics and language as well as my own beliefs around language as a cultural commodity.

Then and now, I have found language to be a currency of power, freighted with a social consciousness that we tend to believe is inborn but actually arises from a feverish human need for hierarchy. In its very essence, language is as much about perception as it is about relation, and perhaps it even favors the former functionally. That is, through speech patterns we arrive at a preset of assumptions about the values of people, and then intuitively decide the appropriate course of interaction given these latent clues. And to the poet, of course, language always possesses a certain lyricism, and within that lyricism, a revelation—a brief but plausible rendering of one's humanness.

But as language wields this undefined power, what happens when it becomes the touchstone for human respectability? Class, race, gender— certainly all these things and their political tensions are embodied in the everyday vernacular we choose to use and disuse. As language mirrors our socialization, how is it even possible to escape the judgments tied to identity as it is outwardly perceived? More consequential, for many of us anyway, is the question of preserving identity and its tenets while navigating a world that stubbornly resists nuance in what it *perceives* to be the correct way of living or speaking. In this particular hierarchy, those who speak or behave with regard for the established formal convention of the time are awarded the power of the benefit of the doubt: naturally *presumed* to be intelligent, pleasant, well-adjusted. Of course, white supremacist logic would have it that even this grace is not afforded to everyone equally, which suggests to me an entanglement between language and the ongoing power struggles of race and class.

I've always thought about these double standards in the reception of literature. Many acclaimed writers and artists have imitated, borrowed, or flat-out lifted from folk culture with universal praise for "candid" or "avant-garde" work. Even with such appropriation, the natural inventors of the cultural canon not only go unrecognized for their contributions, but often face derogation for the same practices that literary elites appropriate as their own. So then, if language truly is a core belonging of identity, what is the mode of non-compliance that asserts self-possession and, more existentially, importance in the world?

"If My Late Grandmother Were Gertrude Stein" is a poem about the fraught tension between spoken language and respectability. Concretely, it is a poem written in the voice of my late grandmother. Structured in four distinct movements, which take the form of distinct, thematic prose blocks, the poem strings together a biographical mediation on my grandmother's life: born and raised dirt-poor in rural Alabama in the early 20th-century with only a 5th-grade education, she moved north to Newark during the Great Migration. She fell in love with my grandfather, who was two decades her senior and a Sicilian immigrant, and later gave birth to a mixed-race child, my mother, in an era of anti-miscegenation sentiments. As a Southern black woman of her time, her language was firmly steeped in a form of English that was non-standard and largely unpopular, a form that would come to be known as African American Vernacular English (AAVE). Her sentences were quite often fragmented or incomplete, auxiliary verbs were largely absent, double and sometimes triple negation, articles often omitted for the sake of pith, and any number of phonological variants were employed. Her style of storytelling relied on a metonymic streams-of-consciousness, as her relaxed sentence structure conducted a special flair for dramatic, free association. She was always negatively judged for the way that she spoke, especially by white elitists of the North who figured that anything black and Southern was intrinsically lowbrow. But she was also a woman of pride and wit who never stood for any insult to her character or capability. I wanted to write a poem that pushes back against the constructs of propriety, situated in the crucial moment of judgment wherein one's spoken language becomes an operable proxy for their whole life's value, the simple way to place humans within the hierarchy.

Equally, "If My Late Grandmother" interrogates a certain irony that I picked up on while re-reading Stein's work in my grad school days: my grandmother's pattern of speech was eerily similar to Stein's paratactical writing style. But, of course, the reception was inconsistent; Stein, who lived a comfortable life as the daughter of a railroad baron, was able to capitalize off of a signature syntax that was not truly hers, but an aesthetic simulation. Her work has been interpreted as a challenge of formal conventions of language, a brilliant exercise of agency in art. Meanwhile, my grandmother never wore a mask: the way she spoke was simply the way she spoke, unabashedly, for her whole life. But she was often labelled ignorant and, even worse, treated as though she were undeserving of dignity and respect. While her authenticity had racialized consequences, Stein's pretension found eventual reward in literary criticism. Disturbed by this extreme privilege, I wrote not only to linguistically engage Stein, but to celebrate my grandmother and her black working-class heritage.

I wrote this piece in the vein of auto-theory as I imagined my grandmother would narrate it. She, like many of us, was never slowed down by the nasty fate of judgment; life went on, after all, forging new struggles from the sinew of the last. The final movement of the poem directly engages with Stein, as promised by the poem's title. I had to only imagine what my grandmother would say had she been told that Gertrude Stein tried to imitate her speech, and I wrote the response, a typical question reframed as an assertion: "Who." This forms the poem's voltaic shift from the speaker's personal memoir towards a propulsive self-reckoning, a realization that her living holds worth notwithstanding the constant rejection and devaluation of her identity. There is a resolution of ignorance, but not an ignorance of the self—my grandmother knew who she was perfectly well. Rather, the defiant ignorance towards Gertrude Stein serves as a testimony to what is truly impressive: not Stein's uninventive imitation of syntax, but my grandmother's undying pride in hers, which she held onto even when it did not benefit her socially, artistically, or politically—a style not for show but for survival.

Language dares to risk in this way. Born from time and isolation, it is only useful should it be the pillar of a culture or community, a tool for shaping and reshaping identity around an assembly of shared values represented in distinct symbolisms. But to stay faithful to it requires both a self-understanding and a sense of how we are understood by others, which is dynamic and ever-changing depending on circumstance. This is the knowledge my grandmother cherished and graciously passed on to me— and so, I write toward and into my inheritance.

Campbell McGrath

The Ladder

The past, a dust-covered shoebox recovered
from my mother's attic, does not open easily.

Webs of duct tape, the ladder one must climb
into the unfinished attic, hot as a coffin—

going up the light bulb shatters
against my skull and the shadows deepen.

But in the end it yields, and photographs spill
across the kitchen table like playing cards.

She in her beautiful wedding dress,
my father in the uniform of youth.

There I am, with a cap gun and cowboy hat
on Christmas morning some geologic age ago.

Further in, deeper down
to the antique black and white images,

yellow-margined, crimped with age,
backed with carefully penciled notes:

my grandmother beside the cottage in Donegal;
my grandfather, newly arrived in America,

on a New York City rooftop with two friends
nobody remembers the names of.

Donegal—that green archaism—
and Manhattan in the 1930s, polyglot dynamo,

all that was great about the Twentieth Century
fermenting in its democratic casks.

And there, in a battered Irish tintype,
is my great-grandmother, Margaret McGuire.

I've never seen her before.
I've never even thought to imagine her.

Widowed young, turned away
by her husband's impoverished people,

with three daughters to raise
and only the needle-work to keep them,

monogrammed handkerchiefs
and lace-edged linen tablecloths, a life

beyond my powers of narrative comprehension,
notations I cannot translate from ancient script.

Donegal derives from the Irish *Dún na nGall*,
Dún meaning fort or tower or castle,

and *nGall*, meaning foreigner, outlander, stranger,
in memory of the conquerors who occupied it.

The Castle of the Stranger.
Which is another name for the past.

In the Castle of the Stranger

Like many of my poems, "The Ladder" springs from the physical landscape it describes, in this instance County Donegal, in the northwest corner of Ireland. Even by Irish standards, Donegal is a remote patch of land whipped by wind and rain off the North Atlantic, a place of sheep-dotted moors and tidal bays bathed in silvery light, and seeing it for the first time, one understands implicitly the tenacity and stubbornness it takes to live there, as people have done for thousands of years. *Donegal* as a word, a name, is a translation from the Irish, as the poem itself explains; it means "the castle of the stranger," or some version of that thought, which, among other things, invokes Ireland's complex heritage of conflict and occupation. It is a simple but haunting phrase, a piece of language at once mysterious, poetic, and rich with history. The difficult beauty of the land, along with the material difficulty of my immigrant grandmother's life, provide subjects for the poem to meditate upon, but its originating moment, the seed from which the poem grew, is that evocative, enigmatic castle.

How does it happen, you might wonder, that a poem's point of origin evolves, by the final version, into its conclusion? I suppose my grandmother is to blame. Writing a poem about your grandmother is not exactly a revolutionary notion, which is perhaps why so many poets have done it, though it would be more accurate to say this poem is "about" three people—my grandmother, my mother, and my great-grandmother—and more significantly about what links them, the ladder of generations which descends into the past, and sometimes rises into a dusty attic. You should not, as the saying goes, "live in the past," but writers end up spending quite a lot of time there. Why? Because we can't write in the present instant, which moves faster than the pen on the page or the cursor on a computer screen. We write from memory, which is the past instantiated within us, or from history, which is a form of collective memory. Language itself—the tool with which we write—descends to us from the deepest human past, and carries historical and cultural reverberations embedded in it, as a castle resounds with the echoes of its bygone builders.

"The Ladder" took four or five years to write, as I put the poem aside and picked it up again, draft after draft. One day I noticed, to my surprise, that there were no longer any sheep or green hills to be found—it had become a poem about history and inheritance, about the ways in which the past defies easy translation. As is often the case, it was only in the act of writing that I came to understand what I was really writing about; more than a form of dictation, or journalistic depiction, the writing process should be a process of discovery. This poem ends with a sudden recognition, a type of discovery, just as it starts with the recovery of those long-forgotten black and white photos, which bring the past to life for the narrator. Formally, the poem employs a similar method, using images to concretize ideas or emotions that are abstract, ephemeral, untouchable. The past is a shoebox, the past is an ancient castle—such images, whether literal or metaphorical, have the curious power to conjure the world into words, uniting reader and writer in an instant of perception. We don't share the same lived experience, of course, but we breathe the same atmosphere, we inhabit the same three dimensions, we rely on the same five senses to interact with the world beyond ourselves. Even death is part of that common inheritance: we move forward through time until the moment our heart stops beating, becoming, in that instant, one more stone in the castle of the stranger.

Dunya Mikhail

The Stranger in Her Feminine Sign

Everything has gender
in Arabic:
History is male.
Fiction is female.
Dream is male.
Wish is female.

Feminine words are followed
by a circle with two dots over it.
They call this symbol 'the tied circle'
knotted with wishes
which come true only when forgotten
or replaced by the wishes of others.

In the town of tied wishes
people feel great anticipation
because a stranger will arrive
today in her feminine sign.
Someone says he saw her
two dots glittering,
refuting another's vision
of a cat's eyes hunting in darkness.
So scary, he says, *how the moon
hides in her red circle.*

Everyone is busy today
listing wishes on pieces
of paper they'll give to the wind.
When the stranger finds them
on her way, she'll collect them
and adorn them to her circle,
tossing off some old wishes
to make space for the new.
They say the dropped ones
will come true.

161

The stranger's lateness
worries those who wait.
Someone says she's searching
for a word to complete
a special sentence,
the gift she'll bring to town.

Another wonders if she seeks
a verb or a noun,
and offers to find her.
A third warns that the stranger
may turn him, with one touch,
into a flower that blooms
for only an instant
before it withers and dies,
her circle throbbing with songs
that cause sadness and elation,
and something so obscure
no one has a name for it.
Will she complete a verb
or a noun phrase—or go solo,
a word complete on its own?
They wonder.

When they finally hear footsteps,
they know the stranger must be near.
Make sure the gate is open,
they remind one another.
They hear clinking—
A bracelet? A chain?

Female Slave Market

In the Arabic language, there's a feminine symbol called taa-marbuta (a circle with two dots above it that determines a feminine word). The literal meaning of "marbuta" is "tied." The tied circle obsessed me, more than any time before, in August 2014 when a market was opened to buy and sell women in Iraq and Syria and elsewhere. The market was called "suq al-sabaya" (female slave market) opened by Daesh (ISIS) members who considered women, namely Yazidis, as spoils of war. I could easily see the tied hands and souls of women who terrorists advertised to their prospective buyers. Later, when I had the chance to listen to some of those women, I felt responsible to have their voices heard, and that's how my book *The Beekeeper: Rescuing the Stolen Women of Iraq* came to be. But, in between the stories, I wrote poems and that's how "The Stranger in Her Feminine Sign" was formed, quietly furious. During that trip to my country (Iraq) after 20 years of absence, I visited the temple of Lalish, where survivors were seeking healing by the spring water. There, I noticed a special tree, which was colorful due to pieces of clothes untied and re-tied on branches by survivors. They believe that their wishes come true when visitors untie their pieces. I wrote a few poems after that special visit back home, and this is one of them.

Robert Morgan

Sigodlin

When old carpenters would talk of buildings
out of plumb or out of square, they always
said they were sigodlin, as though anti-
sigodlin meant upright and square, at proper
angles as a structure should be, true to
spirit level, plumb line, erect and sure
from the very center of the earth, firm
and joined solid, orthogonal and right,
no sloping or queasy joints, no slouching
rafters or sills. Those men made as they were:
the heavy joists and studs yoked perfectly,
and showing the dimensions themselves, each
mated pair of timbers to embody
and enact the crossing of space in its
real extensions, the vertical to be
the virtual pith of gravity, horizontal
aligned with the surface of the planet at
its local tangent. And what they fitted
and nailed or mortised into place, downright
and upstanding, straight up and down and flat
as water, established the coordinates
forever of their place in creation's
fabric, in a word learned perhaps from
masons who heard it in masonic rites
drawn from ancient Rosicrucians who
had the term from Greek mysteries'
love of geometry's power to say,
while everything in the real may lean just
the slightest bit sigodlin or oblique,
the power whose center is everywhere.

The World Made Plumb

My father and my grandfathers and all my uncles were farmers in the
Blue Ridge Mountains of North Carolina. But in the winters, they worked

part-time as carpenters and builders. My dad was a house painter, and he and his brother, Dwight, also worked as stone masons. One of the most memorable events of my childhood was watching my dad and another uncle lay out the foundation for our new house on the mountainside in the fall of 1949. The site was an opening in the woods where my late Uncle Robert had placed a cot for napping, sketching, and reading on summer days after working the hoot owl shift in the cotton mill. He was killed in a B-17 crash in England in 1943. The rusting springs of his cot were still visible in the leaves.

At the age of five, I got to see the bulldozer carve out a level site for the house, pushing down oak trees and making heaps of red clay on either side of the clearing. I was mesmerized by the steam-driven well-digger that clanged so loud its rhythm echoed off the mountains. Trees cut on the slope provided lumber for the house. My parents wanted a dwelling veneered with creek rock, and my dad wrestled thousands of rocks out of the river and hauled them with horse and wagon to the building site.

In the years after World War II, my mother had saved $1700 by working in the cotton mill to build the new house. She kept the money in the post office in town because, having lived through the Great Depression, she did not trust banks. As my dad built the foundation, floor, and began raising the walls, they soon ran out of money. I remember him breaking down and weeping because they had nothing left for buying nails. But little by little the house took shape, in the winters of 1949, 1950, 1951. I studied the plumbers wielding blow torches, electricians stringing wires, and trucks delivering boards, windows, and doors.

I think it was Christmas of 1950 when I was given the best gift ever, a little gray toolbox. Inside were a child's hammer, saw, brace and bit, ruler, level, chisel, pliers, and try square. I would have preferred a cowboy pistol, but I carried the box up to the house, and on winter days while Daddy hammered and sawed and carried boards, I gathered odds and ends of lumber and tried to nail together airplanes, helicopters, and tanks. The Korean War was raging, and on the radio there were many reports of battles.

For the next two years, I spent much of my time attempting to make things—a well-digger with a thread over its tower, speedboats like I'd seen on Lake Summit, a version of the B-36 with its motors turned backwards. I became familiar with the use of the level, plumb line, and knew structures must be four-square, in plumb. A house had to be level as the surface of water, and walls had to stand at a perfect 90-degree angle. However long it took to hang a door or cut the pitch on a rafter, it had to be done exactly. One uncle bragged that, though he'd never gone to school, he could "figure" lumber better than college men. It was said he had a good "idea" of building, meaning he could visualize the finished structure before work began.

When I was invited to teach at Cornell University in 1971, I'd never lived outside the South before. My contract as a visiting lecturer was for one year, and I expected to be back in North Carolina in 1972, doing a little farming and house painting and carpentry with my father. But Cornell invited me to stay on, and in 1973, made me a professor. I was happy to have the position at such an excellent university, but I was also homesick for the mountains, for the place where I'd grown up, for family.

Out of homesickness, with a touch of nostalgia, I began to check out books from Cornell's big library about the Southern Appalachians, about the history and geography of the highlands, the geology and climate, the flora and fauna, the Cherokee Indians, the early explorers like Lawson, Timberlake, and Bartram. I discovered essays and glossaries about the speech and dialects of the region where I'd grown up. In Ithaca, I became a student of my native region in a way I never had been while living there. While working to become an effective teacher of writing and literature, I also immersed myself in the folklore, myths, narratives of panthers and snakes, and recalled the family stories I had heard of Civil War, the Revolution. I became interested in the churches I'd known as a boy, the hymns and gospel music, the rhetoric of sermons, the ballads I'd heard at corn shuckings, homecomings, and clog dances. My grandpa had been a banjo picker in his youth. My great-great-grandpa had been a noted fiddler. My step-grandma loved to tickle her mandolin to delight us kids. It was exciting to recall what I'd known as a child and left.

One of the essays I read in the 1980s about mountain speech mentioned the word "sigodlin," a term for askew, out of plumb. That word took me soaring back to the voices of my grandpa, my dad, and uncles: "Clyde, that stud's just a little bit sigodlin." That one word released an avalanche of associations with cold mornings on the job, the smell of lumber, sentences fragrant with tobacco juice. I hadn't heard the term in decades, but it served as a trigger. Of course, I had to write a poem about the images the word elicited.

But as I began to describe the way old carpenters used the word, I wondered about the origins of such a term. Something about it sounded Welsh. Many who settled our part of the mountains had come from Wales, with names like Jones, Morgan, Williams, Thomas. But my dictionaries did not include the word sigodlin. Because the term was associated with building, I wondered if it might be derived from Masonic ceremonies, from rituals going back to Rosicrucian rites, or even Greek mysteries and hermetic rituals. And I thought of the modern theory of the essential asymmetry of matter and creation. Finally, I remembered what I thought was St. Augustine's definition of God, "whose center is everywhere and circumference nowhere." That the origins of the word were mysterious seemed appropriate.

I included the poem "Sigodlin" in a reading at UNC Chapel Hill and explained that the ending was inspired by St. Augustine's definition of God. A learned friend came up to me after the reading and whispered, "I think it's Tertullian." It was sometime later, at a reading at Guilford College, when I explained my speculations about the etymology of sigodlin. A woman approached me afterward and said, "I'll tell you where that word comes from. My grandma used to say 'side-goggling.' The word is a contraction of 'side-goggling.'" I knew instantly she was right. While I'd been looking for Welsh or Masonic or Greek origins, the obvious derivation had been in the sound. I had been so intent on an exotic source I'd missed what was plain as daylight. I was looking in the distance while the truth was as close as my ear.

One snowy afternoon in February a few years later, the phone in my office rang. The caller explained that he was a builder in northern Saskatchewan. Since it was the depth of winter and he couldn't work outside, he had decided to satisfy his curiosity. The Amish carpenters who did timber frame building for him used the term "sigodlin," and he had wondered for years where the word came from. He'd called the English Department at the University of Saskatchewan. The professor he spoke to admitted that he didn't know the etymology of "sigodlin," but added that there was a fellow at Cornell who had published a book of poems called *Sigodlin*. I explained to the caller what I'd learned about the evolution of the word.

"Are you Amish?" the contractor asked.

I explained that I was not Amish, but from the mountains of North Carolina where the word was common. Since the Amish carpenters were from the mountains of Pennsylvania, they had probably learned the word as it was passed along by other carpenters in Appalachia. We had a long and pleasant conversation about building and language. Twice he asked, "Are you sure you're not Amish?"

"Reasonably sure," I said.

David Mura

South Carolina Sea Island

A purple blush above the marshes; below
on the wooden deck, two boys squeal at the cage
of crabs they've yanked from the muddy inlet.
Each year we come back to this: A heron's white

cross sails towards the sea, the tide crawls out,
and a wasp sputters about the wooden shelter
as I take it in—my boys, the caged crabs, the heron,
the sky; a scent of iodine, salting my tongue.

Once slaves hid in these islands, scions of
of a tongue they kept alive for their own,
foraging boars, fish, crabs and deer,
a teeming Eden just beyond original sin.

Nights over the ocean, did the stars chart
myths they shrouded from their far forest home?
Did they cipher barking hounds hunting within
the tidal winds? Or chant rhythms and songs

to ward them back? Did they holler praise
to the crabs and boars and fish for their bellies?
Pray to their gods to hold their bodies hidden?
And are they still listening, those Gullah ghosts?

Now, ripping thru the inlet, a giant wave
roars up higher and higher and thrashes on—
Two dolphins, fins, flanks churning the current.
We stare at their passing, seething to the sea.

The sky bleeds out its bruise; salt marshes swell
and darken the tide. Trudging off with their catch,
my sons are quieter now; as the night falls
about us quick and black, I tell them again

a history we can't take back.

Walking with Ghosts

This poem appeared in my book, *The Last Incantations*, in 2014. Ostensibly, it describes me and my sons crabbing from a dock on an inlet at Fripp Island, off the South Carolina coast. But, in another sense, this poem's origins go back many years, to my college days.

I met my wife at Grinnell College when she was a freshman and I was a junior. Susie had grown up the daughter of northern liberal white parents in Atlanta, and her early childhood there spanned some of the most violent years of the Civil Rights era. Her parents went to a Unitarian Church which did joint events with Martin Luther King, Sr.'s, congregation, where they heard Martin Luther King, Jr., speak at his father's church. As a second grader, Susie was followed home by a Baptist neighbor who insisted the unbaptized Susie was going to hell. As a child, Susie had nightmares of burning crosses, and she would look into the closets at her white friends' houses for Ku Klux Klan robes.

All this is to say, I, a third-generation Japanese American, married a white Southerner of sorts, or in another sense, a Northerner who grew up in the South (though when I first met her, Susie retained a slight lilt of a Southern accent). Growing up the daughter of liberal Northerners in Atlanta, Susie always felt she would never marry a Southern white boy. In high school, she'd had a crush on a black student when her school integrated, but he moved away and for her, at that time, crossing such a racial line was still taboo. I was the first person she met at college, and with her room across the hall from mine, perhaps our match was fated. We've been together ever since.

Years later, after the millennium, we found ourselves vacationing each summer with her Atlanta family at Fripp Island, one of the sea islands off of Beaufort, South Carolina. We'd gotten connected to Fripp through the South Carolinian novelist Pat Conroy, a family friend of her brother Steve's wife. Conroy even came to Steve's wedding and did an impromptu toast at the rehearsal dinner; he invited my brother-in-law Steve and his bride to stay at Conroy's home on Fripp, and that's how my wife's family started vacationing on the island.

Our family loved going to Fripp Island. The beach on the Atlantic side is several miles of open sand, with warm surf-flecked waters and a horizon so wide one sees the sky going through myriads of changes, as storms conjure up from inland and recede, as the sun rises and sets, as the stars step out in multitudes that one never sees at our home in Minneapolis. The back side of the island features marshlands, and you can see shrimp boats setting out or coming in. This whole coastal landscape has backdropped scenes in *The Big Chill*, Disney's *The Jungle Book*, and the Vietnam scenes in *Forrest Gump*. The area has also been used in films of Conroy's novels, *Conrack*, based on Conroy's autobiographical novel of a young white man who teaches young black kids on a remote sea island, and his two-family dramas, *The Great Santini* and *The Prince of Tides*. In both *Conrack* and *The Great Santini*, the conflicts and tensions of race in the South are clearly present, and since Susie's family often watched these movies while at Fripp, they're associated in my mind with the place.

I also associated Fripp with Julie Dash's *Daughters of the Dust* (1991), that brilliant and beautiful film set on an island just a few miles from Fripp and centered on the Gullah, a group which was able to retain a great portion of their culture and language in spite of the violence and destruction of slavery. The Gullah culture was creolized from West Africans of Ibo, Yorub, Kikongo, Mende, and Twi origins living in relative isolation because of their island location. From a small museum to an art gallery to a restaurant, the presence of the Gullah are part of the roots of Fripp and the surrounding islands. On a more personal level, the cinematographer for *Daughters of the Dust* was the great visual artist, Arthur Jaffa, and A.J. had also directed me and my friend, the black novelist Alexs Pate, in *Slowly This*, a short PBS independent film about our friendship and our lives as men of color that Alexs and I wrote and performed in (we looked at cuts from *Daughters of the Dust* as preparation for our film).

All this is a complicated way of saying that race in the South is both always present and yet so often occluded or muted or politely—or impolitely—moved to the background, whether we are dealing with family histories, with any historical period, and with any locale. The ghosts are there, many unremarked and uncelebrated, like the countless black people who have suffered during slavery and the Jim Crow eras. The ghosts are on public display, with the various monuments of Southern Confederate soldiers and political leaders, scions of a past that supported chattel slavery, a past that people still don't want to examine for its disturbing truths.

And so, for several years, we took our family each summer to Fripp Island, where we sunned and swam on the beaches and at the pool, played golf at the golf course, played b-ball with my boys, and saw alligators near the creeks on the island and on the golf course. We fished off the surf, threw nets at the surf and in the island's creeks. Off a marshy inlet was the little pier where we let down our crab cages; in the corner of the awning over the pier, there was a wasp's nest attached to the roof covering. One day while we were crabbing, a huge wave seemed to roll through the inlet, like some tidal surge, and it took a couple of moments before we realized that the wave was actually two dolphins, winding through the maze of marshes back towards the sea and the shifting tide.

So, I decided to write a poem about crabbing with my boys. That was, to use Richard Hugo's term, the triggering incident. But as the poem progressed, I thought about the presence of the Gullah and the ghosts of slavery all around the area. I thought of the images from Julie Dash's *Daughters of the Dust* and A.J.'s beautiful cinematography capturing the Gullah on the beach—beautiful black women in white dresses riding horses, a communal picnic, a boat of Gullah headed for the mainland to travel up north. I thought about how some escaped slaves hid in these sea islands. I thought of the language and culture the Gullah had fought to retain, the books on the Gullah in the local stores, the cuisine their descendants still cook at local restaurants. I thought how I always tried teaching my children the truth of American history during their childhoods, to go beyond the scrim of lies and occlusions which create for so many Americans a false sense of what this country has been.

The poem's first draft was written in long lines and without stanza breaks. I sometimes like to start with long lines because they give me a sense of freedom and keep me from trying too hard to restrict where the poem might go or to be too worried at first about felicities of phrasing. Several drafts later, the lines were still fairly long, but broken up into quatrains. Here's a sample from that draft:

> They watched the stars rise over the ocean in figures
> they carried in their minds from Africa and longed for home.
> (Home for me is these two boys, the place where I feel safe.)
>
> I know they're still here, in some other fold of the universe, just
> as they suspected they'd mistakenly slipped into an alien time.
>
> My boys come tumbling back, and I mention only the Gullah,
> and not this history I'm imagining, knowing so little, ignorant
> as always of the past and whatever sustains my presence here,
> at home for a moment before I return to that other universe
>
> I sometimes—having given up my prayers?—my only home.

One of the ways I sometimes revise poems is to make myself an assignment which will force me to use fewer words. By rewriting the lines in a loose iambic pentameter, I made the poem more concise (from fourteen syllables to ten syllables a line). I also introduced half rhymes. To shorten the lines, I cut away unnecessary verbiage and introduced a more insistent rhythmic structure, end-stopping the briefer pentameter phrases. Much of what I cut seemed unnecessary commentary as opposed to straight images ("show, don't tell" or say it metaphorically rather than abstractly). The final version possesses more structure and is firmer and thicker in its language texture (more metaphorical verbs—"sputters," "shrouded," "cipher," "holler," "bleeds"—and participles—"churning," "seething"). I make use of assonances and alliteration, and the wording's much more concise and less prosy.

This poem is about passing on our racial history to my sons, letting them know that we don't stand at a remove from the past but that we live within the past, surrounded by the past; we are walking upon the past and with its ghosts, and we ignore all that at our peril. The poem is about the incredible beauty of the South Carolina Sea Islands, a country praised by Pat Conroy in his novels ("my soul grazes like a lamb on the beauty of ingrown tides…" the protagonist, a son of a shrimp boater, writes in a love letter to his wife in *The Prince of Tides*). It is about my marriage to a white Southerner, who was the child of two white Northerners and who came to consciousness about race as a prime area of conflict in her formative years. It is about the beauty and power of the two dolphins streaming through a salt marsh, their flight to the sea echoing other dreams of freedom and escape buried within the past of South Carolina and its beautiful sea islands.

My next book of essays, *The Master's House: The Stories Whiteness Tells Itself*, examines the narratives that white Americans have created, both in histories and in fictional stories and films, about our racial past and present. I argue that whether in history or in fiction, white American narratives still employ the ontological categories of whiteness and blackness that stem from slavery and assumptions of epistemological racial superiority ("our white knowledge is objective and your subjective knowledge is always subject to our judgement and acceptance"). There are other versions of our racial history and our racial present which are still being excluded or rendered to secondary status, and we see this obviously in our justice system, yes, but it's there too in the stories our children imbibe. All this needs to change.

Marilyn Nelson

The Tulsa Convulsion
June 1, 1921

North of Frisco Station, up Archer Street,
was what white folks called "Little Africa,"
the Greenwood neighborhood, Tulsa's Harlem.
On Greenwood Avenue, "The Black Wall Street,"
were drugstores, grocery stores, men's and ladies' fine
furnishings, shoe shops, barbershops, cafes,
hotels, theaters, a beauty school,
brick churches, newspapers, a funeral home.
Greenwood's houses ranged from simple to stately:
Built by black people, on the Rock of Faith.
Some old folks remembered being enslaved.
Some young men were veterans of The Great War.
Tulsa's prosperous black citizens
looked to the future through the lens of hope.

Civilization is a house of cards:
What else explains how all hell can break loose
if a black boy steps on a white girl's toe?
Armed rescuers who believed in justice
freed the terrified boy from the chanting mob.
Then the veneer of community
burst into a gasoline-fueled whirlwind
with a deadly deluge of machine gun bullets.
Carloads of white men robbed the hardware stores
of gun and ammunition; truckloads, armed,
surrounded Greenwood as the night deepened.
At 6 a.m. the city's whistle blew,
and white men carrying high powered rifles
invaded Greenwood, screaming like Huns.

I dressed my little daughter, and we ran.
My sisters and I carried Mother out,
with bullets falling around us like rain.

173

About two dozen armed white men stopped us,
made us hold up our hands. The boys with them,
all armed, were told to go in the houses,
take what they wanted, then set them on fire.
Ten-year-old boys with guns pushed us around.
The fire department came out to protect
white homes on the west side of Detroit Street
while on the east side of the street
white women with shopping bags and white men
with torches stole or destroyed everything they could find.
A praying man, I wondered if God is just.

They dropped turpentine bombs from aero planes.
They shot down fleeing people from above.
They burned the hospital, with its patients.
They stole victrolas and smashed pianos.
They tore up and burned family Bibles.
If atrocities are measured in body counts,
these three hundred dead equal Wounded Knee.
Almost as many dead as at My Lai.
And hundreds wounded, thousands made homeless,
widowed, orphaned, indelibly traumatized.
The possessed rioted for one day.
Then laws were passed against rebuilding;
insurance companies found reasons not to pay;
the city auctioned off the burnt-out lots.

Ladies batting lashes around blue eyes
wide as #who-me? accepted gifts
of fine garments still reeking of smoke.
Some white granddaughters must have inherited
jewelry forfeited by a lady who ran
barefoot, in her nightgown, wild-eyed, dragging
her children by their wrists, as a white man
squinted one eye, bit the tip of his tongue, and fired.
What forms groups into mobs of the possessed,
ordinary until struck by seizures?
Other American cities succumbed
to epidemic xenophobia
a hundred years ago: East St. Louis;
Washington, D.C.; Omaha….

Because honkies think they're a superior race.
Because crackers, ofays, whiteys, and peckerwoods
believe Creation's best work leads to them.
If you're offended by these epithets,
think of a lifetime of equivalents.
Invisibility is a privilege.
White America forgets histories

like a blond child screamed awake from a nightmare
and patted back to sleep by a dark hand.
Our system hosts an anxiety disorder
characterized by irrational fear.
Reconciliation is not simple.
I saw men, women and children treated like beasts.
The white Red Cross workers were angels of mercy.

Family Trip to Oklahoma, 2018

It's not easy to trace a poem fully back to its source, but my poem, "The Tulsa Convulsion" sprang from my mother's pride in her having been born and raised in Boley, Oklahoma. Boley was established in 1903 as an all-black pioneer town on Creek Indian land. It was named for J.B. Boley, a white roadmaster who convinced the Fort Smith & Western Railroad that blacks could govern themselves. He arranged for the town, Boley, to be a stop on the railroad line. Boley soon boasted a population of more than 4,000. Booker T. Washington often mentioned the town as an exemplar of Negro success. Declared as a National Historic Landmark District by Congress in 1975, Boley has hosted one of the few all-black rodeos in the nation every Memorial Day weekend since 1903. 2020 was the first time the Boley Rodeo and Barbeque Festival was cancelled. In 2018, I decided to write a poem about the Boley Rodeo and convinced my sister and my niece to accompany me to our mother's hometown, a return to our roots.

We arrived in Tulsa a couple of days before the rodeo, rented a car, drove around a little bit, walked up and down every aisle in a huge Oklahoma souvenir store, ate some *coneys*, a traditional local specialty of wieners in buns covered with chili and cheese, found our hotel, relaxed, and made plans: one day for Tulsa, one day for the Boley Rodeo and Barbecue Festival, and then home.

We had come to Oklahoma to go to Boley. The history of Tulsa was, frankly, far from my mind. But driving through the area which was once Greenwood, we saw a sign directing us to the Greenwood Community Center. I was not prepared for the wrenching lessons we learned together during the shocked time we spent there gasping at photographs and wiping our eyes as we read eyewitness accounts, and then, later, walking quietly and meditating before the thought-provoking plaques in the John Hope Franklin Reconciliation Park. Why didn't I know this history before? I'd known that white race riots happened, but that's all I'd known of them. I'd never been taught about them, and I'd never given them any serious thought. Even in the year when I devoted my thinking time to the theological question of radical evil, I had never asked what race riots say about the human capacity for evil. In my mind, those riots were filed under the general category of lynch mobs, when individuals surrender their rational selves and are dissolved in the irresistible currents flooding up out of their brutal forebears.

Yet, the firsthand accounts we were reading and discussing as we walked through the museum seemed to indicate that what happened in Tulsa in 1921 wasn't simple mob violence. The white population of the city seemed to have undergone something like a moral convulsion: a brief, violent, uncontrollable, red-eyed spasm of racist greed, of supremacist envy. Yet, the reactions seemed to have been organized, coordinated, almost as though they had been considered ahead of time, almost as though they had been planned. The city's whistle ringing at 6 a.m. as a starting signal, the ax-wielding piano-destroyers marching from house to house, the ladies with their shopping bags filling with fashionable dresses and jewelry, the airplanes dropping fire-bombs on businesses. It was as if part of a community had been possessed, had been caught up in a communal orgasm of well-planned evil. And, while the violence lasted only one day, the injustices perpetrated by a corrupt Jim Crow system insured that the well-to-do black community that had lost so much so suddenly would find it extremely difficult to rebuild.

That image stayed with me through the drive to and around Boley, through the rodeo, to my return to my New England home and my desk. Although I was still determined to write the rodeo poem I had originally planned, it was clear to me that I had to first write a Tulsa Massacre poem, another of the lyric histories I've been writing. This one had already in my mind acquired a title: "The Tulsa Convulsion." I felt this poem needed only to bear witness. To tell the facts, and to capture the voices of some of the people who lived through the attack—that's all I wanted the poem to do. No "interpretation" of the story seemed necessary, though I couldn't help wondering, as I had in an earlier poem, "A Wreath for Emmett Till," how people who seem "normal" and "civilized" can suddenly erupt in murderous violence against their neighbors. If "civilization" can evaporate so quickly, is it only a veneer over the inheritance of savagery? These American convulsions of people mad with killing-fever seem to have been limited to explosions within the white population and aimed against the Black, but we've seen people in Yugoslavia writhe in such spasms, and people in Rwanda. I was driven repeatedly to ask why and how these outbreaks occur.

I find myself asking similar questions now, one hundred years after 1921, watching inexplicably passionate and mindless crowds of wild-eyed, hate-filled, mostly white Americans cheer on our malignant President. Twenty years ago, when I wrote "A Wreath for Emmett Till," I struggled to encase its argument within a formalist envelope which would serve as insulation for its young adult readers, protecting them from the blazing pain of its factual history and demonstrating to them the potential—the probable—consequences of a nation's allowing its president to turn its population into a lynch mob. This is what I thought then President George W. Bush was doing at the time: cheering us into accepting an unjust and illegal war.

In some ways, the form itself, a heroic crown of Petrarchan sonnets, was responsible for the poem's turning in that direction: its tight metrical structure, rhyme scheme, and repeated lines exerted a great deal of control over the unfolding of the poem's argument, and I was racing to complete it in time to present it to our librarian First Lady at a White House day of poetry to which I had been invited. My secret hope was that Mrs. Bush would read the poem, follow its argument, and convince her husband not to start war with Iraq. Unfortunately, some other poets invited to the White House announced their plans to openly protest the threat of war, and the event was preemptively cancelled.

The last of the unrhymed metrical sonnets which make up the "The Tulsa Convulsion" asks questions and posits answers to them, possible ways to understand the passion and mindlessness we see of late, on naked display in our national news. This poem suggests that at its deepest level, perhaps the current president's base desperately subscribes to the deadly myth of superiority which places white male humans at the pinnacle of Creation, living with the irrational terror of being pulled down. Invisibility and forgetfulness are white privileges in the USA.

However, holding to Mr. Rogers' mother's admonition that we must "look for the helpers" in even the most desperate situations, I did take note among the eyewitness accounts of several grateful mentions of white people who did not succumb to the epidemic xenophobia. Mary E. Jones Parrish, editor of the collection of eyewitness accounts of the 1921 Tulsa Race Riot, published in 1923, praised the "State troops who so gallantly came to the rescue of stricken Tulsa. They used no partiality in quieting the disorder. It is the general belief that if they had reached the scene sooner many lives and valuable property would have been saved." Another witness quoted in Mrs. Parrish's book, Richard J. Hill, tells of being taken back to his damaged home by white friends, and finding "a White gentleman in charge of the house, who related to us that himself and son and a few neighboring White friends had prevented any further molestation of our home. They stated that they were ready to stay with us all night if we thought it necessary to ensure that we would not be molested." Another witness describes a farm outside of Tulsa, where refugees were welcomed, fed, and allowed to sleep in the barn.

While I do not want to place too much emphasis on these rare instances of normal decency and kindness, I do feel strongly that those who exhibited such ordinary humane behavior must be credited for the tenacity with which they held on to their values. There may have been only a few of them in white Tulsa that day, but their existence proved that humanity can be stronger than cruelty, that, in spite of all evidence to the contrary, there may still be reason not to despair. Mrs. Parrish remembers, and reminds us, that the white Red Cross workers were angels of mercy. My offering her observation as the last line of the poem is intended to close the poem with a small sense of hope.

Laura Newbern

Novella

On the last day of summer
    there was a man by the river.
We were the women, gathered
    for wine on the rocks: there were three
or four of us; we were women
    with plastic cups, passerine, on rocks—
our eyes on each other and
    on the rocked river, last day of summer. Sunlight
dotted the water, small golden urns
    pitching those final drops
into the rush and void. We talked,
    we made noise; we had things to say—
and then he was there, the man
    by the river, behind us, crouched
on the slatey shelf at our backs,
    drunk, we could tell, but not frightening;
drunk in the way of the true drunk,
    sullen and silent; his body
its own hood—regret might sit up
    but sadness slouches and broods—;
as I said he was sullen, and pale,
    and silent until he said, quite aloud,
he had a *girl*, who was *lonely*,
    back at the motel; so maybe, could she
join you ladies. All of us
    looked in the same direction; we all
whispered, without saying words.
    And we all looked across, to the river's
bar: small, sandy, bedraggled island,
    summer-gray, uninhabited, ashen—

There was a man, we said of it later,
      in our bright kitchens filled

with glass, *down by the river*, though in the
      moment, no one said what she thought;

someone acknowledged him, yes; there
      was a man, but there was no man; we

were like nymphs with lighted limbs
      and our faces in shadow, under our hats,

and the man a shepherd, or lion—who
      among rocks is hidden, these days; what

is a sadness enough to look at, to turn
      and see, hand at the brim, squinting, the light

dazzling: a thousand cuts he so easily came
      and went in, man in a dream, not wounded

but bearing the wound. And then, softly, quietly,
      gone. I am thinking

not that he was a god, though gods,
      like the man, are at once presence

and absence—there
      the story would end; I am thinking instead

of our heads, bowed as we left, in careful file,
      our eyes cast down, and of how

the last of us in her balancing spied
      a blue sweater, snagged on a rock.

On "Novella"

The poem took a while to find. Its origin is a warm Labor Day after-noon four years ago that I spent perched on a rock in the middle of a river in a remote part of Maine, with some women who kindly invited me to join them. Sometimes it's easier to talk to strangers about your life than to those you love; I found myself complaining to one of them about my lack of time to write, the space it takes, how hard that can be to find. She looked at me very seriously—likely she found me a little ridiculous. Mainers tend to be pretty no-nonsense. She waved a hand around in the air. *Write this*, she said.

She must've said that before the man appeared behind us, because once he was there, we grew quiet. Her words, all the sunlight, and all the shadows stayed in my head. I tend to let things turn in my head for a long time, until I can really see them. Two years later I finally sat down and wrote the first lines and in them immediately heard a storytelling voice, the cadence of cause and effect, of *this, then that*; this led to the couplets, indented for looseness, to accommodate a sense of talk, a halfway-lilting, almost hyper-telling voice.

At the same time, the loose couplets began to open up the poem's landscape. I don't usually write long poems—and this poem isn't even really long; but it is spacious—it needed room to look forwards and back, and then up and then down, to chase its larger subject, to find the spot where telling and describing begin to turn or lift or discover. At that point I called it "Novella" because of its storytelling bent, but more so because a novella is an in-between thing, smaller than a novel and bigger than a story, but no less focused, and a little ornate, kind of like a viola, which is a violin with an alto voice.

It stalled for a while—I got to the hands at the brim and the squinting, and felt, appropriately, blind, and stuck. And I walked away—it's very hard for me to trust a poem that's not coming easily, that doesn't spill out whole—I think it was Marina Tsvetaeva who wrote that the poet's role in composing a poem is "to let the ear hear and the hand race, and when it doesn't race, to stop."

And perhaps I should've stayed away, but I went back, months later, and typed it from the top, asking myself, as I went, what I was writing about. Scenery? No. Fear? Not really. Re-typing often will bring out things that were already there but not yet visible, like the small island; I became more conscious, too, of the sense of aftermath, adding the "kitchens filled with glass." Was I writing about sadness? Yes, and distance—the often-terrible distance between people, which is what nagged at me, from a day that was memorably dazzling and gray all at once. So I aimed for the liminal space and tried to push into it—not too hard, but enough to create a moment of speculation and emptiness, a kind of hollow, shattered place, where someone was, and then was not.

I wish I could say that the final image surprised me. The rhythms of the ending lines, where there are a lot of monosyllabic words, were hard to get right—my ear and I are constantly pulling our hair out. But the blue sweater, snagged, was a flag I saw from a distance, a remnant, across four years of making my shaky way out of the river. I was the last in that twilight to scramble up the steep bank.

Annemarie Ní Churreáin

Six Ways to Wash Your Hands (Ayliffe 1978)
for the Irish Mother and Baby Homes Commission of Investigation

1
Wet hands, apply soap and rub palm to palm
until a white lather forms like the spit and rage of women,
who, having lain among waves, were dragged back up again
by the hair and stripped of their names to pay for the wrongs
in their bellies, as they stitched lace, pressed linen sheets,
and each week bowed their heads to the postpartum girls
all lined up at the font like a row of roots half-pulled
out of the earth and still holding on to their young.

2
Rub right palm over left dorsum and left palm over right dorsum
to ensure the scent of infant leaves your skin: the sour fumes
of bottled milk, triangled terry cloths, ice-cold smears of cream.
The scent of sin can cling for years as potent as a bad dream
of trade-deals, needle pricks, poppies bloomed on the skull.
The scent of a child in an unmarked grave may get in beneath
your fingernails and cause all sorts of problems in later life.

3
Rub palm to palm, fingers interlaced and around the wrists
to erase all trace of fathers. Never mention cuffs.
Never mention scars. Raise your head against the sky
and let the violet clouds overfill your eyes as the names
of these men become again unknown as birds.
When you see a wing, like a realm of thumbed pages
fluttering, take this as a sign: the fathers are no more.

4
Rub backs of fingers to opposing palm with fingers interlocked
and loosen the joints of wards, nurseries, bolted pantries
stocked with canisters of warm milk and cheese sold
by the yellow quart as the imagined cream of it dripped

182

from the mouths of hungry, swollen girls. Rub out the halls,
statues, sills. Leave only a rusted nail in a cemetery wall.

5
Rotational rubbing of right thumb clasped in left palm and vice versa
to disimprint the memory of files. Wash clean the data
until days, months, years signed by clammy hands run
like slip-streams into a great shaking lake. This means
that, even should your lips part to release a holy word,
all that will spill out is a wet pulp no one understands.

6
Rotational rubbing back and forwards with clasped fingers
of right hand in left palm and vice versa to wear thin heart-lines.
Be a sister and repeat the law like a hymn into the sink.
Do not commemorate: Do not remunerate. Do not let
the wounded woman or her child speak in a bare tongue.
Wash in this way and rid your hands of Mother, Baby, Home.

In the Shadow of Men Who Wanted to Conquer Wildness

"You go up a mountain and down the other side / To find out who you are." I often quote this line by the Irish poet, Madge Herron, as important to me. I grew up in northwest Donegal on a piece of Irish bogland named Cnoc Na Naomh (or, in English, "Hill of the Saints"). Legend tells that on this hill, four men once convened to decide who among them would convert the local area from paganism. It's a legend I heard all throughout my girlhood, and one that remains popular, not least because it contains all the best ingredients of a good story: conflict, strong characters, and of course the divine intervention of God.

When I dream today of that hill, I dream of a landscape in motion; of sheep scuttling through heather; of muck-streams tumbling from the peak where a clear view of the Atlantic Ocean can be inhaled; of light shifting like shale across dark pleats of water and out towards Tory Island. I think of the way the bog wants to carry the human voice. I think of the fact that I was raised in the shadow of men who wanted to conquer the wildness around them. From a young age, I had the sense of myself as not merely *in* this landscape but as *part* of it. In my poetry today, this understanding of my physical self as an extension of the environment keeps certain questions alive in my mind: what is the relationship between landscape and lyrical control? Between control and imagination? Between the place that I physically come from and the State in which I, as a woman in Ireland today, now exist?

In 2017, my debut collection of poetry *Bloodroot* was published by

Doire Press. It's a book of poems in English haunted by my mother tongue of Gaeilge. The book is dedicated to my foremothers, particularly the women of my family whose voices were silenced in a country once deeply influenced by the strict moral codes of the Roman Catholic Church. The poem "Six Ways to Wash Your Hands (Ayliffe 1978)" is, at least partly, a found poem. But it's also a poem that arises out of the journey my paternal grandmother took in the spring of 1951 from Northern Ireland to County Westmeath, where she gave birth to my father at a place formerly known as the Castlepollard Mother and Baby Home. It was here that, like many other unmarried Irish women over the past 100 years, my grandmother was forced to relinquish her child to adoption. It was at this point in my family history that poetry, as a form of protest, began to write and rewrite itself into the DNA of who I am.

"Poetry," James Joyce said, "even when apparently most fantastic, is always a revolt against artifice, a revolt, in a sense, against actuality." For me, the urge to speak a truth aloud is so bound up in an ancestral grief that by the time I learned to write a word on a page, the sensitivity for poetry was already fully formed. To grow up in 1980s in Ireland was to grow up inside a country of rupture, where all around me, the atmosphere of church and State was as potent as the scent of mink on the hill. I eavesdropped on family conversations about adoption records, legal rights, and the search for family roots. I observed registered letters, secret numbers, pensive moods. When you live with someone who might be anyone, you learn the mixed-up language of shame and expectation. You learn that—like a bogland—a person is the sum of buried and unburied things. I watched my family roots traced out of one county, over the border, and into Northern Ireland as the news stories that I would later, in adulthood, begin to explore in poetry, made the TV headlines.

The year 1984 in Ireland was particularly bleak. In January 15-year-old Ann Lovett died after giving birth alone to a stillborn son at the Virgin Mary grotto in Co Longford. In February, teacher Eileen Flynn lost her appeal of unfair dismissal against the Holy Faith Convent in New Ross, Co Wexford; she had been living with a married man at the time and had had a baby with him. In April, two infant bodies were discovered in Co Kerry and the wrongly accused woman, Joanne Hayes, found herself at the center of a bizarre investigation and a national media debate about the lives of women and children in Ireland. The household I was raised in was not bookish, and there was no library in the local town. But we did have a television. We did have a radio. And through these mediums the stories of Irish women entered my life, to hang in the air around me like shadows, like ghosts. When I look back now, I don't need to ask myself why I started to write. The only question is: how could I not?

In the 1990s, a woman identified as my paternal grandmother was found. Overnight, the family was catapulted onto the tricky path of adoption reunion. In 1994, Ireland's first female president stepped forth and I, a sulky teenager, was packed up and sent unhappily over the Derry border to the meet my new "real" family. I was an unlikely olive-branch and much overwhelmed by the new currency, the strange accent, and the emotional dynamics of the experience. I have a vivid memory of standing in a phone-box one day, on a call back to the hill in Donegal, and pleading *"Please, I want to come home."* Years later, on the day of my new grandmother's funeral, I stood outside the church and realized that it had been a doomed reunion from the start. Nobody had the language to talk about family loss. Nobody had the words. For some years I could not shake the feeling that I, personally, had failed in my role as messenger to bring any healing to the wound.

In 2016, the manuscript for *Bloodroot* was almost complete. Still, I had one more poem to write and it involved a pilgrimage. On Easter Friday, I packed up the car and travelled down into the flat midlands of the country. It was raining and almost dark by the time I arrived. I located the tall, imposing stone walls outside Castlepollard, passed through the gates, and rolled up along the tree-lined avenue. Here it was, finally: the building which had troubled my family for decades. The former Castlepollard Mother and Baby Home is now a mostly derelict and out-of-use building. I found the doors locked, windows boarded up and gardens run into neglect. In the courtyard stood a chipped statue of Jesus with his palms upturned.

Over the next hours, I circled the building I could not enter, listening to the hollow sounds of distant farm-animals and thinking of the women who'd spent time here over the years. Often, they were made to shave their heads. They were given new "house-names," uniforms and a tough schedule of domestic chores. I was standing outside a building known in historical documents as "the screaming room"—so called because it's where women in labor were sent to howl—when I spotted in the long grass a piece of scrap paper. When I picked it up, I realized that it was an old, discarded set of health-worker instructions. The title on the instructions was: "Six Ways to Wash Your Hands (Ayliffe, 1978)."

Back at the local bed and breakfast, I propped the instructions on my desk and began to write. Ordinarily, my style is methodical and slow. But I now found myself gripped by an energy that felt urgent and old. At great speed the lines came to me, extending to the end of the page margins. The tone of the poem was one I did not fully recognize. Darker and darker images emerged. It's almost as if the poem, like an undiscovered lake, had been lying inside of me all this time, waiting to written. Truly, it seemed that I was being guided by voices and echoes that were not my own.

For me, poetry is not only about language, it's about control. Poems come out of the desire to excavate and restore, to figure history out in relation to space, power structures, and the unsaid. To make a mark on a page, or carry sound on breath, is a way of navigating an otherwise uncertain world. And to the business of hope, poetry brings not only a mysterious radio but also a high regard for brokenness and repair. As poets, we count syllables, break lines, separate verses; we strip, part, and pare to free a new meaning that moves us backward and forwards in time, alive and embodied. One of the great joys of my life is the chance to read poems aloud. Many times, poems have connected me to others whose lives have been impacted by familial trauma, loss, and separation. When the poet recites, attention returns in towards the body, the mouth, the lungs, the air. When the poet recites, some boundary between physical environment and self becomes blurred, placing human experience back into the landscape, placing landscape back into the story of who we are.

Alicia Ostriker

Listen

Having lost you, I attract substitutes.
The student poets visit, think me wise,
Think me generous, confide in me.
Earnestly they sit in my office
Showing me their stigmata
Under the Judy Chicago poster
Of her half-opened writhing-petalled
Clitoris that appears to wheel
Slowly clockwise when you gaze at it,
And I sympathize. Then they try on their ambitions
Like stiff new hiking boots, and I laugh
And approve, telling them where to climb.
They bring me tiny plastic bags
Of healthy seeds and nuts, they bring me wine,
We huddle by the electric heater
When it is snowing,
We watch the sparrows dash
And when they leave we hug.

Oh, silly mother, I can hear you mock.
Listen, loveliest, I am not unaware
This is as it must be.
Do daughters mock their mothers? is Paris
A city? Do your pouring hormones
Cause you to do the slam
And other Dionysiac dances,
And did not even Sappho tear her hair
And act undignified, when the maiden
She wanted, the girl with the soft lips,
The one who could dance,
Deserted her?

Do I suffer? of course I do,
I am supposed to, but listen, loveliest.
I want to be a shrub, you a tree.
I hum inaudibly and want you

To sing arias. I want to lie down
At the foot of your mountain
And rub the two dimes in my pocket
Together, while you dispense treasure
to the needy. I want the gods
Who have eluded me
All my life, or whom I have eluded,
To invite you regularly
To their lunches and jazz recitals.
Moreover, I wish to stand on the dock
All by myself waving a handkerchief,
And you to be the flagship
Sailing from the midnight harbor,
A blue moon leading you outward,
So huge, so public, so disappearing—
I beg and beg, loveliest, I can't
Seem to help myself,
While you quiver and pull
Back, and try to hide, try to be
Invisible, like a sensitive
irritated sea animal
Caught in a tide pool, caught
Under my hand, can I
Cut off my hand for you,
Cut off my life.

"Listen": A Mother-Daughter Poem and How It Grew

The beloved oldest daughter had been in San Francisco on leave of absence from college, living with the boyfriend, working at the Tower Records, learning to play the bass guitar. In other words, she had dropped out of college to do sex, drugs, and rock and roll. This could have been okay, except the daughter wasn't writing or calling, wasn't sharing the juicy details with the mama, who would have loved to hear about the music, or the boyfriend, or the LSD. The mama was tangled, clotted up, hogtied by her own confusion. There was the distress stemming from the daughter's personal coolness to her, which had been creeping along like a mist for—what was it, a year or three. Or was she inventing it? An equal and opposite distress was the anxiety that the daughter was, in fact, still too attached to the mama, appearing to drift but actually tethered, unable to set her own course, though the mama had thought she was raising the girl toward freedom and autonomy. The mama had thought she was unpossessive. She wondered exactly how self-deluded she might be. Racked by fear, she was uncertain what she feared. If everything was going just as it should, the daughter properly freeing herself and finding a path, or if everything was going all wrong, the daughter wasting herself, how would the abandoned mother know, knotted in good intentions and greedy need?

I had already, in back pages of notebooks, begun several poems that never lifted off the ground. I had attempted angry epistles, pleading ones, love poems. I cannot begin a poem with forethought. Words or lines appear in the mind, and the hand writes them until they stop appearing. Sometimes the words are worthless, or too skimpy ever to become a poem. Sometimes, I find I have something substantial to which I can return. Then, I can add and subtract, revise and pursue. The poem becomes a problem I hope to solve, and in so doing, to discover what I mean. Clarify a confusion, find the pattern of a turbulence. What *is* the truth? I will revise endlessly in the hope of finding out.

On this occasion in the late fall of 1983, I received thirteen lines, beginning "Having lost you, I try to attract substitutes." When I returned to that scrap, I deleted "try to," for compression and candor. The thirteen lines described, with what I hoped was some vivacity and wit, my warm relations with my students. *They* like me even if you don't, was the gist. To that scrap I added, under a cloudy doodle at the bottom, the words "Trying to Leave You the Fuck Alone," obviously a caption or summary of what I thought the poem was supposed to be about. That sentence never went into the poem. The rest arrived over a period of months in interpolated chunks. One chunk elaborated on the student-teacher description. A second developed the idea that the daughter's abandonment of the mother was healthy. Lastly, came the chunk in which I say "I want."

The first finished draft was, in fact, chunky. I had been writing lately in unrhymed couplets and triplets whose elegance and coolness I liked. They had an interesting tempo, tended to turn corners sharply, the ghost of Wallace Stevens breathed in them, and it pleased me to use these esthete tricks to my own contrary purposes. Here, in contrast, was something lump-like, heavy, unrefined. I tried putting it in triplets for distance and coolness. Wrong. I returned to the original form, and when I did so, a final piece formed. The poem did not wish to be elegant; it wished to push past the censor; it wanted to make me say more and more of the unsaid, the unsayable, and it wanted to retain a sense of the difficulty of coming at these truths.

Having lost you, I attract substitutes.

The opening is straightforward: I boast and am grateful that my desire to mother people through sympathy and support seems needed and used by students. It is ironic that they confide in me more than my own children do, but I am convinced I successfully strengthen them. There is some light sense of erotic connection here. It remains light. The poet's voice is not uncomfortable.

Oh silly mother, I can hear you mock.

Second section: Daughter mocks mother; I "can hear" her = I am sure she does or would, that she no longer values what I value, if she ever did, and she would dismiss my boast, thinking I fool myself. I submit to this hypothetical mockery as natural and proper; the daughter must separate from the mother just as she must obey her own body. I try to be good-humored about this, keep the levity afloat. Likewise, it is natural for the mother to feel pain at this predictable event. Tone of slight exaggeration, slight self-mockery: tearing one's hair is a bit of a joke.

Mentioning Sappho as precedent, however, does several other things. First of all, it invents. Who knows if Sappho was undignified in "real life?" The poems in which Sappho mourns being rejected are "art," but is it not undignified to reveal desire and pain? Does art purify humiliation, make it acceptable and less embarrassing? Apparently, I am in this poem engaged in a parallel artistic act. Although, if Sappho is my precedent, I will have to cut the comedy, the hijinks, such as they are, which constitute armor, and let the poem go deeper, find what is at the core and say it, which I will try to do in the rest of the poem. But to invent, and to make the Sappho comparison, is already to take the *self* more seriously, to begin to make claims and seize space. Now the erotic element is stronger. It implies that I "want" my daughter as Sappho wanted her favorite girls. This is pushing rather far and is, in fact, an exaggeration, but there is a core assertion of eros here, and I am also, not incidentally, implying that Sappho, that any mother, wants the same.

I am unsure of the word "rejected." It is the accurate word but has that awful aura of psychobabble about it. A soap opera word. A *Psychology Today* word. A word my own mother solemnly likes to use. Ah well, then. I reject "rejected." "Deserted" alliterates nicely with "dance." What next?

Do I suffer? Of course I do. I am supposed to....

In its third section, the poem pushes yet further into the reality of maternal desire. It is not that the mother wants the daughter to "succeed" or be "happy." No, what she wants is far more aggressive, more willful, more laden. She wants the daughter to excel her, specifically. She wants to have launched the daughter, to have sent her forth, further than she herself hopes to go.

This longing is deeper than sex. I have felt it for ages and was never before able to articulate it. The sequence of metaphors, *apparently*hyperbolic, *apparently*comic, says precisely what I mean. And there is a sweetness to these wishes; there has to be a sweetness. I recognize them with a smile when Anne Sexton says to her daughter "You've picked my pocket and left me empty" or "I'm an old tree in the background." But there is also all that pushing (to launch is to push), the will to direct and control, that unconscious seeing of the daughter as an extension of the mother's self instead of another being whose direction will not be tied to the mother's direction. And so, the poem descends to its final section, to its dreads. There are two of these.

First, that I cannot seem to stop myself from begging my daughter to excel me, and that far from having successfully escaped me, she is still beneath the shadow of my monster hand, shrinking from my wishes, trying to protect herself from me and becoming smaller instead of larger! Weaker instead of stronger! And all because I cannot quit *desiring* her to grow and strengthen. And the other dread, at which the poem can only hint: that the daughter's life depends on the mother's death. That if the mother were suddenly removed, the daughter would become immediately stronger. Would suffer, of course, because of the love between them—and would burst into flower. In the closing ten lines, the poem abandons its leavening levity, the grammar yields to run-on blur, and lastly the question mark, which would imply the possibility of an answer, is eschewed in favor of an abrupt and numb full stop.

Why is it important that the poem ends where it does? It was written decades ago, in the 1980s, yet the issues unresolved then remain unresolved today. There exists a large and continually growing body of poetry by women who write as mothers and who are making clear, if anyone would care to notice, that our culture's sanitized idea of what "mother" signifies is absurdly reductive, that we have many more questions than answers, and that to re-think the myriad meanings of "mother" would mean re-thinking everything else we suppose we know, from the meaning of sex to the meaning of history. "Listen" is a small contribution to a large body of—I believe—necessary work.

Frank Paino

Swallow

Spring again, and outside our hotel window swallows raise
their raucous cries between branches that bear only
the faintest blush of jade. I watch you, still lost to dreams,
a knife-edge of sun slicing the length of your perfect neck,
and I'm back to yesterday, to the Mutter's two dwarfed
galleries, their brass and polished cases hung with human grief:
a young man's throat flayed and pinned wide to unveil
the tumor that finally choked back his last breath;
twins molded pelvis-to-face in a grotesque parody
of pleasure; the toothless woman, mouth agape,
whose corpulence turned her to soap inside her grave;
countless rows of yellowed bone eaten to lace by syphilis,
and varnished drawers filled with objects swallowed
then later retrieved—dental work, buttons, children's toys,
and a puzzling host of unclasped safety pins.
We passed an hour or more amongst the wreckage of
so much flesh. Long enough to remind me
why I don't have faith in any god. Long enough
to make the lovers who moved ahead of us press
so close I knew their night would end sooner
than most in the comfort of their rumpled bed.
What better salve for sadness than such bliss?
And we, having had our fill of things unsound, stepped back
into the street where the seemingly-whole wrapped their coats
against early evening's chill and carried themselves to the places
strangers go while we drifted, arm in arm, back to the hotel
where you opened your thighs, luminous as x-rays
in the fallen light, and I swallowed the damp gathered there,
then entered you as a swimmer enters a warm, solemn lake,
and we slept, limbs entwined, while the Milk Moon moved
across the sky until morning swallowed it whole, just like
the light that vanishes halfway down the throat
of that nearly-bottomless cave in Mexico where swallows rise
in unison each dawn, unspooling from darkness in a fluttering iris,
until, at last, they spill into daybreak and disappear

toward the far horizon. I think their swift ancestors
must have mesmerized Cortés and his men, made them
draw back their reins and watch a while in wonder. I want
to believe the sight of those thousand-thousand wings lifting as one
made the soldiers stay their torches a heartbeat or more before
they wicked the forest into a second sun to burn their way back
into paradise. And I want to believe they wept to see those birds chase
cinders they mistook for prey until their flight became a smolder,
then a stillness, as they fell back to this earth which, however broken,
beckons us to drink deep. Swallow. Deeper still.

Writing My Obsessions

When I was invited to contribute to this anthology, I wanted to choose a poem that embodies as many of my obsessions as possible so readers could get a sense of who I am as a poet. After no small amount of consideration, I determined "Swallow" satisfies that desire completely, even if, in some instances, briefly. So, here's a poem with at least a hint of: the curious/obscure; the ekphrastic (admittedly, that's a bit of a stretch); the erotic; the dead (death); the secular—as opposed to the theistic (again, a slight stretch, but there it is); the ways we mistreat the Earth and others; and our good fortune in being alive, despite the drawbacks.

So ... how did this poem come to be written? When I sat down at my computer, I had no idea the piece I'd create would fire on all of the cylinders I just mentioned. Instead, I meant only to revisit the things I'd seen at the Mutter Museum in Philadelphia. It's a strange and wondrous place filled with a host of anatomical specimens and medical instruments, all housed within highly-polished cabinets of wood and glass. Walking through, I was stuck not only by the astonishing complexity of the human body, but also by the plethora of things that can wrong with it, and how science has sought methods to alleviate pain and to heal.

It was these considerations that haunted me during my time among the exhibits, in the nights and days that followed, in the long hours I sat composing and revising ... until today, as I sit here to tell you about it.

So, the Mutter was the *occasion* for the poem, but I am a poet who never restricts himself to any one subject when writing. Often, my unconscious mind will make associations I'm not immediately aware of, and this, for me, is part of the real magic of writing.

This particular poem begins with the contemplation of a lover's throat. I wasn't thinking about it at the time I put those words onto my computer screen, but the throat is, of course, an organ designed for, among other functions, swallowing. The poem then moves into the museum.

After, it opens outward—first to another couple, then an erotic act of swallowing. From there, it travels to The Cave of the Swallows in Mexico, then to Cortés and his slaughter of indigenous peoples, the pillaging of their cities and rich forests. Finally, the poem concludes by recognizing the beauty of our world, despite all we do to destroy it and each other.

But "Swallow" didn't spring to the page in its current form. That sort of "gift poem" has arrived only two or three times in my writing life. Instead, my process is long, messy, and most often mentally exhausting. Many of my poems require a great deal of research as they are based on curious, little-known events or people. In the case of "Swallow," I didn't need to sit down to study much of anything, but even so, it took hours to get to the point where I had before me what I indecorously call a "blob," that being an extraordinarily rough draft of the poem. Once I had that, as with all my poems, the fun began.

Revising!

I'm an insufferable reviser. Indeed, if I had my way, I'd likely never submit a poem to a journal because, for me, Valery's pronouncement that "a poem is never finished; it is only abandoned," is exactly the case. As it is, I eventually abandon each piece and let it out into the world to be whatever it will be. To refuse to do so would mean I'd never get anything published, and while publication isn't the be-all and end-all of writing, I would be lying if I said I didn't want my work to be read by others.

But back to the "blob."

What is it, exactly? Well, it is, as I mentioned, a rough draft ... but the emphasis is on "rough." Yes, there are line breaks, but at this point they exist wholly arbitrarily and simply so the thing doesn't metamorphose into a paragraph of prose. It's at this point I begin playing with lineation. Does the poem suggest it wants to be in couplets? Tercets? Quatrains? Does it even *have* stanzas, or is it all of a piece? And, if I go with stanzas ... does each take shape on its own, regardless of length or form? The answers to these questions are things I spend quite a bit of time experimenting with, all the while listening to what the poem wants to be.

When I say listening, I mean that literally. For me, a poem is meant to be read aloud. The words are exquisitely important as they establish the music and rhythm of the piece. Line breaks, enjambment, diction— these are all critical to the poem's symphony. Where might one best draw a breath? Where hold? Assonance? Consonance? An occasional rhyme? All of these questions (and more) are considered, during which the poem will go through a host of versions.

In the case of "Swallow," it demanded to be one long stanza. I didn't think about it consciously at first, but as I pondered, it became clear that form would lend itself to the topic in a multitude of ways, e.g., the suggestion of breathlessness or something large enough to choke on when swallowed (like the objects described in the Mutter's collection), something suggestive of the way time itself swallows us, something imitative of the swallows that rise as one from that vast Mexican cave, and, finally, the way so many of us (most?) thirst for life. Even when it isn't exactly lovely ... we "rage against the dying of the light."

In addition to sound, I am keenly aware of, and interested in, images. I've long said if I had the skills to paint or sculpt, I wouldn't write. In other words, I'm a frustrated visual artist. My poems must become my palette or my block of marble awaiting a chisel to chip away at ... reveal the shape within. I want my readers to be able to *see* whatever it is I'm writing about as much as hear its music.

I also spend a lot of time weeding out lazy language. I don't want my poem to suffer clichés, and I certainly don't want the language to feel flat and uninspired. So, while reading aloud, I'll listen for areas when a simile or metaphor might be too pedestrian, or instances where I've taken an easier route instead of fighting for something more striking, more unexpected.

Lastly, I have long recognized my tendency to overwrite, offering too many examples, too many adjectives, etc. "Swallow" is probably a case-in-point, but I leave it as is for two reasons: first, to underscore a point I made earlier: "A poem is never finished; it is only abandoned." Second, as a caveat to other poets/writers who may be reading this. And here, I'll quote some wise advice I received (years after writing "Swallow," I might add) from the poet Lise Goett, whose work I deeply admire:

> "...question every adjective you use and try the line without it. Polarize your opposites, meaning not every adjectival slot can be filled. Allow the pageant of the poem to move with less freight. The tendency to elaborate on a figure with two or more examples must be resisted and balanced by places where the language cuts to the quick without embellishment."

Sometimes I manage to heed that advice. It's something I'm perpetually working on.

Sara Pirkle

What Hurts

Maybe what hurts should always hurt.
The throbbing thumb, the achy joint,
The tender foot in thorn-filled dirt.
Maybe forgetting is not the point.

The throbbing thumb and achy joints
Are needling griefs we need to feel.
Maybe forgetting is not the point.
Maybe what heals should never heal.

These needling griefs we need to feel
Remind us where we tend to fail.
Maybe what heals should never heal.
The naked skin snagged on a nail

Reminds us when we tend to fail
To spy sharp edges we should fear.
Like naked skin snagged on a nail
My heart was snared by a poet's sneer.

Despite sharp edges I should've feared,
His words were little, pretty stings.
My heart was snared by the poet's sneer.
He'd strum his guitar, strum and sing.

His words were little, pretty stings.
I loved him though. I loved his hands.
He'd strum his guitar, then strum me.
His threatening lust plucked every strand.

I loved him though. I loved his hands.
His fingers tangled in my hair
Made threats of love to every strand,
Each greedy tug a teasing dare.

His fingers tangled in my hair
Unhooked my body's modesty.
Each greedy tug, each tease, each dare.
Yes, a constant state of agony

Unhooks a body's modesty.
But we forget the bites, the burns.
A constant state of agony
Could save us all from future spurns,

But we forget the bites, the burns.
Like tender feet in thorn-filled dirt
We stay exposed to future spurs.
Maybe what hurts should always hurt.

Listing and Listening

I was having dinner with some artist friends at a residency, and the conversation turned to having children. Most of us sitting around the table had never had a baby, but one woman, slightly older, had two. "You know, what's funny?" she asked. "I thought going into the second birth that it would be easy, because I was remembering the first time not being so bad. But when the delivery began and the pain was excruciating, I suddenly recalled how painful the first birth was. Why didn't I remember the pain?"

She went on to theorize that she forgot the pain because it was traumatizing and that humans had evolved over thousands of years to forget childbirth pain between pregnancies, because if women always remembered it, they would never choose to have a second baby, and the species would die out. As we were musing over this idea, we began sharing our own stories of pain that we'd forgotten, or that had dulled over time. At some point I said, "Maybe what hurts should always hurt!" As soon as I heard myself say that sentence out loud, I realized I had a good line for a poem.

A good line is as good way to trigger the writing of a poem. Richard Hugo speaks of "triggering subjects" in his book *The Triggering Town*. He says, "A poem can be said to have two subjects, the initiating or triggering subject, which starts the poem or 'causes' the poem to be written, and the real or generated subject, which the poem comes to say or mean, and which is generated or discovered in the poem during the writing." What I had after that dinner conversation was both a good line, and a good idea: the notion that if we could recall with perfect accuracy the pain of a certain experience, we might avoid it at all costs.

Though the poem I wrote became a pantoum, which is one of the strictest poetic forms, when I sat down to write, I did not have this form in mind. Instead, I just began to free-write on the topic of pain. I made a list in my journal titled "Things that Hurt" and tried to think of as many things that I could, ranging from mild to severe: a paper cut, a wasp sting, a finger pinched in a car door, muscles after a marathon, a double-mastectomy.

As I listed physical "hurts," I found myself also thinking about emotional pain—experiences I'd had that really hurt my feelings: unreturned phone calls, lies, insults, betrayals. As I made these lists, I realized that the *triggering* subject about physical pain really was leading me to the *generated* subject of emotional pain.

Once I'd compiled my lists of experiences, I made a list of words that related to pain: throbbing, biting, aching, agony, inflamed, raw, sore. As you can tell, I like making lists. Listing is one of the primary ways that I generate content for a poem. I love making word banks and even on days when I have no other idea in mind for a poem, if I can fill a page with words, I feel like I've generated the building blocks of a poem. I have often likened *listing* to *mining* when speaking of it to my students. In order to make art, one needs raw material to work with. Sculptors need a block of marble before they can carve a statue, and for my process, I need a block of text to carve a poem. The block of text tends to be a combination of free-writes and lists about the topic that I pare down and rearrange, cutting the dull phrases and words and leaving only the sharpest images.

After making my lists, I went back to the line that triggered my idea: "Maybe what hurts should always hurt." The line had a nice rhythm—I liked the repetition of the word "hurt" in the line, as well as the symmetry of the line (three syllables, *hurts*, three syllables, *hurt*). There was a musicality to the line that appealed to me, and I've always thought that the main difference between prose and poetry is the musicality of the language. As I started drafting the poem, I tried to write lines that had the same meter as the initial line (tetrameter), and I made another list in the margin of my journal of words that rhymed with the words on my list of painful words. By the time I had all of my lists and ideas generated and sitting in front of me, I realized I could turn them into a pantoum.

My grandfather was a Southern Baptist preacher, so I grew up reading the Bible before breakfast, going to church, sitting through sermons every Sunday, and my favorite part of church was always the music or the responsive reading—the moment in church when I could participate, throw my voice into the sanctuary. Hymns and bible verses rely on a lot of poetic devices: repetition, rhyme, imagery, alliteration, anaphora, and after years of weekly exposure to those devices, I internalized them. This may explain why repetitive poetic forms are so appealing to me—my favorite form is the pantoum, a poem that relies heavily on repetition and order. Every line is used twice in the poem, and the first line of the poem becomes the last, completing a full circle of thought.

Drafting and revising this poem was like putting together a complicated jigsaw puzzle; I could see all the pieces but needed to fit them together to make the bigger picture. Sometimes the best way to do that is to spread everything out on the table and make sure that you can see everything you're working with. And another bit of advice—you should never sit down and say, "I'm going to write a pantoum" (or a sonnet, or a villanelle) because it's nearly impossible to generate a poem in form in a first draft. These forms are easier to achieve when you have a different poem (often in free verse) that needs a shape.

Because I was at an artist residency when I wrote this poem, I had unlimited free time for a month to write. This poem took about two days to draft and revise in my studio, but that's because I was solely focused on it without any distractions. Very few of us are afforded the luxury of uninterrupted time to write a pantoum, and I have found that free-verse poetry is easier in my day-to-day writing. The main advice that I give my students (and that I have to remind myself) is that none of the rules of poetry matter when you are drafting. Setting yourself up to produce a complete poem in one sitting is a recipe for disappointment. Rather, approach the page with curiosity and playfulness. Be honest, be flexible, and allow your mind to make connections on the page, and perhaps you will stumble upon an idea that reveals a small truth about being human.

John Poch

Denzel Sestina

In the background, Denzel Washington,
who preferred not to come ashore with his fellow celebrity.
—Caption of photograph in Naples newspaper, *Il Mattino*

I wish you would have come ashore this morning
to Lacco Ameno for the sfogliatella
and selfies with the locals. I jogged past
the port and suffered on my three-mile race
with time. Almost fifty, I slogged up the hill
that overlooks your monstrous yacht. Which one?

I bet that new two-story silver one
that looked like a destroyer yesterday morning.
We saw it from another mighty hill,
Castello Aragonese. Sfogliatella
is a shell-shaped, stuffed, and layered-leaf treat. No race,
no hurry, six times the baker folds her past-

ry, crafting this confection unsurpassed.
I'm not much into movie stars, not one
for the latest hype. A poet, I erase
much better than I write. Most Texas mornings
I eat my toast, and I dream of sfogliatella
and cappuccino on someone else's hill

above the sea, some steep volcanic hill
now looking out on Saint Paul's shipwreck past,
perhaps these very waters. Sfogliatella,
like a sun-stuffed seashell, pleases everyone.
Your pal, Will Smith, on Ischia this morning!
Your two yachts moored there are in a kind of race.

Of wealth. You float. I run. I sidestep *race*,
though half the world in which we live, the hill
we climb, the sea we sail, is words. Morning
has cast its jasmine over the slave trade past.
But Africa's not far, whence gusted one
dusty scirocco last week. Sfogliatella

is rich. You really should try the sfogliatella.
I've changed again our theme from precarious race
to pastry, privilege, taste. As I, for one,
can taste in the candied orange this local hill
terraced with citrus trees, the ancient past
in the blood orange, the orange's blood like morning.

On heaven's hill, Denzel, no death, no mourning,
our bodies shift, our mortal races passed.
And breakfast: sfogliatella for everyone.

Denzel & Me

Travel is essential for poets. You don't *have* to travel (you have to do a lot more of it with your imagination, anyway), but it is probably the primary thing that you can do to open up your imagination to new possibilities, especially through seeing your own language and self differently. If anything is needed for a serious poet, it is a kind of objectivity that allows one to escape the blind subjectivity suffered by bad writers. They like the sound of their own voices, and they think that people might *get* them. Writers in the midst of their writing often think they are being clear, but the picture in their own heads of what they are concocting mostly remains in their heads. It is better to find some distance (literally) with your own writing. Get out of your own head, at least into your body, and take that body elsewhere to see and know where you were and who you are.

For the past fourteen years, I've been traveling quite a bit, off and on, to Spain, teaching numerous study abroad courses in Sevilla, as a Fulbright Core Scholar to the University of Barcelona, and on a one-month residency to Fundación Valparaíso—a residency program below the cliffs of the little white seaside town of Mojácar. I'm a lucky guy, yes, I know. I've written and published other books during this time, but little by little I've put together an entire manuscript of poems (mostly love poems) that have Spain as their place, their source, and their inspiration. The Spain I have experienced, especially the south, is a place of deep beauty and passion, involving suffering and blood (see Lorca), and maybe in the next year or two I will publish these poems in book form.

But, in more recent years, I have been traveling to Italy, and it is my plan to focus my writing on her landscape and culture rather than the other side of the Mediterranean. Three times now I have traveled to the island of Ischia with my friend, the poet Chad Davidson, and each time have come away with good handfuls of poems. Chad and I explore the island; we swim; we run; we eat (some of the best food I've ever eaten); we drink; we catch up on our lives; take walks down memory lane; and we write almost every day. Chad writes in one room, or out on the patio, and I write somewhere else. An hour or two later, we come together and share what we have gotten down on paper. We listen, and we criticize and praise. Then we go for a swim or something. "Denzel Sestina" is a result of one of our writing sessions.

This poem (obviously, a sestina) in particular, was inspired by seeing in a local newspaper that Denzel Washington and Will Smith had come through Ischia, briefly, parking their yachts the next town over from where we were staying. Denzel and I happen to share December 28 as a birthday, and I love his acting, so I was particularly happy to see that we had almost met! I fantasized briefly of running (literally, maybe?) into him on one of our outings. I thought maybe I'd write a poem for him, so I began this one, thinking there was no way to pull it off, but if I could I would call it "Denzel Sestina" and I further fantasized that he would one day read it, and we would share a drink or a meal, or even a breakfast involving *sfogliatelle*.

In graduate school, one of my professors suggested to me that a good sestina often has one odd teleuton (the repeating end-words). Think Anthony Hecht's teleuton "Rochester" or Elizabeth Bishop's "almanac." The writer should vary the use of other teleutons in the sestina, because homonyms or word fragments (past, passed, surpassed, past-/ry) might spark the reader's interest in the craft and keep them reading until the end of the 39 lines. You don't want to be too obnoxious about it; you want the poem to do its work with meaning being clear. Is "past- / ry" too obnoxious? Probably. This poem is all about Denzel and my imaginary *sfogliatelle* breakfast with him—I just couldn't help myself. I used *sfogliatella* as an end-word because it is so strange, as a word, the *sf* and *gl* sounds something we never use quite the way the Italians do. *Sfogliatelle* is the plural, and I sweated over whether to use that or the singular for a long time. I settled on the singular.

One of the teleutons I thought to use from the very beginning was "race." I knew I would use it in the context of running and also in that I am not African American and Denzel Washington is. So, what of it, especially in a time of racial strife in America where Black Lives Matter protests have been drawing our attention to violent injustices? How am I going to get THAT into a sestina in which I'm living this privileged existence for a week on an island, writing poems? Denzel has his own privilege, obviously, what with the yacht, but it's not the same. We know this. So what of it? What could I say? In "Denzel Sestina," I attempted to address race, and then, maybe I'm commenting on my failure to do that. Do I fall into the imitative fallacy? Also, am I anointing my own white privilege? I do think about Rodney King lamenting back in 1992: "People, I just want to say, you know, can we all get along?" At some point, one wants this kind of wide civility and for people to "not be judged by the color of their skin but by the content of their character," as Dr. King so profoundly put it.

I thought of heaven, where we are all equal and loved. Certainly, I try to do my part here and now, but I'm not so romantic to think that a poem can enact racial justice or change anybody's mind about behaving better. As well, I don't want to be charged with escapism. But, I figured that's my prayer, that men like Denzel Washington and I might have something more in common than we have differently. Not yachts, not skin color, but the love of film, of poetry, and the Word of God (see *The Book of Eli*). I want heaven on earth, which brings us back to *sfogliatella*.

Denzel, give me a call. I'm easy to find.

Paisley Rekdal

Wild Horses
Seraph Young Ford, Maryland, 1887
First woman to vote in Utah and the modern nation, February 14, 1870.

I am known, if at all, for a moment's
      pride: *first American woman*
in the modern nation
    to vote though at the time

I wasn't considered American
      by all. Not modern, either,
but Mormon, one
    the East Coast suffragists had hoped

would vote Utah's scourge of polygamy
      out. But plural marriage
was on no ballot
    I ever saw. Why would it be,

my mother asked, when men
      make laws and shape
their women's choice in freedoms?
    And how changeable

those freedoms are
      denied or given
certain women, she knew, who saw
    a Shoshone woman one day selling ponies

from a stall: watched, amazed,
      her pocket all the earnings
without a husband's permission.
    I wouldn't be a white girl

for all the horses
    in the world, the woman scoffed
at her astonishment: my mother
    who never sold an apple

without my father's
           say-so. Like my mother,
I married young, to an older man who believed–
           like certain, stiff-backed politicians—

to join the union, Utah
           must acculturate, scrub off
the oddities and freedoms
           of its difference, renounce

some part of politics and faith:
           our secrecy and marriage customs,
and then my woman's right to vote. All gone
           to make us join

the "modern" state—
           And so perhaps I might be known
for what I've lost: a right, a home,
           and now my mother, who died

the year we moved back East.
           How fragile, indeed, are rights
and hopes, how unstable the powers
           to which we grow attached.

My husband now can barely leave his bed.
           As he's grown ill, I've watched myself
become the wife
           of many men, as all men in the end

become husband
           to a congregation of women.
When he dies, I'll move back West
           to where my mother's buried

and buy some land with the money
           that she left—
To me alone she wrote,
           who loved me,

and so for love of her
           I'll buy a house
and marble headstone
           and fill my land with horses.

On Wild Horses

In early 2019, I was commissioned by the Academy of American Poets
and the New York Philharmonic to contribute a poem to *Project 19*, a pam-
phlet of poems by 19 American women poets that would commemorate

the passage of the 19th amendment to the U.S. Constitution. As Utah's poet laureate and a longtime resident of the West, I chose to write a monologue in the voice of Seraph Young, the first woman to vote in Utah and the modern American nation.

Many readers may not know that the fraught and complex history around women's suffrage in the western territories reflected the larger conversation the nation as a whole was having in the late 19th century around assimilation, states' rights, gerrymandering, and racial and ethnic identity, a conversation that often turned white women into symbolic figureheads of larger forces they themselves could not always control, even as they benefited from them. Nowhere was this more apparent than in Utah.

While the United States did not nationally legalize women's suffrage until 1920, many western territories did, in order to both generate publicity and bolster local conservative voting blocks. Wyoming was the first territory to give women the vote, in December 1869. Utah followed two months after, granting women suffrage on February 12, 1870. The state held its first elections in Salt Lake City two days later, and Seraph Young, a schoolteacher and grand-niece of the Church of Jesus Christ of Latter-day Saints (LDS Church) President Brigham Young, was the first in line to cast a vote.

At the time Seraph Young cast her vote, the Utah Territory was considered by many East Coast activists to be a testing ground for the national case for women's suffrage. The hope was that Mormon women like Young would vote out polygamy, which the vast majority of Americans opposed, thus demonstrating that suffrage could give women a voice different from their husbands' and fathers' as well as provide definitive evidence to skeptical politicians that women's votes could be of significant social use. Polygamy, however, was never on any Utah referendum, thus Utah women had no opportunity to vote plural marriage out, if indeed they would have.

When Utah women did not vote out polygamy, some lobbyists argued to Congress that not only should polygamy be abolished, but women in Utah be stripped of their voting rights. In 1887, Congress passed the Edmunds-Tucker Act, punitively taking away the voting rights of all Utah women, Mormon and non–Mormon. Utah women, furious at losing the right to vote, lobbied hard for re-enfranchisement; however, when Utah became a state in 1896, it entered the union with women's voting rights firmly intact.

I happened upon Seraph Young's story and the problems of Utah women's suffrage while doing research for another poetry commission, this time to commemorate my state's 150th anniversary of the transcontinental railroad's completion. While researching for my multi-media poem "West," I read numerous travelogues by East Coast journalists traveling to Utah that focused on what D.C. politicians once called "The Mormon and Indian Problem," a phrase I found fascinating in its casual elision of so many distinct cultures into one monolithic (and racialized) threat. In our current moment, we tend to portray Mormons as the epitome of American conservative whiteness, but in late nineteenth-century America, Mormons—by dint of their practice of polygamy, their large number of immigrant practitioners, the novelty of their faith, their insularity, and their (often well-founded) hostility to non–Mormon outsiders—were racially and nationally suspect. Cartoons in magazines popularly depicted withered-looking Mormon men holding hands with women from other polygamous or conspicuously non-white cultures, implying that Mormons were not only racially "other" and "primitive," but inherently un–American.

On top of this, the 1857 Mormon-led Mountain Meadows massacre of the Baker-Fancher emigrant train in southern Utah only fed East Coast fears that the Mormons, and Utah, posed a physical threat to civic peace and national unity, fears that only increased in the wake of the Civil War.

The Mormons and the LDS Church presented a cultural and political problem similar to that posed by the sovereignty of Native Americans. Could Mormons and Utah be assimilated into the growing American nation? Would they be harmful or beneficial to the building of the transcontinental railroad and would they impede the nation's martial, westward expansion? Would the nation be forced to fight a war with Utah, as it had with the South and also with American Indians, or could the state be subdued with threats and trade? But while many Americans might have seen Mormons as "like" Native Americans, Mormons did not see themselves the same way.

The travelogues I read about the transcontinental focused almost exclusively on the "exotic" aspects of Mormon culture, more so even than on the cultural presence of American Indians and Chinese in the West. At the heart of this focus, naturally, was the question of what Mormon women themselves were like. Were they pretty? Were they naïve, uneducated, or stupid? What kind of white women would allow themselves to be treated as interchangeable chattel? Why were these women given the vote at all, unless their husbands believed they fully controlled them?

Into this fray stepped Seraph Young, whose very name—and whose contemporary cartoon image I've now seen plastered on billboards across my state—suggests angelic white femininity. Not much is known about the real Seraph Young, unfortunately, especially not her thoughts and feelings about her ethnic upbringing. The few details I could find are included in the poem, and certainly the poem itself is meant to memorialize her complex historical meaning in the women's rights movement. "Wild Horses" isn't a typical poem for me as the poem isn't even *for* me, which is how I like to think about my poetry in general. I wrote this poem specifically for younger students to engage them in a larger conversation about American history, and in that, I care less about whether the poem is "good" or "truthful" and more about whether the poem connects the reader to a larger conversation around American history. As a state poet laureate who teaches in K–12 schools, I've tried to re-imagine the place poetry might hold in a classroom, to enlarge poetry's place in students' lives. Why do we only read poetry in English classes? Why can't we also see—and teach students to create—poems as critical engagements with other humanistic fields, thus expanding poetry's reach through its expanded pedagogical application?

Poetry, of course, is not history, as it does not make the same claims to factual accuracy. I certainly have no idea what Young really thought about polygamy, though I do know her own husband (an ex–Civil War soldier) never took a second wife, and in fact wasn't even Mormon. I have no idea how close Young really was to her mother, and I certainly don't know what interactions, if any, Young had with the Shoshoni. That said, I was also never interested in duplicating any strict biographical narrative nor easy hagiographic renderings of her as suffragist heroine. Young's Mormon background may be unique to the average contemporary reader, but it presents another kind of challenge to a reader steeped in western history. The Mormon relationship to the Shoshoni is deep and also violent, as many Shoshoni lived on lands the Mormons later seized.

The Shoshoni are a matriarchal and itinerant tribe of four cultural divisions or bands, whose lands altogether traditionally extend from Wyoming and across northern and western Utah, Nevada, and southern Idaho. Settler colonialism in the nineteenth century meant Mormon encroachment on the Northwestern Band of Shoshoni hunting lands, forcing some Shoshoni to raid farms and ranches for food. In 1863, soldiers from Fort Douglas in Salt Lake City attacked a group of the Northwestern Band of Shoshoni near Bear Creek, located in southern Idaho, massacring over 400 people, mostly women and children. In 1875, after a decade of starvation, many Northwestern Shoshoni converted to Mormonism and settled on a farm near Corinne, Utah, before being driven out again due to unconfirmed rumors of a planned Shoshoni attack on white farmers. The remaining Northwestern Band of Shoshoni were then forced onto the newly founded Fort Hall reservation in Idaho.

While I've invented the details about Seraph Young's mother and the Shoshoni woman, there are a number of nineteenth century letters and diaries from white women noting the rights of ownership and self-sovereignty that native women possessed at the time that white women did not. The most famous example of this might be Elizabeth Cady Stanton's recounting of witnessing a Haudenosaunee woman in 1820 selling her own horses. In 1891, the writer Emma Borglum noted a similar event in South Dakota. According to Bridget Quinn in *She Votes*, when she told the native woman that she herself could not sell horses without her husband's permission, the woman replied, "I would not be a white woman."

"Wild Horses" may be sympathetic to Seraph's unique ethnic and gendered position, but an acute reader may notice that the presence of the Shoshoni woman makes the poem implicitly critical of her racial one. Suffrage was something *white* women in Utah had, not all women, and if white women's political awakening came in part via interactions with native women, it also came at their expense as well. Rights and powers may be "fragile" for women like Seraph Young, but they were even more fragile for those whose tribal sovereignty was threatened and sometimes eradicated by the U.S. government. A reader interested in Utah native rights might want to read about Zitkála-Šá, a Yankton Dakota Sioux woman, musician and writer who moved to Utah in 1902, founded the National Council of American Indians, and actively fought for both native citizenship and women's suffrage.

My poem, like all persona poems, is a fabrication of a self, not a biography, but what I lose in a completely accurate rendering of Young, I hopefully gain in presenting a larger truth of the era in which she lived. That, for me, is one of poetry's unique strengths: its ability to compress and encapsulate broader moments of time and to place potentially contradictory narratives alongside each other. While readers do not need to know all, or even part of the history I've detailed here, when reading "Wild Horses," it may be helpful to consider the issue of women's rights within the larger national conversation happening during the 19th century around citizenship, race, ethnicity, assimilation, power, and gender, a conversation that twenty-first-century Americans are still very much engaged in now.

On a final, more personal note, I'd like to say that as a biracial woman who has become Utah's representative poet, I felt it was important to complicate the symbolic figurehead that Young has become at this moment in time in Utah. Oftentimes, we choose artistic and historic figures to represent non-threatening institutional values. Young, and I, might be unwitting accomplices to a version of western history that wants to ignore the more questionable, ethnically suspect or even violent histories that we also represent. In that, while I want to celebrate and sympathize with Young, I do not want to humanize her without some acknowledgment of what her humanity also historically cost or was finally denied.

Alberto Ríos

Refugio's Hair

In the old days of our family
My grandmother was a young woman
Whose hair was as long as the river.
She lived with her sisters on the ranch
La Calera, the land of the lime,
And her days were happy.

But her uncle Carlos lived there too
Carlos whose soul had the edge of a knife.
One day to teach her to ride a horse
He made her climb on the fastest one
Bare-back, and sit there
As he held its long face in his arms.

And then he did the unspeakable deed
For which he would always be remembered.
He called for the handsome baby Pirrín
And he placed the child in her arms.
With that picture of a Madonna on horseback
He slapped the shank of the horse's rear leg.

The horse did what a horse must
Racing full toward the bright horizon.
But first that horse ran under the *álamo* trees
To rid its back of this unfair weight,
This woman full of tears
And this baby full of love.

When they reached the trees and went under,
My grandmother's hair, which had trailed her
Equal in its magnificence to the tail of the horse
That hair rose up, and flew into the branches
As if it were a thousand arms
All of them trying to save her.

The horse ran off and left her,
The baby still in her arms,
The two of them hanging from her hair.

The baby looked only at her
And did not cry, so steady was her cradle.
Her sisters came running to save them.

But the hair would not let go.
From its fear it held on, and had to be cut
All of it, from her head.
From that day on my grandmother
Wore her hair short, like a scream
But it was long like a river in her sleep.

The Story Is Relative

Some poems are remembered into being; some poems are needed into being. This poem should have been a memory but was instead the profound disruption of a memory—a "new" memory, if such a thing is possible.

This poem is predicated on family history, on stories repeated so often through the years at the kitchen table after a Sunday meal. I spent many hours there with my grandmother, whose name was Refugio, her sisters, and, my great-grandmother, whose name was also Refugio, and all the permutations of a large family. However, this recounting is not the family history I thought I knew.

The poem has in it my great-uncle, Carlos. Even though I knew him all my life, in this poem, because of what happens, he appears as a new-found relative to me. He is not the man I knew.

Growing up I thought he was a wonderful man. That sense of him changed so dramatically just after he died. I had come home from college and was sitting in the living room when my father got the phone call from family in Mexico. He spoke for a bit, listened, then blanched a little and finished the conversation. When he hung up, he said to me, "Son, you probably don't remember him, but my uncle Carlos died."

Don't remember him? I had already been writing about him and remembered him quite specially, though in that moment I realized I had probably never said that aloud. He was internal to me, internal to my experience, which felt very large. He seemed like a big part of my life, at least my imaginary life, and I had already mentioned him several times in early poems.

When we were quite young, we visited the family rancho in the northern Mexican state of Sonora, just south of Arizona. Mexico is an agrarian country, and virtually everyone has a family rancho or a farm somewhere in their background. Ours was called La Calera. In its later years, Carlos had become its caretaker, and it had become a place that grew fruit trees.

When we visited, it was during summer vacation when all the fruit trees were perfectly in their moment.

As we approached and before we went inside, Carlos said to me and my brother, "go ahead, go get whatever you want"—and off we went running. We climbed into those trees and stuffed ourselves with all sorts of fruits, all perfect—it felt like the Garden of Eden. When we were done, we went into his house, which was one room and made of adobe. The whole thing was so old and weathered that it leaned a little, and the window, which was now distorted, had no glass, so that one could get in through the window, which my brother and I thought was fantastic. Of course, it was abject poverty, but I wouldn't know to recognize that for many years.

About a week after hearing that he had died, I was visiting with my aunt Norma and I expressed to her how sad it was that he was gone.

"*Sad? Sad?*" she practically shouted. "He was the meanest man who ever lived."

In that half-second, my whole sense of our family history was about to be profoundly changed. I had brought my own childhood into the mix of this man's memory without considering what others might have gone through—as kids are wont to do. To me, he had seemed to live an aspirational life, idyllic, close to nature, timeless.

She proceeded to tell me story after story of what life was like for my grandmother and her sisters as they lived on the ranch with this Carlos. There were so many, and so defining, how, for example, he taught them to swim by throwing them in the river while carrying a stick that he poked them with repeatedly when they tried to get out.

She told me one story in particular, about my grandmother's hair, which simply glowed in narrative neon as an exemplar of something singular, something especially cruel and lasting.

I quickly sat down to recount her story and I cast it in the form of a family legend, something mythic, starting with what sounded to me like a kind of standard opening for these kinds of stories, "In the old days of my family…." I wanted something traditional to start what I knew would be as far from traditional in my own life as possible. I wanted to get out of its way. The poem, in so many ways, was simply there, waiting to be told, or, rather, to tell itself.

That is the story of the poem, but its narrative brought along something more, something of its own. Understanding what I had told came to be another thing.

Something else happened, something beyond the story, something for me as a writer and a thinker. After I wrote and published the poem, it was pointed out to me that I had ascribed agency to inanimate objects in the poem—particularly the hair, characterized as feeling fear. The narrative, near the end, indeed gives the hair itself very real and crucial voice. The poem allows the hair to be a full participant in that moment, rather than being relegated to merely one more imaginative detail.

The hair and its moment had a quiet economy of purpose—not in themselves showy, but simply one more logical part of the telling of the event. True and necessary to the moment, the hair's speaking parts are workaday words, not performative actors. They do their job and get out, narratively speaking. In this simple way, these words suggest a quiet magical realism, something intrinsic to the moment but spoken my way and through me.

This felt true to the moment but extraordinary as well.

I've never tried to write magical realism, always relying on the idea that it derived from lives lived, not lives imagined. This small note in this poem brought that idea home to me in a very personal way. It helped me to understand that I am only ever part of the story.

Tim Seibles

Movie

It was already on when you came in:

a two-lane road, the car's high beams
blaming the dark. In the rearview mirror,
the downtown of a city—familiar, but not.

Because you have found yourself
cast in the world without your consent,

you think you must be something
like other people—like the dude
two rows back with his face lit by a phone

or maybe like the star behind the wheel:
one eye swollen, the other tight in a squint.

You want to know what happened,
what's happening and where the road
will go and when and soon

she's standing outside a *7–11*
filling up her dusty, dark-blue Mustang.

Early sun steams the back window.
Maybe she drove all night—

her voice: part sorrow, part wind
under the overhang. *Why didn't I*

see it before, she asks aloud
for everyone, flexing the engine,

ready to go.
This is the story of what

happens when what
has seemed one way

turns out to be *another* way:
like a priest.
Even when the day is sprung,
and you wake up trapped
in everything, you want this face

on screen: cool, without a flinch.

Even the way she steers
is a declaration—you want to drive
like that.

You could drive like that:
like somebody in charge,
somebody who "knows the deal."

On the passenger seat,
half-stashed in her scarf, a .38.

Your mind moves to revenge: how
your circumstances just don't
make any sense. You want

to know who made it this way

and one chance to make them
back down and beg: the reversal,

sizzling with drama and music
that means *you were right*

all along. That's why you

keep watching—like everyone else
holding their sodas in the dark.

She could be a friend,
A nice person who deserves

some goddam *justice.* You
can tell she'd like another life:

without so many
hard decisions adding up

to only one. Maybe
you really are the character
other people think you are,

even though they can't hear
what's playing in your head.

After the movie, you walk
back into the mall wondering

if you could do what
she did. *That was*

pretty good, you mutter
with no one nearby

and light all over your face.

The Making of "Movie"

Like most human beings, I think of myself as a peaceful person,
someone who'd rather engage others through kindness rather than anger

or violent confrontation. However, over the years, I have sometimes found *payback* movies hard to resist. I started this poem after watching *Rosewood* and *V Is for Vendetta,* then a few days later, *Alita: Battle Angel.* I had not planned to write anything, but this poem emerged as my curiosity about the pleasure taken in such films became a persistent itch in my brain.

Stumbling into a poem's subject is normal for me, so at first, I had no solid sense of intention, no idea what I was chasing. This is what makes revision crucial; it is rethinking and rewriting that reveals the fullness of what is at hand. In the early drafts, I thought the poem might be a spoof of the revenge genre. I think this notion still shows in the opening stanzas. When I felt the poem take a serious turn toward the vengeful impulse, I was uncomfortable. The old parental whispers, "Be nice, behave yourself," were causing me to hesitate. Over the years, I have come to accept that this anxiety is part of any work that confronts a cultural taboo. Violence, even when it might appear justified, is rarely seen as a good thing.

Coming to grips with the poem's real subject usually demands a shift in my perspective, a widening of the aperture through which I *see* the poem. In this case, the revelation of subject helped me gain a clear sense of the tone and structure that would sharpen the ideas and emotions central to the poem. I had tried a few different ways of starting the action, but they felt off, too simple, too *thin.* When I understood that this poem had to involve a story within a story, that the re-telling of the movie was going to be a slant re-telling of the speaker's life, I also realized that the figure who was watching the movie (the *you* in the poem) could be me or anyone.

In finding the poems we are driven to write, I think we are also *found* by those poems. While working on this one, a vein of my own jagged anger came to light, but writing fueled by anger requires extra discipline. If not brought under the governance of craft, hard feelings can lead to blurred vision, bad choices. If you've ever tried to have a careful conversation while enraged, you know that it's virtually impossible. I had to resist the urge to write *with anger,* but anger *is* unruly. To treat it honestly, some of its threat must be present. Without it, the poem becomes a yapping poodle rather than a Rottweiler starting to bare its teeth—and I wanted that low growl of warning.

If a person is lucky, they are raised in a home where fury is rarely expressed—is, in fact, seen as a terrible loss of self-control, a complete failure to live up to the standards of respectable behavior. However, much of what society demands of us and *projects at us* is maddening. Acting like nothing's wrong—*playing it cool*—requires a kind of make-believe which, bit by bit, becomes a mandate (if we'd like to keep our job and our friends). In large part, the *workday* shifts our attention to work and away from the concerns and emotions that define our personal lives. No matter what else is going on, we must also live with the constant shove: *do your job—make it to the weekend.*

Consider the American ideas of race, for example, and the racialized thinking that has grown from those ideas and the various torments suffered by those who've been targeted by such thinking. Consider the various daily affronts that women sustain as they live—or what it means to be poor or *working poor* in this country. There is very little true relief for these groups of people. Lastly, think of the bile almost everyone has to swallow in a society that generally values profit over human fulfillment.

It's clear that movies of the wronged getting revenge speak directly to my own *felt* predicament. Few of us ever say it aloud, but it's easy to believe that our lives have been damaged by societal forces that show no regard for what we wish, so there's some short-lived satisfaction in watching somebody *get even* with those who've done harm. This may not be admirable, but it does reflect something undeniable about a prevailing sense of chronic frustration, and isn't this the sort of straight-shooting—pardon the pun—that we want from art? No matter how displaced I may feel, it helps when a film (or a poem) offers proof that my take on reality is, in fact, *shared.* In thinking through and writing "Movie," I realized that my own simmering dissatisfaction with life in America is probably just one marker of the aggravation shared by many of my fellow citizens.

By the ninth and tenth drafts, I knew there had to be a clear approximation of a revenge narrative, something that would call the genre to mind without being overly specific. I wanted this poem to point to all such movies—and the star needed to be an avatar for anyone who's felt bullied or beaten up by the rough aspects of *getting along* in the world. The images in the poem—of both the movie theater and the movie—had to be poignant enough to draw readers in, call up specific memories of such films, and nudge readers to reflect on their own recurring grievances.

The most difficult thing was shaping the half-story, which had to be spare but evocative. I wanted the reader to feel what I felt as the poem took shape, not merely *interest* but visceral anxiety, creeping desperation, and that touch of rage. In the early stanzas, I tried to sow the seeds of righteous anger and curiosity—the elements that drive the suspense that make a revenge story irresistible: the woman's wounded face, the driving through the night until dawn, her wondering aloud about what she should've known, and the suggestion that she'd been in some way ambushed. Once those things were in place, it was simply a matter of using *my own* anger and disappointment as fuel—particularly for the speaker's *voice*, the voice that narrates the poem and moves beyond the action to address the predicament of the *you* directly. By the seventeenth and eighteenth drafts, I felt my own ire becoming tightly braided with the star's sense of things, and I believed her story could operate as an emblem of any reader's story. With this, the poem seemed about finished.

I first fell in love with poetry because it struck me as a magical form of transportation—much like movies. You enter a poem and, by its closing, you have traveled in some immeasurable way from ignorance to knowing, perhaps from equivocation to a kind of certainty. Maybe, in this case, a repressed emotion, a previously hidden perspective, was revealed and—for better or worse—I stumbled into a not-so-polite view of the human interior, a different understanding of who we are behind the smiling mask.

Vijay Seshadri

Trailing Clouds of Glory

Even though I'm an immigrant,
the angel with the flaming sword seems fine with me.
He unhooks the velvet rope. He ushers me into the club.
Some activity in the mosh pit, a banquet here, a panhandler there,
a gray curtain drawn down over the infinitely curving lunette,
Jupiter in its crescent phase, huge,
a vista of a waterfall, with a rainbow in the spray,
a few desultory orgies, a billboard
of the snub-nosed electric car of the future—
the inside is exactly the same as the outside,
down to the m.c. in the yellow spats.
So why the angel with the flaming sword
bringing in the sheep and waving away the goats,
and the men with the binoculars,
elbows resting on the roll bars of jeeps,
peering into the desert? There is a border,
but it is not fixed, it wavers, it shimmies, it rises
and plunges into the unimaginable seventh dimension
before erupting in a field of Dakota corn. On the F train
to Manhattan yesterday, I sat across
from a family threesome Guatemalan by the look of them—
delicate and archaic and Mayan—
and obviously undocumented to the bone.
They didn't seem anxious. The mother was
laughing and squabbling with the daughter
over a knockoff smart phone on which they were playing a
video game together. The boy, maybe three,
disdained their ruckus. I recognized the scowl on his face,
the retrospective, maskless rage of inception.
He looked just like my son when my son came out of his mother
after thirty hours of labor—the head squashed,
the lips swollen, the skin empurpled and hideous
with blood and afterbirth. Out of the inflamed tunnel
and into the cold room of harsh sounds.
He looked right at me with his bleared eyes.

He had a voice like Richard Burton's.
He had an impressive command of the major English texts.
I will do such things, what they are yet I know not,
but they shall be the terrors of the earth, he said.
The child, he said, *is father of the man.*

Senate Bill 1070 and "Trailing Clouds of Glory"

The first ideas for "Trailing Clouds of Glory" anticipated the writing of the poem by almost two decades. They came to me in a birthing room at New York Hospital, in 1992. My son was being born and the labor, as the poem says, was hard, very hard. Urgency was swirling around me without taking me up. I was the fifth wheel of that human agony, peripheral, insignificant, nothing more than the guilty party, while everyone else in the room—the nurses, Dr. Cox, our ob-gyn, who came in and went out regularly, and, centrally and heroically, my wife, Suzanne—was fixed on the tremendous task at hand. I was exquisitely conscious of my uselessness; and doing the things I'd been told to do—rubbing Suzanne's shoulders and what was available of her back, feeding her ice chips, telling her to breathe—actually made emphatic rather than mitigated that uselessness.

Occasionally during those long, heaving hours, with all my time on my own hands, I would warehouse images and ideas in my mind. (I was going to write about this, of course.) Fragments of relevant literature floated around in my brain: the birth scene from "Anna Karenina"; imperious Caesar and Macduff untimely ripped from his mother's womb (at a moment of crisis, the question of a Cesarean came up; Suzanne said no); Anne Bradstreet's delirious parturition in John Berryman's "Homage to Mistress Bradstreet." And, also, I kept hearing Wordsworth's lines about birth and infancy from the Immortality ode: "Trailing clouds of glory did we come/From God, who is our home"—beautiful as lines but now, also, more than a little complacent-seeming in the face of the actual fact of a woman pushing eight pounds and fourteen ounces of fully articulated human flesh and bone through the tiny passageway and aperture of her birth canal.

Wordsworth's lines gave me the title of a poem, and the first line of the famous epigraph ("The child is father of the man") gave me the ending. The complacency gave me a working irony, a way to contrast fact and dream. That was as far as I got thinking it out sporadically in the birthing room, but I was sure given time I could do something with this frame, so a little while after we brought the kid home, I tried to work the frame into a poem. I couldn't get beyond those first ideas, though. I didn't have, for lack of a better word, a theme, and I couldn't find one then, and long after. For many years, I had the depressing experience of knowing you have great material but not being able to deliver it.

I always tell students never to give up on an idea, to keep all their ideas with them somehow—in their heads, in notebooks—and I use composing "Trailing Clouds of Glory" as an example. It took eighteen years to get from the idea to the poem. As well, I always tell students to pay attention to current events. The last place you might think of finding a poem might be the first place you find one. "Trailing Clouds of Glory" was rescued from my notebooks by current events, specifically, and incongruously, by the legislature of the State of Arizona, which in 2010 passed the Support Our Law Enforcement and Safe Neighborhoods Act, also known as SB (Senate Bill) 1070, an anti-immigrant bill. One of its provisions allowed Arizona law-enforcement officers to demand of anyone that they produce papers establishing their identity and immigration status if there was "probable cause" to think that person was "undocumented" and on Arizona soil without the authorization of the federal government.

When I read about SB 1070 in the *Times*, I felt the indignation a lot of people felt. The provision was blatantly unconstitutional (the Supreme Court eventually struck it down). It violated jurisprudence about the hard-won rights of the human person that went all the way back to the Magna Carta. It invited, it tacitly encouraged, in fact, racial profiling, profiling that I, as a brown person, would be subject to if I found myself within Arizona's borders. Would I ever be able to see the Grand Canyon again without exposing myself to unreasonable search and seizure? Strangely though, and maybe perversely, I also felt a surge of happiness when I read the *Times* story. It mysteriously and immediately triggered the solution to "Trailing Clouds of Glory." The story of SB 1070 immediately, by means of a leap I couldn't comprehend, attached itself to the ideas from the birthing room. As the first line popped into my head, I forgot my political indignation entirely, and the poem slid out that morning (after eighteen years) with almost no effort, just the way the baby slid out, with a shocking surprise and suddenness, after thirty hours of contractions and agonized pushing and rhythmic breathing and groaning.

Migration was the theme, the binding element, I'd been looking for. The migration of the soul into the body, and its slow imprisonment there, which is what the Immortality ode is about. My own complex immigrant status, extending back to the Eisenhower era, always with its ambiguity and privations and confusing middle-class privileges. The inception that is birth. The inception that is migration. Immigration, often thought of as quintessentially American, as a part of the American myth, but now an issue inciting hypocrisy and demagogy. Migration understood as metaphysical, as fundamental. All these things crowded around and then took their inevitable places in the rapidly developing poem. I remembered a Central American family I'd seen on the subway the week before; I recalled an image from somewhere—maybe a dream; maybe a science magazine—of Jupiter seen from one of its moons; I thought about how powerful and present and enraged my son seemed when Dr. Cox yanked him out of the womb and held him up. The turns came automatically. Everything suddenly fit, without needing my intervention. Everything seemed to write itself, and this after a long time when nothing in the poem would write itself or let me write it. I didn't have to force a thing. All I had to do was take dictation.

A lot has been written about moments of inspiration like this one. Most artists have experienced them. Some ascribe them to luck, some to grace. I've had a few of these moments (not nearly as many as I would have liked), and they leave me filled with wonder. How did that happen? How could I, of all people, have come up with something like that? Of all those moments, I would have to say the one out of which "Trailing Clouds of Glory" came is the one I think about the most, that is the most gratifying to me. The pregnancy was so long, the birth so short, and the midwife was the legislature of the great state of Arizona.

Patricia Smith

Coo Coo Cachoo

The boy doesn't trust his own skin. He paints his neck and forearms
with sugary scent, dabs a smidgen on his testes just in case.
He razors sprouting hairs until chest and chin are effortless as water.

I am drawn to that stinky willow, his preoccupation with leg day
and the bellies of Mustangs, how he assumes that I am primed for his
peppermint sigh to shift a pathway in my chest. Some trash,

I believe, is too luscious to discard. So I snap a fierce scarlet sheath
to my stride and hook a manicured forefinger under the lid of his left
eye. I'm a jukebox of slow drag songs, and that poor boy is gobbling

my lyric, clawing through his pockets for quarters. I am his mother,
his magic and his Magdalene—no mouth has thirsted for mere
skin this much. I toy idly with his air, watching his soft-grizzled

cheek spurt blood where my patient patent stiletto has snagged.
For a second, I pity, consider loosing him. But then he snickers
with particular oil, arranges the most potent angles of his pout.

Are you trying to seduce me, Mrs. Robinson?

I have studied all the ways there are to fall dramatically beneath
a hunter. So no, I'm not *trying* anything. We are oh-so-thickly
in the midst of this, and he knows that he knows how it will end.

He has all the time I don't, a complicated purplish tat riding high
on a bicep, and sweat sparkling his landscape. In a voice not unlike
his mother's, I plead with him to *stop/please don't* as if the very

bigness of him is a hurt I would beg for. He believes that once
he has dispensed of me, I will crumble, babbling of doomed love
and bellowing the nickname of his thrust. Instead, I press the full

of my hand against his chest and come away with his heart.
The writhing thing, still insistent upon itself, is barely worth
the bother. But still I lift it to my mouth. And I feed.

A Badass Woman Revises, Never Compromises

   I originally wrote a poem for a themed program at Hugo House
entitled "Leading Ladies"—several poets were asked to create new work

featuring strong women in film, television, and (although they never said this, I *assumed*) literature. I wrote about Alice Kramden, Ralph's droll, long-suffering spouse; Lady Frankenstein, just because her story has always fascinated me; and Mammy Two-Shoes, the black maid whose shuffling feet constantly appeared in early "Tom and Jerry" cartoons. At times, you heard her voice. Yes, she has a name, such as it is. Yes, she has a *website*. And yes, she was eventually replaced by a thin white woman.

"Coo Coo Cachoo" (from the Simon & Garfunkel song, remember?) was my "Mrs. Robinson" contribution from the film *The Graduate*. I'm sure you agree that she was undoubtedly a manipulative, uncompromising badass. I set out to write something that was sensory-driven, tantalizing, and stark, with the Lady Robinson, of course, in complete control. It's a persona poem in her voice as she studies her young admirer, reveling in his youth, touting how easy he will be to subdue and capture. She tricks him into believing that he wields the power, but ultimately—well, you know.

Yum.

First of all, I absolutely love writing poems on commission—I am obsessed with the pressure of writing something others are actually waiting for. Sometimes I imagine a ticking clock following me throughout the day. Sometimes it's the Sword of Damocles whistling just above my hairline. I often say I do my best poet-ing when I'm pressed. Actually, I think that's when I do my *fastest* poet-ing. There's no such thing as perfection. Sometimes I've written poems for an event *at* the event, crouching with pen and legal pad in the loo while program introductions begin blaring outside.

Of course, after the dust has settled (and the event is over), I always intend to pull the work back for careful review and revision. *Intend to.* But sometimes the initial piece, with its ink still drying, is relatively successful, and I fool myself into thinking that it's done. NO POEM IS EVER DONE. When I move from performance and begin to visualize the poem in a book or journal, I know I owe it a critical second look.

The poem that eventually rises from the ashes is crafted using a three-step process:

- **Story:** I have to make sure the story in my head is the one that's eventually told in the poem. All of it. What I loved. What scared me. What keeps me from forgetting. My poems tend to be heavily narrative, with rising action, a climax, falling action and, hopefully, a unpredictable conclusion. I believe I'm a storyteller who identifies as a poet.
- **Language:** As I tell my students (over and over and over), "If you've heard it before, take it out." There are so many comfort spots in

our language, so many places to sink into normalcy. If I can't find a fresh way to say something, I'd rather not say it. However, that's also a danger—sometimes my quest for "fresh" leads me into questionable, cringey territory. Unfortunately (or fortunately, considering the reason we're here), there are a few of those moments in the original attempt at this poem.

- **Music:** Sound in poetry is of the utmost importance. It's why I read every poem (actually everything) out loud, why I'm obsessed with poetic meter, why I guess dedicated two whole years to studying how the sound of a poem touches the air.

This is my first second look—the difficult birth of a new poem. Here's how the very flawed "Coo Coo Cachoo" became "Coo Coo Cachoo 2," or "Coo Coo Cahoo Two," or, at last, "Coo Coo Cachoo," too.

At 41 lines, the poem was too long. I knew it, you know it (if you know me at all), we all know it. I'll be the first to admit that I have a tendency to overwrite—especially since I come from a "get up on stage and do it," background, which often makes one talky and frantic for backdrop and more backdrop. There are some beautiful, deftly-crafted poems out there that deserve every one of 41 their lines. This is *not* one of them.

Some of those 41 lines included gems like "...his ribs float in some incarnation of a cheap suit" (I can just hear myself chastising my students for that fanciful phrasing) and "Oh, I am intrigued by that one," which is utterly too precious. I called the lanky young man, who was doused with too much cologne, a "fragrant willow," which makes me shudder even as I type it instead of "smelly." He wasn't "fragrant," he was "smelly." I also like the idea and surprise of "smelly willow."

"Rollicking assumption" just took up too much unnecessary room, and what makes an assumption "rollick" anyway? "Primed for" just sounds meatier than "ready for." "Idly stalked, then consumed," was really the whole poem in four words, and why let on so early?

Arrgggghhhh! The second stanza began with this catastrophe: "Crossing mile-high gams, my expression barely flickers."

See anything out-of-whack there? Anything? Anything at all?

AN EXPRESSION CAN'T HAVE MILE-HIGH GAMS!

"Coo with an overload of circumstance in my nouns"—*What?* I can't even imagine what I had in mind with that jumble of nonsense, although it flew by quickly during first performance and the audience seemed dazzled. Probably because they were trying to figure out what the hell I could possibly mean.

There was a line I loved in which the Lady Robinson described herself as "a thousand layers of my own daughter"—I was really thinking about the film there, but I wanted the poem to be more universal. Something for everyone. I considered pulling back on references to the actual film. I wanted every woman who read the poem to see themselves as the badass in question.

Oh, and there's more. What in the world is "improbably young"? I had a stiletto slashing the young boy's cheek, but maybe that stiletto was best doing something else. I needed to do something else with that stiletto, but what?

In stanza three, there was a tense problem. All of sudden, the speaker was at the beginning of the day? NOPE. Tense issues just go whizzing by when you're on stage, but the page is much less forgiving. I decided that I didn't want Mrs. Robinson's breasts to droop. I doubt she wanted them to droop either. There was a lot of misplaced throat-clearing, which happens when you're writing (1) on deadline, and (2) for a performance in which the audience will have no access to the actual written work.

I got to work, adding the unpredictable and trimming the downright weird.

I liked making a tattoo "complicated" and shortening "tattoo" to "tat" like the young'uns do. I had NO IDEA what I was doing with "ingrown hairs" ("He has youth on his side—/purple tattoo riding high on a bicep, those ingrown hairs/ sparkling his landscape"). "Golden boy sweat" wasn't really working. And "They dream incessantly of that drum" felt out of tone with—well, everything. I decided to simplify the language, especially zeroing in on the end of the poem. There was no need to repeat the sweet phrase "doesn't trust his own skin" from the first stanza, although I thought it was cute at first.

How about tercets? I write in big, long blocks until I decide not to. Hence, tercets! I carve and aim for conciseness and clarity. Engaging language, a surprising end. Still, a definite sexual undercurrent. This is what usually happens with these poems—they say what they say faster and better. I stop clearing my throat and wasting the reader's time.

Virgil Suárez

The Cotton Ball Queen

In 1970, Havana, Cuba, my mother
took it upon herself to inject

B12 on the butt cheeks of as many
neighbors as brought her doses

and paid for her service. My mother
wanted to be a nurse but was not

a nurse, but the house filled with women
waiting for their shots and I, at eight,

watched them lower one side of their
pants or shorts or pull up a dress

to expose their flesh to the needle.
The needle disappeared into the flesh.

My mother swabbed their skin
with a cotton ball drenched in alcohol

after each shot and threw it in a bucket
by the kitchen door. When she was

not looking I reached for a handful
and went outside to look at how

the blood darkened. I wrapped my
toy soldiers in the used cotton.

They were wounded. Cuba
was sending military personnel

to Viet Nam. My mother shot up
more people, "patients," as she called

them. When my father came home
there was no trace of anyone ever

been over. My mother expected
me to keep her secrets. On the mud

fort I had built in the patio all my
soldiers lay wounded, bloodied

and dying. At night I dreamt
of the house filling with mother's

pillow cases full of cotton balls.
In the United States, my mother

worked in a factory, sewing zippers
at 10 cents a piece. 25 years.

She never looked up from her machine.
Her fingers became arthritic....

Every time I cut myself shaving, I reach
for a cotton ball to soak up the blood.

Blood is a cardinal taking flight
against the darkening of the sky.

Nursing People Back to Health

I write from memory. I cannot help it. That is to say that I write from
the moment I remember something in particular about my childhood,
or people from another time and place, and certainly, I write about those
early years I spent in Cuba waiting for my parents to be granted entry visas
to come to the United States. Of course, I did not know any of this at the
time, but I heard things and I learned things, and as an adult, I started to
piece together what must have happened. I cannot blame my parents for
wanting to take their only son to a place that promised a better life and
a chance at a good education instead of taking the risk of that same son
being conscripted into the military and sent off to fight in a civil war in
Angola. Cuba was involved in both Vietnam and African conflicts during
those early years of my childhood.

My poems begin with the tendrils that connect me to a specific
moment in time. In this case, I remembered my mother's cotton balls and
the image of her stash, which she kept in the bathroom cabinet my grandmother and I shared—triggered by my own use of a cotton ball when I cut
myself shaving one day. The memories work their magic, but often it is
the case that I must drop whatever I am doing and sit at the computer and
connect these fragile tendrils or they will be gone forever. My first drafts
are often manic and scattered as I try quickly to put down everything I
remember. Both of my parents have always been such inciters, but most
certainly my mother with whom I have spent the most time in my life. My
father worked outside of the house when I was a child, and later, he died
rather young.

To say my mother is quite the character is to simplify matters in her
life. Nothing about her life and the way she carries herself is simple. She's
always been a fighter. I've tried very hard in this poem to show that, at

the same time, she was performing a task she tried her best to be good at. She wanted to be a nurse (I can only surmise she did not have the means nor the family support why not a doctor) but she never made it. Instead, she became a seamstress and a homemaker, but she has always dabbled in nursing people back to health, via standard practices or with her *remedios caseros*, as she calls her sorties into superstition and apothecary work. She is a fighter, and I often try to honor her spirit in my work without trying not to be too casual or sentimental. More often than not, I fail.

"The Cotton Ball Queen" sets out to capture the memory, but also paint a portrait of my mother and my life in a time and place I try my best not to forget. I tend to think my childhood in Havana circa 1960s and 70s was idyllic, but also fraught with pain and emotional scarring. My erotic meanderings began quite early for me as a child, so to see countless women pull up their skirts or lower their pants so that my mother could give them an injection thrilled me and filled with such longing that I still can close my eyes and see the needle enter the flesh.

All of the things I describe in the poem came to me in a feverish flash, and so I wrote it all down on the page. Then, I began to arrange and rearrange things. The wounded soldiers came later when I realized a lot of these women were married to men who had either gone off to serve as military advisors in Vietnam or were laboring in work camps run by soldiers. These were snippets of adult conversation and gossip I became privy to along the way.

The poem evolves from those connections, rooting deep and out of my psyche. I don't ask too many questions of my work as I am writing, but I do return to the poem over and over to make sure that I am being truthful to the craft and to the spirit of how most of my work arrives in my consciousness and evolves through its insistence that I get the details right. The right details always capture the truth and shed light on the universal. Without them and the right images, the poem cannot exist.

Mai Der Vang

Prayer to the Redwood

Senescent and dwelling
　　In your tower with sorrel

　　For shoes, I come to you fleshed
With intention,

A muted engine
　　　　Dismantled at your coastal throne,

　　In doubt and daring
Intuit from you:

　　　　　Tell me if you've
　　　　Heard of the Apis dorsata *and I*
　　　　　　Will affirm
　　　What I know of its innocence.

　　Take this confession to your
Wildlife, mahogany limbs

Grasping the upper
　　　Avenues of your genius memory

　　　　As readily there a
Nursery for hemlock and new firs.

　　How would you have guarded your pine?
These sudden flecks, you would have

Known its taste as factory-born far from organic consent,
　　　You would have deemed its

　　　　　　False footprint.
　　Here in your globe's

Fluent echo, you exhale the words:
　　Stockpile, degrade, human subjects.

230

I make sentient
My palm over your bark of suede,

Dense as it were to defy
A passing inferno.

Stockpile, degrade, human subjects.
No secret must ever be singed of your knowing.

Ever More Poems: A Poetics of Creation and Abundance

When I sense the urge to write a poem, the anticipation will pester me for days if I do nothing about it. I might evade the poem, perhaps even attempt to sidetrack myself for as long as I can. But the longer my postponement, the deeper my frustration and the stranger my body reacts as it starts to manifest physical symptoms: headaches, excitability, sweaty palms, and an overall somatic restlessness.

Maybe this behavior is embedded in some inherent need to "channel" an energy beyond myself. Or, more likely, maybe an external stimulus has activated a part of my *unconscious* mind, and through that activation, my unconscious mind has already written the poem. This happens unbeknownst to my *conscious* mind which still frets the act of having to write the poem and which lacks the sophistication to realize the poem is already done and out there, perhaps hovering around in some parallel plane of thought.

My charge as the poet is to go within, find the poem, and slog it through the unwieldy forest terrain of my unconscious self in order to cast the poem headfirst into the present moment. Maybe that's why my body will at times respond with a sense of eagerness and panic if I choose to do nothing. Something inside of me already senses the poem is within reach. The process of actually writing it then turns into an outpouring of adrenaline, a deep carving into and battling with my own creative interior to slowly draw and coax the poem out. When I was an MFA student, I encountered long days sitting with my poems, always at first staring for hours into a blank document screen (I still have days like this), and refusing to go out, leave my house, or do anything else until I had produced one line of poetry with which I was content.

So why do all of this to myself? Why bother if writing poetry can at times feel like a crisis of the body and mind, of the conscious and unconscious selves? For me, perhaps it's rooted in the idea of an individual and collective potentiality. Every poem I write humbles me and allows me to truly appreciate the depth of my own potential and the potential of all poets, artists, and writers—to participate in an act of artistic creation that happens because of our agency and will to create, because of the numinous miracles we manifest into this world when we craft something we did not initially think ourselves capable of. Where did that sudden potential for creation come from? From where did we pull the will to be capable?

Creation grants us the opportunity to experience the possibilities of our own abundance and to surprise ourselves every time we accomplish a piece of writing we did not expect to create. Anaïs Nin writes, "Perhaps I have loved the artist because creation is the nearest we come to divinity," and I, too, share in that belief. To excavate my own light and shadow as well as my potential for literary transformation is perhaps why I choose to create. Three days ago, the poem did not exist on a piece of paper, and my life, at that time, was all the lesser and deficient because of the poem's non-existence. But because I chose to write the poem and I chose to pursue the potential of having it in my life, the poem now exists, and I am made all the more abundant. It is sometimes as simple as that.

I wrote "Prayer to the Redwood" a few years ago and I recall experiencing that initial frenetic feeling—this poem would torment me if I ignored it. At the time, I was visiting the Mendocino area of California, surrounded by cathedrals of old-growth redwood trees all along the Pacific Ocean. I had seen redwood trees before, but I had never seen them in their full coastal majesty, groves of massive trees coming together as a kingdom, poised as Earth's ancestral sentinels, each individual redwood sheltering animals and other plants within its own distinct micro-ecosystem.

At the same time, I was working on poems for my second book on the subject of "yellow rain." As a daughter of Hmong refugees from Laos, I was born shortly after they arrived to the states. They escaped Laos like hundreds of thousands of other civilians who fled the region, and they settled in this country just after the U.S. Secret War in Vietnam and Laos came to an end. During the period of escape starting in the mid–1970s, many Hmong refugees recounted stories of a mysterious substance that fell mostly from planes in the sky, which caused severe illnesses and even death. This substance, known as "yellow rain," prompted a global investigation into allegations that a chemical biological weapon had been used against the Hmong in breach of international treaties. Culpability was pointed at the former Soviet Union, which had been charged with aiding the communist governments of Vietnam and Laos. Denials and accusations were thrown about. And then to the world's amusement, a group of scientists argued the substance was simply the feces of honeybees defecating en masse. An international political scandal erupted, wrapped in with partisan debate around arms development versus control. The truth of what happened to the Hmong was never entirely discovered nor fully told.

This book had been and would prove to be an exhausting project, specifically due to the extensive archival and declassified research I undertook in order to write the poems and offer another version of the yellow rain events. I had arrived to Mendocino steeped in all of this documentation and research, overwhelmed and without a clear sense of where to start my digging. But as I spent time in the northern California forests and learned about the coast redwood, *Sequoia sempervirens*, discovering that this incredible species can live up to 2,000 years, I realized that if someone possessed the answers to yellow rain, it had to be the ancient all-knowing redwood.

That's when the poem clicked for me: intuiting from the coastal redwood as a means to re-examine yellow rain. If there had been some manmade breach against nature inflicted by way of a biological weapon, the coast redwood would know and feel it deep down in its sagacious roots (even, I suspect, if it happened thousands of miles away and across bodies of water). In fact, if there's anything we need to know about the history of the world and our humanity, we can probably learn it from the redwood, whose resiliency and endurance have been witness to the evolution of our existence, and who has been here on this planet long before we came along and will remain here long after. I could not rest nor shake off this connection, as my unconscious mind had already begun scribbling out the lines, perhaps had even finished the poem. So without delay, I took to the page.

I prefer to write at night, especially when starting a new poem. This normally involves me sitting for hours with my laptop, talking out loud to myself and turning words and phrases over in my head so as to reorder them in a way that might intrigue my ear. Night one is entirely dedicated to generating that first line that will set the tone and serve as a launchpad for the rest of the lines to come. At least that's what happened in the case of this poem. I knew the word "senescent" was going to figure somewhere in the first line, but I did not immediately think it would be the first word. After much anguish and contemplation, "senescent" found its way to the poem's beginning, and as such, riffing off this one word came other words that shared a natural sonic consonance of the "e" sound: "dwelling," "fleshed," "intention," "engine," and to some extent, even the word "sorrel." To get this far in a poem for me can elicit feelings of satisfaction and relief. It might not appear as though I've done much, but in my mind, I've already completed 60 percent of the work.

The rest of the poem comes over the next few days. I prefer not to get wrapped up in the intricacies of enjambment or line breaks just yet, so I'll write the poem in a simple paragraph form, allowing the lines to flow across the page for however long they want. The language, diction, and word choices might be all over the place. The syntactical inversions and rupturing of phrases are given free rein. The voice is permitted to shift up and down. The images are encouraged to flip themselves inside out. Nothing is required to make sense at this point, if ever.

But as I'm working through the poem, there is one significant feature that consumes me and where I remain entirely attentive: sound. In the poem's grasping toward a sonic rigor, I am always attempting to recreate for the reader the syllabic musicality I hear in my head. This is why I read aloud and work alone most of the time. And if I'm tuned-in well enough, I can sometimes hear the sound and resonance of the line before I even know what the words will be.

In this particular poem, I felt a shift in the cadence nearing three-quarters of the way down. Starting with the line "I make sentient" which directly follows a three-clause list, my ear registered a sudden sonic break from the lengthier lines and more inquisitive language of the prior sections. Just after the list, I sensed the need for a sudden turn as the poem prepared its leap toward finishing, hence "I make sentient," a moment that returns the emphasis and ownership back to the "I" and the poem's speaker.

The draft is almost there. At this point, I am ready to integrate line breaks, explore enjambment possibilities, consider stanzaic form, implement delineations, rupture the page with negative spatiality, or whatever might move me to fully depict the poem's visual potential. I might also rearrange the lines, switch them around, and resituate them in a place that allows for the most unexpected effect. The title comes at the end of the process.

"Prayer to the Redwood" is a favorite for me, having allowed me to experience the work full circle from the point of disillusionment, to the moment of conceptualization, into the throes of creation, and then to completion. I've learned that writing poetry is one of the most powerful ways to connect with my unconscious mind, compelling me every single time to go deeper than I did before. To experience the outcome of my own work and have it surprise me, and then tell myself, "I didn't have this poem last week, but I have it today, and next week, I might be one more poem wealthier than I am right now," is just all the reason to celebrate and keep writing.

William Walsh

Why Otters Hold Hands

I want to live in a small town like Lakewood,
where the fastest thing is a sailboat without wind.

I want to know the world is safe for my daughter,
that I never have to share my failures, a place,

where, if I ever lose my religion again, someone
will return it to my house, ring the bell

and if I am not home, they'll leave
it on the mat. I want a kid selling scout popcorn

or Christmas paper to stop me at the grocery store,
and I want a kid on every corner selling Kool-Aid

from a card table, and a kid asking to rake my leaves.
I want the woman down the street to wear her bikini

while pushing the mower. I want a parade through town
every Fourth of July, and I want Friday fish fries

at the church. I want to hear my daughter singing
in the shower while I'm cooking spaghetti, straining

the angel hair while she crows like Iris Dement,
lost to herself, having forgotten the rest of the world can hear her.

I want to sit at the kitchen table, listening, just listening.
There's so much, and yet, I can never have it again:

Dora the Explorer, helicopter rides, or watching a documentary
on *The Life of Otters*, how we laughed

at the *Dog Fails* on YouTube, scrunched up together on the sofa
eating popcorn with too much salt, dripping with butter

and drinking Cokes on a school night.
I want my daughter to walk with me

in the mall and not down the other side
like I am an alien, the family embarrassment

who mortifies her. Because,
this morning, at the cross-country meet

235

my daughter shooed me away when I stood too close
to the school tent, talking to the other parents.

Loosening up, the girls stretch, run wind sprints
toward womanhood. There's no chance of her winning this race.

I told her—just work on your best time. She shooed me away again.
I know this is the future, what I haven't quite prepared for.

There will be other, more important races, I want to say.
The field is stacked with nearly two hundred girls,

most giggling about something parents don't understand.
As she pushes forward through the crown of girlhood,

I remember the otters holding hands while sleeping
so they won't drift apart.

When a Young Woman Must Run

A few years ago, while teaching poetry writing at Reinhardt University, one of my students asked if I would show the class a step-by-step process of how I write a poem, from beginning to end. This was a way for this student, and subsequently, the others, to see first-hand the impetus and then my process, however ugly it might be in the beginning.

That weekend, I found some quiet time on Sunday morning before my kids were up and the house was buzzing with activity, but something was bugging me from the day before, an incident with my teenage daughter, Olivia. I wrote some notes down and tossed in random thoughts and ideas about my place in the world. Then, I wrote a horrible first draft about my daughter at her cross-country meet from the previous day, where, because I was standing too close to the school tent, she shooed me away, as if embarrassed to be seen with her father. Although we have always had a wonderful relationship, something was in the air, and she did not want me nearby. My two boys never shooed me away, but Olivia shooed me away from the tent twice that morning, which became the impetus for the poem.

Because I had not written any poetry in a few months, I had a warehouse of ideas, lines, thoughts, and pieces of poetry rolling around in my head, but nothing was written down. I simply piled everything into the first draft to see what came of it. Once I had a draft, I did not edit it; however, on Tuesday, I brought the poem to class and showed the draft to my students. I apologized for it being such a bad draft, but I assured them that this is exactly how many poems begin, as a series of random thoughts and images, unconnected nonsense, just an inkling of an idea, an emotion, or a story, the triggering image or event, such as Richard Hugo might discuss. There were between ten and fifteen possible directions the poem could have navigated, but I left it up to the students to gauge what was strongest and critique it as they would in any workshop. In class, I talked about Anne Lamott's essay *Shitty First Drafts*, and said, "Well, here's your proof." It was quite terrible, which was perfectly fine because it was a throwaway poem, an exercise to demonstrate the process of writing a poem from beginning to end. Nothing more.

I allowed the students to workshop the poem, and without hesitation, they told me what was not working and what might be salvageable. Maybe it was a touch of revenge. They were not tentative, diving right in with their opinions. They weren't brutal, either, but proved their skill at being steadfast editors. I took their suggestions and returned home to edit the poem over the course of the week. I returned each week with my revision. They spent about ten minutes workshopping my poem, comparing the previous versions to the more recent. They were curious about why I deleted certain lines and words and how I navigated creatively through the process, why things were added that had not been discussed in class. I explained my procedure and what I was intending to accomplish with each edit.

This activity demonstrated *how I write a poem* and allowed the students to have some ownership in the editorial process by providing suggestions and comments. It provided insight into *how I did it,* and they had the opportunity to see the poem develop, which is an important element in the creative process. For the longest time I felt this was simply an exercise, a poem I would completely dismiss and throw away after the semester ended. Most importantly, I wanted to demonstrate to my students that most poems are not finished in one or two drafts, that time must be invested for thinking about the ideas, the possibilities, deconstructing everything, reassembling it, then returning days and weeks, and sometimes years later with a clearer perspective. I emphasized the idea that poems often take months or years to complete and used Elizabeth Bishop as an example.

Around the tenth week into the poem, about the twentieth draft, the poem took some shape. Later, when the poem began to have merit, I worked on it steadily, sometimes a few hours per day. One of the last things to present itself was the form. Up until the end, it was free verse, staggered lines and stanzas. The couplets developed around the last two drafts, and as soon as I had the couplets, I knew that was the form I wanted.

When it was *finished*, one of the students gave the poem to another professor, who, upon reading it, began to cry. This student then gave it to his father to read that same weekend, and he, too, cried. I had no idea anyone outside of the class had read it, but I soon began to notice that I had struck a chord. I continued to tweak the poem and ended up loving it enough to add it to the new collection, *Fly Fishing in Times Square*, which was the last poem included.

In class, we always identify the *Subject, Conflict*, and *Metaphor* in a poem in order to understand it as fully as possible. It helps to immediately break through all the other problems if we can or cannot identify those three things. "Why Otters Hold Hands" and the process of writing it, demonstrated how to take a first draft and work towards the subject, infuse conflict, and attempt to realize a metaphor.

Oddly enough, "Why Otters Hold Hands" has become the seminal poem in the collection, something I never imagined occurring. What I would like the reader to experience is the father-daughter relationship and how the father is there to support his daughter running the high school race, but, in truth, he knows she's running away from him. She must. She needs to run, needs to grow, and the only method by which she can fulfill that journey is to run away. It hurts the father deeply, but he must stand there and take it because there is more of the same thing in the future.

The father does not want his daughter to drift permanently away, so he must allow her to run, with the hope that she will return. As in the beginning of the poem, what the father wants are all the things in his life that are simple and quiet and known to him, such as his daughter's love. He wants everything to be the way it was. Unfortunately, the daughter has different plans for her life. The father must allow his daughter to have her freedom, which is a difficult situation for any parent. The consolation remains that otters hold hands so they will not drift apart, and thus, the father has hope that he and his daughter will continue a strong relationship despite her new freedom.

Afaa M. Weaver

Thelonius
for Gene F. Thomas

It's as if you are given the sky to carry,
lift it on your shoulders and take it to lunch,
sit in McDonald's with it weighing you down,
this business of being black, of staying black
until the darkness of some eternity kisses you.
Birth gives you something other folk thank
God for not having, or else they pray for it,
to have its gift of a body inclined to touch,
inclined to sing. Yet they will not give back
to God the paleness of being able to touch
absolute power. They envy only for so long,
as being black is being bound to danger.

Among us there are masters like Monk,
who understood the left hand stride
on a brick. In his rapturous dance beside
the piano, he was connected to knowing
the scratch and slide of the shoes leaving
the ground, the shoes of the lynched men.
He carried the truth of who we are,
as the mystic he was, reveling in its magic,
respectful of its anger, mute and unchanged
as the hate and envy surround us.

One day we learn there is no sky above
this trapped air around the earth.
The sky is but a puff of smoke from
this giant head smoking a Lucky Strike,
pretending not to know the truths.
We learn sometimes in this life,
sometimes in what comes after, where
there is really nothing but everything
we never knew. We learn in silence
the dance Monk knew. We find
secrets for pulling the million arrows

from our souls each time we move
to sleep, to forget that we are both
jewel and jetsam, wanted and unforgiven.

Liner Notes for "Thelonius"

In noting the pleasantries of Boston and the greater area around it, I think of autumn with the gorgeous weaving of trees on the walkway along Commonwealth Avenue, the euphoria of sitting on a bench in the Public Garden eating ice cream, strolling up Newberry Street gazing at the tourists, or taking the turn on Mass Ave in Harvard Square to walk down to the Grolier Book Shop. I moved to greater Boston from Philadelphia in 1996, the year black men who found themselves on the wrong side of the law were mislabeled by Hillary Clinton as super predators, a mess of liberal misspeaking that became infamous as one of a few liabilities in her loss of the 2016 presidential election, one that would unleash the toxicity of America's underbelly, an unleashing millions of Americans would celebrate as a long overdue victory.

In writing "Thelonius," I tried to show the embodiment of that feeling of having to live inside the psychic projections of the nation's ongoing denial of the consequences of the enslavement of millions of Africans, the country's original sin. Watching Thelonius Monk perform in videos from time to time, I am always touched deeply by the moments where he stood up from the piano to do a few dance steps, followed by a graceful return to the keyboard to hit the notes exactly where they should be touched. It is as if he performed the full embodiment of jazz, the African American art form that, I believe, includes a full sweep of its predecessors, from field hollers and shouts to spirituals and the blues enslaved Africans brought with them during the bloody passage over the Atlantic, along with their languages and belief systems, ranging from Arabic and Islam to Yoruba, with a universe around and in between those three.

Embodiment is, I think, a keyword in understanding this country, as everyone who lives in this society carries the angst of it in their bodies, where the soul's struggle to survive is the unwritten axiom in the refusal to grant a social contract to black people. I experience this axiom as a litany of acts ranging from the sinister to the malicious to the ludicrous. In Baltimore on the way home after an evening shift in the warehouse, I saw an older couple standing near their damaged car, looking very afraid. I stopped to help and offered to wait with them until the police arrived, which they did, one black and one white man, both in blue. Seeing them I assumed, however wrongly, that I could then leave, but the white officer shouted "Halt!" twice, even as the elderly wife began to plead. Angry, I nonetheless stopped and walked back until he decided to release me.

In my first few months in the Boston area, a policeman in Melrose rides his motorcycle over to where I am standing, waiting for the regional train. He dismounts and walks over to stand close to me, saying nothing, trying to intimidate me in the space of silence, making mental notes for profiling, before slowly riding away. Some years later, walking down the street next to my apartment in Somerville, I sense someone is close behind me, and when I turn, I am shocked to see it is a white woman leaning toward me, sniffing in an effort to smell me, looking for an odor. The shock was more that she was someone I knew, a poet married to another poet, an older couple I knew. She made some awkward excuse I cannot remember, an excuse mumbled under a smirk. Never mind the endowed chair, or the publications. Never mind those things. They do not matter in the mind of racism.

The ancestral voices that spoke to me as I was composing "Thelonius" include the unknown whisperings of Phillis Wheatley growing as a child bereft of her family of birth to become the mother of all black poets, as well as Jupiter Hammond, a poet with a fine sensibility who could not write his way out of slavery, Paul Laurence Dunbar and Alice Dunbar, Frances Harper and Langston Hughes, Margaret Walker and Owen Dodson, Gwendolyn Brooks and Robert Hayden. However, in the case of metrics, of the meeting of pacing and tone pattern, it is Paul Laurence Dunbar's "Sympathy" that gave me the emotional framing for what happens inside my lines, and inside my heart as I composed "Thelonius," and as I continue to read and think of it. It's the feeling of being trapped, and while trapped enduring expectations to perform according to racism's code of compliance.

Demands for compliance in society occur in polite spaces, such as academia, where humiliation takes the place of the scars on beaten backs and stumps of amputated parts. If that seems too harsh a comparison, think of the cost to the health of black Americans. Compliance is written in the unpublished documents of America's refusal to grant its black citizens a social contract, after all these years, as the concept of race, as artificial as it is, has given black people the weight of its social and political reality, while the cultures that traveled the Atlantic with enslaved Africans were beaten down in an attempt at erasure and ensured dominance. However, black resilience has formed a culture that continues to shape and define not only our lives, but the lives of other Americans.

Moving into Boston, a city of legendary standing in its embodiment of the hierarchy of whiteness and supremacy, I came to see a denial of the same hierarchy rooted in the area's overwhelming academic presence, a denial that emerges as liberal pretense. To me, it seemed so oddly ironic. Massachusetts was the first slave-holding colony, and Boston was the center of slave trading in colonial New England. In this city where enslaved Africans lived under the harshest of conditions, I came to write this poem about how it feels to be black. It was the late 1990s, before white militias, some of whom are in Massachusetts, were acknowledged as a major threat to this country. The time in which some would come to believe in the realization of a post-racial America was ahead of us, and American poetry was on the verge of seeing a steady stream of award-winning younger black poets, some of whom were my students in my time as first faculty at Cave Canem. I had begun to feel, in an intensely personal way, the pain of the challenges black folk faced each day, as I wrote "Thelonius" in a city where I would be doubted, by blacks and whites, more often than I cared to notice. We are given the sky to carry, the sky with its unbearable weight, the trick of an otherworldly irony.

Whitman celebrated himself and the whiteness Melville had enough courage to critique, as in the former's *Leaves of Grass* he assumed the voice of Americans as his own, saying they/we would assume what he assumed. The challenges to his hopefulness are now descending on us in full force, just as African American poets are reshaping the literary landscape. We celebrate ourselves by claiming our humanity over and against the denial of the same, we celebrate ourselves by claiming life over the structures of death created by the system that was designed, in the early years of the republic, for the propagation of wealth at the expense of our lives. We celebrate ourselves by witnessing the truth of how we feel.

I embrace that truth in the music of Dunbar's lines, citing how we struggle in a world of beauty where "...the wind stirs soft through the springing grass," a world where "...we are both/ jewel and jetsam, wanted and unforgiven," while faith in the ability to forgive and love, especially as we seek justice, is, I believe, what we all need in order to live.

Artress Bethany White

Vibrio Cholerae
In 1830, amid* a cholera epidemic,
recently freed slaves await passage to Liberia
under the auspices of the American Colonization Society.

The face will turn as blue as an ocean
lips spew foul over a roiling stomach
Liquefy bowels no quick cure can slow.

How adjacent to death freedom can be;
the ship that would steer us to Africa
moored as cholera's death mask fills a city.

Sulky musings while stranded in Norfolk
generations removed from shackles and chains,
and a ship's bowels full of waste-drenched slaves.

Port a cemetery of anchored boats,
every downcast visage a coy scythe raised,
and suspicion peaked by death's azure shades.

We idly drink cup after cup of tea
await solemn word of others stricken,
while nurses tend bowels doctors can't cure.

Jupiter waits, bound for Liberia
land my American feet never knew.
This face won't pitch as blue as an ocean
my cure is freedom, bondage now over.

*Amid its better-known symptoms, medical journals of the period often referred to a blue or blackish tint to the skin of cholera victims.

Documenting Freedom at the Intersection of History and Disease in "Vibrio Cholerae"

The poem "Vibrio Cholerae" stems from research into my family's enslavement in America. I initiated this investigation in the summer of

2018, when I began to examine university archives related to the planter family who once enslaved members of my own. As I sifted through folder after manila folder of personal correspondence and plantation ledger records, one letter in particular captured my attention. In the letter, an agent for the American Colonization Society writes about the status of a group of slaves who appear to have once been the property of Samuel Hairston, a man who at one time owned thousands of slaves. These several slaves, however, had recently been emancipated and provided with transport to Liberia aboard the passenger ship *Jupiter*. The attraction of this story, of course, was the possibility that a branch of my own family was related to members of this small packet of ex-slaves bound for the continent of Africa, a serendipitous voyage that would distance their ties with the shackles and land mass which once enslaved them.

As part of the historical recolonization process, select enslaved persons were emancipated by their enslavers or purchased from planters under the auspices of the American Colonization Society and booked passage on a ship bound for Africa. Agents retained for this purpose often served as go-betweens to make sure that the recently freed did not meet with any difficulty before embarking on their voyage. Specifically, these agents handled any funds or materials the newly freed might need: these materials included farming tools or money to buy seeds to begin their agrarian lives abroad.

My first brush with the history of the American Colonization Society took place during my graduate studies at the University of Kentucky, where I discovered an archival letter written by the nineteenth-century ex-enslaved person, Moses Jackson, to his benefactor, Mrs. Fishback. The letter seemed to indicate that Jackson's one-time mistress had responded to the call of abolition by emancipating a number of her slaves and repatriating them to Africa. In fact, a colony even carried the name of their one-time home and was referred to in the letter as "Kentucky in Africa." The letter was dictated by Jackson and written by his clerical patron, the Reverend H.W. Ellis. In it, Jackson strives to strike a balance between hope and hardship; a balance which would have been critical to paving the way for continued financial patronage of emigrants. The hardship is conveyed in the illness suffered by African American emigrants as they strove to acclimate to a new region and climate.

In his letter, Jackson asserts, "You have perhaps been informed previous to this intelligence concerning the large numbers of Kentuckians besides those of your family of blacks who embarked with me, some of who have fallen victims of the African fever, but we who survived, are doing very well." This telling statement conveys the poignant reality that freedom still required challenges that were often fatal for new arrivals from

America. It is highly likely that the fever being referred to is the result of malaria. Jackson's letter was penned in 1848, more than two decades after the first freed African Americans were relocated to the continent of Africa by the American Colonization Society. Still, the living conditions over time had not advanced to the point where resettlement was a risk-free endeavor. Data reveals that many ex-enslaved persons gained their freedom only to have their lives robbed by diseases like malaria after emigration.

Despite the reference to the very real hardship faced by the recently freed, Jackson lends hope to the situation of repatriation by detailing his own good health and gainful employment: "I usually perform the duties of the sexton of the Presbyterian Church, for which I receive a stipend." Making the dramatic shift in condition from enslaved person to paid employee was not lost on him. Still, this change in condition may or may not have made him state that "Liberia is unquestionably the happiest territory for the black man that could be selected on the globe, we enjoy liberty and lives in a degree which it is impossible in the order of things for the negro to enjoy in any other country." Even if his benefactor and letter writer, the Rev. Hines, may have suggested this laudatory line that reads like a public service announcement for the recolonization effort, Jackson still manages to temper this enthusiasm in his postscript where he considers how at least one other may seek to follow in his footsteps without understanding what he might be stepping into: "P.S. Tell Absolom Woodfork that I cannot as a friend recommend him to come out here until I have seen more of the place."

The rhetorical content of Moses Jackson's letter immediately came to mind as I contemplated the destiny of the ship *Jupiter* and its prospective passengers—the recently freed Hairston slaves discovered during my summer 2018 research. The poem I would eventually write about their journey began to take shape in my thoughts as I imagined what it would feel like to depart an America that once only offered either enslavement or a form of freedom that required black freedmen and women to register as free at the county clerk's office in their home counties in order not to be wrongfully re-enslaved. The impending adventure of the once enslaved, however, also carried a bitter taint; many African American emigrants to Africa would leave behind family members on American soil. This was one of the primary reasons African Americans were adverse to the recolonization project in the first place. Additionally, it would not have been easy to leave behind their nation home, which had been cultivated with their blood, sweat, and tears: they considered themselves Americans. Yet, despite these concerns, freedom still came with its own psychological and physical rewards.

When I began the process of writing "Vibrio Cholerae," I wanted to articulate the complexity of threads comprising the narratives of the enslaved in America. It was important for me to point out that the African Americans being repatriated to the continent would not have been the same people who comprised the original cargo of slaves who once experienced the Middle Passage; these newly freed people would be their descendants. The United States international slave trade was legally outlawed in 1808. At best, these descendants may have been raised on stories of the Middle Passage. Still, this reverse migration would have carried notes of history. In some way these new migrants must have felt they were serving as history's corrective for the captured and bargained-for bodies of their ancestors.

As I read the backstory of these newly freed men and women being outfitted for their voyage to Africa, I became fascinated by the local cholera epidemic that would delay them. My thought was that they might interpret this as one more ill-fated circumstance separating them from true freedom. After all, how many slaves had waited for years for their planter master or mistress to die because they had been promised freedom in a will, only to learn after the will was read that they would become the new property of in-laws? Along with the anxiety of being allowed to make the trip at all from a city and port where slavery still thrived, the threat of illness lurked. I began to imagine the cholera outbreak in more graphic detail after reading about the nineteenth-century interpretation of the disease and found it a fitting framework for the poem. The "blueing" of white bodies as part of the disease progression allowed me to play with color in the poem. In particular, I was able to capitalize on the irony that blueing would not be a tell-tale sign of the disease in the black body.

Form was really the clincher for the success of this poem. I see the villanelle as a great form for historical content. The repetitive nature of the lineation allows the poet multiple opportunities to reiterate important information in fresh language. The villanelle form allowed me full coverage of the layered history I sought to examine over the course of the poem. The additional historical notes serving as epigraph and endnote also allowed me to frame the poem with subtle backstory that would not interfere with the more direct narrative of the poem itself.

Carey Scott Wilkerson

Summer's End

We were boys somewhere between Star Wars
and the swarm of girls on purple bicycles
buzzing in driveways and knowing far more
than us about the world—these oracles
of the neighborhood, who had begun in spring
a coordinated campaign of whispering
sundresses and secret plotlines, quoting
made-up love songs and explaining nothing.
John Chancellor warned that Skylab was falling
out of its orbit, so we searched for fiery signs
together, forgot our names and our parents calling
us to our homes among sleeping roses, silent pines.
NASA said the wreckage rained over Australia,
but I swear we saw it blazing over Alabama.

Poetry and Paradox and the Oracles of the Neighborhood

Poetry is a style of speaking and a way of knowing. For me, poetic language translates the mysterious texture of lived experience into a legible form and delivers to us an understanding of the world that transcends the kind of knowledge available through mathematics, biology, or even physics. I feel pretty certain about this. And yet, I want to make clear that it's not so much a precise definition of poetry. I wouldn't presume the accuracy of my intuition about what poetry does, or what it can do. So far, I believe these are all defensible, foundational philosophical statements. However, when speaking about my own poetry, as this present project requires, I turn reflexively to that which comes more naturally to me: absurd conjectures and outrageous claims.

In this sonnet, "Summer's End," from my poetry collection *Cruel Fever of the Sky*, the narrator recalls the summer of 1979 when his life was framed by two crucial events: Sky Lab falling prematurely out of its decaying orbit, mesmerizing the world in fearful fascination, and his discovery of girls—with quite the same fusion of dread and delight. Of course, I remember these moments, but they were decidedly not contemporaneous. First, there was *Star Wars* (1977), then Sky Lab (1979), and then somewhat later, girls, romance, heartbreak, and all the rest. But in the crucible of imaginative experience, that is, in the poetic moment, Sky Lab falling and the first leap into desire must necessarily occur together as they are linked to the poem's basic insight that *love* torques the given world and shapes reality itself. Poetry creates its own reality. I believe that to be unambiguously the case.

At the same time, I'm equally certain that it's a trivial observation about this sonnet and brings me to my first absurd conjecture: poems are not reducible to summary or explanation and our attempts to understand them perhaps threaten poetry itself. On the other hand, to say so is also undeniably an explanatory gesture. Thus—and here is an outrageous claim—all discussions of poetry are both doomed and saved by paradox. Or, to put it another way, all of our clever talk about poetry will ultimately fail to crack the code, but that same zone of weirdness and indeterminacy is the *natural state* of poetic discourse. Nothing to see here, but amazing to behold!

This sonnet's narrator answers poetry's seductive paradox with an idiomatic flourish by speaking in the first-person plural; the declarative "we" is a cover story for the confessional "I." In this game of imposters and double agents, a casual observation about several becomes an epiphany about the *self*. And in the peculiar dynamics of paradox, a revelation unfolding of the *self* becomes a vision of the world, or even the cosmos. To be sure, none of this complex machinery works at all if the poem has no story to tell, no labyrinth to explore. Story, puzzle, and solution are all contained and resolved in the image of the final couplet. The narrator, having spent the summer navigating the maze of the human heart and searching the "sky for fiery signs," at last finds himself with a girl he probably imagines will love him forever—a delusion that will surely go down in flames by summer's end. And though they have already heard the nightly news report that Sky Lab broke up in the atmosphere and rained harmlessly down over Australia, he swears "they saw it blazing over Alabama." He's not wrong. He says it in poetic language and therefore *knows* it in the poem's luminous world of paradox. Poems don't need to be factual. They only have to be true.

William Wright

To a Minor Chinese Poet of the Kunlun Mountains

In your ancient and final hour,
when the moon scraped the horizon,
no longer a white fire
to guide you to the village of willows,

the ink had run dry,
your blood heavy, your spine
curved as the arc of distant lanterns.

When you sat, then collapsed into snow,
your strange verse fled
unperturbed down glacial streams
and into the starlit valley,

teeming with the glowing red fish
that drifted through your dreams.

So it is true no politicians ever championed
your scrolls that flashed
like dying stars
on which the eight immortals cast
their narrow immutable gaze.

So the villagers of Xianjiang
still swing their lanterns
against the dark woods, hungry.

Personal Grief as Empathetic Imagination

I wrote "To a Minor Chinese Poet of the Kunlun Mountains" in January of 2020. I recall the source of inspiration and also the emotional catalyst that led to the poem: I had been reading Jorge Luis Borges' *Selected Poems* (translated by Alexander Coleman), and I noticed some of his work was written to and for obscure figures, some fictional, all long dead, but that his odes contained a reverence that emanated with a universal warmth, a gratitude that any open-hearted reader could appreciate.

Situational depression hit me hard at the beginning of 2020 and seemed to worsen as the months went by—for reasons we all know about—COVID-19—and for another reason: at the end of the summer, my employment situation changed for the worse after years of hard work and lots of productivity. I knew I needed to write about this issue, but I refused to write a poem that literally transcribed my problem; I realized (having made the mistake of ranting before) that the metaphorical potential of such an approach would prove a failure.

Before writing the poem, I remembered my first mentor, the late Stephen Gardner. I was a nineteen-year-old idealist, and he was a likable fatalist damaged by personal familial issues, but one day he told me in his office that the real challenge for any poet was taking the painful circumstances and recontextualizing them to *give* the reader something. "Out of pain comes wisdom," he'd say, along with "the literal truth is an obstacle to quality." This latter bit of insight struck me as epiphanic: a poem that is about one's pain does not have to be scrawled on the page as navel-gazing victimism.

After losing my job, I felt victimized, dismissed, discarded, just like the Chinese poet about whom I wrote in the poem. How could I use this motif to indicate my sadness, but not in a blatant way? I decided, not fully aware of how the poem was going to go, of course, to offer the subject of the poem, and, by extension, the reader who interfaces with that subject, something to take with them. That "something" did not have to be the pain the writer might feel. Indeed, that intangible essence might very well be the antithesis of sorrow—a sense of hope, joy.

Had I come to write this poem equipped with all these notions *consciously*, it is doubtful that I would have written a poem worth reading. The clarity of hindsight can be so radiant and clear that looking into it is akin to staring into the sun for hours, then stumbling through the next few months with intense glare obscuring responsibilities, loved ones, opportunities. I had to wait a while for the pain to subside.

The result is that I *unconsciously* projected my circumstances onto a "minor" Chinese poet who lived long ago in a vastly different place. I explored the poetic imagination by dreaming of *another's* imagination, one whose works were rarely read, and one who only now—by the villagers who live today in a Chinese village—is appreciated, even if the elements that justify that appreciation remain mysterious, anonymous.

Technique

In the first stanza, my goal was to offer a bit of contrast immediately through the "ancient" and "final" adjectives, to express the idea that the moon itself was no longer a beacon for this poet, and that somehow upon his journey, he had been burdened by something insurmountable, whether physical or otherwise. His hopes, once moon-luminous, were now dimming to embers. In retrospect, of course, this mirrored my own experience: the notion of working hard, making an arduous journey, only to "collapse."

One of the difficult but necessary techniques I attempt to embed in all my poetry is a simultaneous sense of stasis and dynamism: let the image hold in the mind, but allow the flow of time, too. In the second stanza, I emphasized the former quality: the fact that this poet is slowing down, lumbered by the weight of age (and, perhaps, a search for something eternally lost). In his act of dying, however, his poetry is "freed" into the world, but finally lands in water, where luminescent red fish, creatures that exist only within the poet's dreams and a motif with which he had been obsessed when healthy, glide around his sinking scrolls. The circumstances of my depression seemed similarly dynamic and static: while I attempted to produce work, depression flattened the motivational impulse, no matter how hard I tried to disentangle it from the creative process.

In the remaining stanzas, my hope was to acknowledge the Chinese poet as someone who, though unnoticed in his life by the "politicians," those who were deemed most important in his culture, the poet's eight gods did not neglect his work and that now in our contemporary moment—villagers walk the bridges at night, swinging their lanterns, not quite satiated for reasons that might escape them—but that ultimately connect across time and space back to this minor Chinese poet. Though once considered "minor," his resonance persists, now "major"—his work, though undervalued and perhaps read by a very few—rings plangently and eternally for the few who *have* encountered him. This is the ultimate hope I have for my own work.

My goal was not to connect myself to this poet, but to give reverence to him and others like him. Still, I cannot escape the fact that this poem's existence depended on recontextualizing my own notions of feeling dismissed, pushed to the peripheries. My hope is that the poem offers a counterpoint to this feeling for readers—to provide a sense of courage.

My friend, the late poet Arthur Smith, said that most of the important work is written in complete obscurity. It is now a truism to note that most poetry is written for an extremely limited audience—mostly this audience is comprised of other poets. However, relative even to that microcosmic few, there are those whose work might never be read. In "To a Minor Chinese Poet of the Kunlun Mountains," I wanted to give thanks to these folks, no matter how few they are, no matter how obscure the places they might wander.

Jenny Xie

Melancholia

The black dog approaches?
I pry open the crooked jaw.

Inside?
A heady odor, elemental.

And then?
I spin through my life again.

How so?
Slow and fast, fast and slow.

What follows?
Time, the oil of it.

What direction?
Solitude throws me off the scent.

And what lies ahead?
Even the future recoils, long as it is.

What points the finger?
All of my eye's mistakes.

And what were they?
Level.

Probing Opacity

In "Mourning and Melancholia" (1917), Freud traces the distinction between the psychological state of mourning, a normal response to loss that is finite, and that of melancholia, a pathological mourning whose labor is endless. In mourning, the object of loss is clear and can be released by the mourner with time. Whereas in melancholia, what has been lost can remain hidden and becomes internalized—"devoured" by the ego, as Freud writes. The ego absorbs the lost object and feeds on it interminably. Doubtless this understanding of melancholia gets highly romanticized, but reading Freud, I felt provoked to write something in response to this concept of melancholia and how it suggests a fecund relationship to loss. There was something, too, about the voracious pull of appetite in the act of devouring loss that struck me.

As is often the case with my writing, an encounter with another's thinking or language quickens my poetic imagination prior the slow, nonlinear work of depositing and shaping language on the page. I found myself drawn to the ambivalence buried in Freud's concept of melancholia, but initial attempts to write into it, or fashioning lines around it, felt unsatisfying. The kinds of lines and stanzas I'd been employing previously didn't have enough movement or torque to them. At the same time, writing directly about melancholia through metaphors of ingestion, or by means of seizing a particular moment in the past, fell flat. These approaches were perhaps too glaringly obvious and deliberate, or too self-consciously frontal in their direction of approach, when what the poem needed was more play, more swerve, and more sidelong glances.

Usually, when my creative process stalls, the diagnosis is that my will is overexerting itself, thereby blotting out the unconscious, along with the kinds of arresting, unwieldy impulses that might pave the way for a refresh—or destabilizing—of perception. In my own experience, accidents and wanderings can yield surprising insights more reliably than stubborn pursuit. I looked at the half-drafts, and the fragments, which didn't move with more attention, more deliberation. Instead, I stepped out of the way, in the hope of inviting in fortuitous accidents that might jostle my imagination some more.

I set my earlier drafts—which mainly consisted of lines, fragments of language, notes from reading Freud's essay—aside for many weeks. Then, as it happens, I was leafing through a collection of translations one evening and stumbled on a poem titled "Came to me—" by the Persian poet Rudaki, which had been translated into English by Basil Bunting. The poem took the form of an alternating exchange of question and response between unidentified interlocutors. This formal structure, the mode of interrogation, held a certain charge. I felt a sensory jolt at having encountered the form and decided to re-enter to my old drafts and play around with the concept of *melancholia* some more. It turns out the dialogic structure was the formal engine I'd been waiting for.

You can hear the etchings, or echoes, of an analysis session in Rudaki's "Came to me—," but I was drawn to the dance of riddling there, too. In riddling, the slant ways of describing or approaching an object seem more pleasurable than arriving at an answer. What animates the exchange is the deferral of understanding, with descriptive lines revealing but also further obscuring the object. The back-and-forth, and the feeling around the shaded contours of something, felt like the right form for a poem aiming to locate the nature of a loss, which remains concealed and unknowable. Riddles, similar to melancholia, necessitate a kind of search, a process of decoding. I wrote most of "Melancholia" in one sitting after experimenting with the push and pull of riddling. There was a vital energy in drawing out the tension and in the process of probing opacity. The questions open to answers, which keep opening.

Monica Youn

A Guide to Usage: Mine

A. Pronoun

My.

Be-
longing

to me.

> *how should I define the limits of my concern the boundary between mine and not-mine the*
> *chime of the pronoun like a steel ring cast over what I know what I name what I claim what*
> *I own the whine of the pronoun hones its bright edges to keenness because there is power*
> *in the categorical that prides itself and plumps itself and proliferates till there is no room*
> *in here for anything but power till there is no air in here but there would be no need for*
> *air if you could learn to breathe in whatever I breathe out*

B. Noun 1

A pit or tunnel in

the earth
from which
precious

stones or ores or coal
are taken

by digging
or by other methods.

> *because the earth does not gleam with the shine of the noun to dig into the earth is*
> *imperative to use my fingers or else to fashion more rigid more perdurable fingers that cut*
> *or delve or sift or shatter because we are more evolved than animals because to mine is*
> *not to burrow because the earth is not for us to live in because the earth is not precious in*
> *itself the earth is that from which what is precious is taken the earth is what is scraped*
> *away or blasted away or melted away from what my steeltipped fingers can display or sell*
> *or burn*

C. Noun 2

A device
intended

to explode
when stepped upon
or touched,

or when approached
by a ship, vehicle,

or person.

> *my devise my device redefined by intent so thinskinned this earth is untouchable a sly*
> *simulacrum of innocence concealing an infinity of hairtrigger malice the cry of the noun*
> *sealed in a concentric sphere that sheaths its lethal secret in silence unapproachable it*
> *sings its unspeakable harvest in this field I have seeded with violence*

D. Verb

To dig
away or otherwise remove

the substratum
or foundation
of.

To sap.
To ruin

by slow degrees or secret means.

> *to dig is to build dark dwellings of negative space to knit a linked network of nothing the*
> *seams of the seemingly solid unravel the itch of erosion the scratch of collapse each*
> *absence the artifact of specific intention an abscess a crater a honeycomb of dead husks*
> *the home of the verb is founded on ruin the crime of the verb hollows out prisons and graves*
> *the rhyme of the verb tunnels from fissure to fracture from factory to faction from faultline*
> *to fate this foundation is equal parts atom and emptiness this fear invades fractally by*
> *rhizome and root what cement could salvage this crumbling concrete should I pledge my*
> *allegiance to unearthing or earth*

Mining the Word

I've never thought of myself as a "hot take" poet. I've always stood in awe of poets who can take what's speeding at them through the air and crystallize it into image, tone and form. Adrienne Rich once wrote of "an instrument in the shape / of a woman trying to translate pulsations / into images for the relief of the body / and the reconstruction of the mind." I'm sadly no such instrument—I'm more of a ruminant, a true Taurus. I like chewing on things for a long time, digesting and redigesting them, extracting maximum nourishment from even unpromising material.

But after the 2016 election, that slow-mo mode started to feel like an unwarranted luxury. In the days and weeks after the election, I felt helpless, panicked. Every morning I would wake up in a cold sweat, heart racing, obsessed with yet another priority—migrant families, Syrian refugees, police shootings of Black people, climate change, mass incarceration, voting rights. My son was about to turn two, and on my worst nights, I would tiptoe into his room, rest my hand on his warm tummy, and listen to his breathing. But even that solace seemed suspect to me—what right had I to bask in my son's safety when other mothers' children were at risk?

At panels and at gatherings, people kept asking me and other poets, "What can poetry do now?" Sometimes they would follow up by asking whether I regretted giving up lawyering. Guilt and shame—at my privileged, passive position—added to my fear. When I was a public-interest lawyer—faced with systemic injustice, I could at least file a lawsuit. But now what could I do to protect the vulnerable? I joined marches, called Congress, donated what I could, but it all felt like drops in the bucket.

Some of my friends suggested that I pick my battles, focus on a single cause and trust others to handle other issues. Pragmatic advice for sustained action, for maintaining my mental, emotional, familial and financial health. But I couldn't help thinking that this would be circling the wagons, a defensive move just short of surrender—narrowing my focus to a small circle that would include only what was most important to me. It seemed to differ only in degree, not in kind, from the deep-rooted selfishness that led to capitalist excess, to the gated community mentality, and eventually to Trumpism.

A few weeks after the election, the literary magazine *The Boston Review* asked me to contribute a poem to an anthology they were creating of poetic responses to the election. I had never accepted such a commission before, but I thought now was the moment for me to step up, to write towards and into my fear, my uncertainty, my shame. And I wanted to join in conversation with other poets, my friends, to see whether a group response seemed more adequate than our individual efforts.

But where to start? What to prioritize? It was like trying to find the end of a thread that led into a nightmarish mass of knots and tangles, of fears and facts and emotions inextricably intertwined. How to find a lyric thread that would pull me through?

Often when I find myself at an impasse in a poem, I find myself turning to the medium itself, to the words. I turn to it instinctively, the way the painter turns to paint or the composer to an individual instrument. Frequently it ends up throwing me a curve ball, an unexpected angle. I tell my students that in a poem you can't surprise the reader unless you also surprise yourself, and I often find the source of surprise buried deep in the material with which I'm working.

As I thought about the election, Trumpism, and all of the cavalcade of catastrophes we were facing, I found myself obsessing over the word *mine*—the piercing whininess of its long I, at the same time babyish but also creepily mechanical. It seemed like the keyword of the brand of toddlerish grabbiness that exemplified Trumpian capitalism. Surely it couldn't be coincidence that the word "mine"—as in a place where metallic ores are stripped out of the earth—was the same as "mine" as in the marker of possessiveness, the coppery scent of urine on a tree, the flag planted on the moon, the ring on the finger. Not to mention landmines, undermining ... there had to be some common denominator, some root that would assist me in diagnosing the ills of our time.

Since it was hard to get quiet time while sharing a home with a toddler, I went to Poets House, which was walking distance from my Manhattan apartment and offered 70,000 volumes of poetry, quiet, and comfortable chairs. I was also happy to discover that they had multiple hefty dictionaries, which I lugged over to my desk, only to find that my initial hypothesis had been wrong—"mine" (the possessive pronoun) did not, in fact, share a common root with "mine" (the noun). The possessive pronoun was derived from the German for "my," the noun from the Latinate for "metal." Clearly my idea of a common denominator wouldn't work out.

But perhaps I could forge my own connection between the disparate meanings of the word, a connection that would be as circular and metallic as the ring of a snare, something that would expand outward and inward in concentric progression. I knew I'd have to harness sound as well as meaning in order to make that connection resonate, reverberate like the terrifying bells of Poe's poem. I leashed together anapestic and iambic rhythms to create a pace that speeds up, the way a spinning coin will speed up as its revolutions flatten out, take up more space. And I wanted the carrying sound of the long I to serve as the shining thread on which the poem was strung. The result, dear reader, was the poem "A Guide to Usage: Mine."

Contributor Notes

Kim **Addonizio** is the author of a dozen books of poetry and prose, and most recently the poetry collection *Now We're Getting Somewhere* (W.W. Norton). Her memoir-in-essays, *Bukowski in a Sundress*, was published by Penguin. She has received NEA and Guggenheim Fellowships, and her work has been widely translated and anthologized. Her website is https://www.kimaddonizio.com.

David **Baker** is the author of 19 books, including *Whale Fall: Poems* (W. W. Norton, 2022), *Swift: New and Selected Poems* (Norton, 2019), and *Show Me Your Environment: Essays on Poetry, Poets, and Poems* (University of Michigan Press, 2014). He lives in Granville, Ohio, teaches at Denison University, and works with *The Kenyon Review*.

Aliki **Barnstone** is a poet, translator, critic, editor, and visual artist. *Dwelling* (Sheep Meadow Press, 2016) is the most recent of her eight books of poetry. She is a professor of English and creative writing at the University of Missouri and served as poet laureate of Missouri from 2016 to 2019.

Erin **Belieu** is the author of five poetry collections, all from Copper Canyon Press, including her most recent, *Come-Hither Honeycomb* published in 2021. Her other works include *Slant Six, Infanta, One Above and One Below, Black Box*, and co-edited the anthology, *The Extraordinary Tide: New Poetry by American Women*.

Richard **Blanco** was selected by President Obama as the fifth inaugural poet in U.S. history. Born in Madrid to Cuban exile parents and raised in Miami, cultural identity characterizes his many collections of award-winning poetry and prose. Blanco is an associate professor of creative writing at Florida International University.

David **Bottoms** is the author of nine collections of poetry, two novels, and a book of essays and interviews. He most recently published *Otherworld, Underworld, Prayer Porch* (Copper Canyon Press). A few titles are *We Almost Disappear, Waltzing Through the Endtime, Vagrant Grace*, and *Shooting Rats at the Bibb County Dump. Scraps in the Blessings Jar: New and Selected Poems* is forthcoming from LSU Press.

Earl Sherman **Braggs**, a UC Foundation and Battle Professor of English at the University of Tennessee at Chattanooga, is the author of 14 collections of poetry. Braggs' prizes include the Anhinga Poetry Prize and the Jack Kerouac

International Literary Prize. His latest poetry collections are *Hat Dancing Blue with Miss Bessie Smith, Negro Side of the Moon,* and *Cruising Weather Wind Blue.* His memoir, *Boy Named* Boy, was published in 2021.

Fred **Chappell** retired in 2004 after teaching for 40 years in the English Department of the University of North Carolina Greensboro. He is guilty of 30-odd books of poetry, fiction, and literary commentary. The recipient of numerous awards, his latest book of verse is *As If It Were* by Louisiana State University Press (2019), and his novel *A Shadow All of Light* was published in 2016 by Tor Books.

Chen **Chen** is the author of *Your Emergency Contact Has Experienced an Emergency,* which is forthcoming from BOA Editions fall 2022. His first book, *When I Grow Up I Want to Be a List of Further Possibilities* (BOA Editions, 2017), was longlisted for the National Book Award and won the Thom Gunn Award.

Marilyn **Chin**, whose newest book is *A Portrait of the Self as Nation: New and Selected Poems,* was awarded the Ruth Lily Prize for lifetime achievement in 2020. She serves as a Chancellor of the Academy of American Poets. Her poems are considered Asian American classics and are taught internationally.

Ama **Codjoe** is the author of *Bluest Nude,* forthcoming from Milkweed Editions in fall 2022 and *Blood of the Air* (Northwestern University Press, 2020), winner of the Drinking Gourd Chapbook Poetry Prize.

Stephen **Corey** retired in 2019 after 36 years with *The Georgia Review.* He is the author of *Startled at the Big Sound: Essays Personal, Literary, and Cultural* (2017), as well as ten poetry collections, including *There Is No Finished World.* In 2022, White Pine Press will publish his new-and-selected poems, *As My Age Then Was, So I Understood Them.*

Chad **Davidson** has published four collections of poems, including in 2020, *Unearth,* from Southern Illinois University Press. *Terra Cognita,* a collection of his travel essays, is forthcoming with LSU Press in 2022. He serves as professor of literature and creative writing at the University of West Georgia near Atlanta and co-directs Convivio, a summer writing conference in Postignano, Italy.

Denise **Duhamel** recently published *Second Story* (Pittsburgh, 2021). Her other titles include *Scald, Blowout, Ka-Ching!, Two and Two, Queen for a Day: Selected and New Poems, The Star-Spangled Banner,* and *Kinky.* She is the recipient of a Guggenheim Foundation fellowship and an NEA and teaches at Florida International University.

Camille **Dungy** is the author of *Guidebook to Relative Strangers: Journeys into Race, Motherhood and History,* and four collections of poetry, most recently *Trophic Cascade.* She has edited three anthologies, including *Black Nature: Four Centuries of African American Nature Poetry.* Her honors include a Guggenheim Fellowship, NEA Fellowships in both poetry and prose, and an American Book Award.

Stephen **Dunn** is the author of *The Not Yet Fallen World: New and Selected Poems,* forthcoming from W.W. Norton in 2022. His awards include the Pulitzer Prize for Poetry, the Academy Award for Literature, the James Wright Prize, and fellowships from the National Endowment for the Arts and the New Jersey State Council on the Arts. Stephen Dunn passed away in June 2021.

Cornelius **Eady** has published several volumes of poetry, including *Victims of the Latest Dance Craze*, winner of the 1985 Lamont Prize; *The Gathering of My Name*, nominated for a 1992 Pulitzer Prize; and *Hardheaded Weather*. He teaches at the University of Tennessee–Knoxville. He is co-founder of the Cave Canem Foundation.

Martín **Espada** has published more than 20 books, including *Floaters* (2021), *Vivas to Those Who Have Failed* (2016), *The Trouble Ball* (2011), *The Republic of Poetry* (2006), and *Alabanza* (2003). He's the recipient of the Ruth Lilly Poetry Prize, the Shelley Memorial Award, an Academy of American Poets Fellowship, and a Guggenheim Fellowship.

Beth Ann **Fennelly**, the poet laureate of Mississippi, has won grants from the N.E.A., United States Artists, and a Fulbright to Brazil. Her sixth book, *Heating & Cooling: 52 Micro-Memoirs* (W. W. Norton), was an *Atlanta-Journal Constitution* Best Book and a Goodreaders Favorite.

Annie **Finch** is the author of seven volumes of poetry, as well as books of poetics, poetry translation, the anthology *Choice Words: Writers on Abortion*, and solo and collaborative verse theater performances. She earned her Ph.D. at Stanford and offers classes on scansion, meter, and Magic of Rhythmical Writing at PoetryWitchCommunity.com.

Gregory **Fraser** is the author of four poetry collections, most recently *Little Armageddon* (Northwestern University Press). His poems have appeared in *The New Yorker*, *The Paris Review*, and *Ploughshares*. The recipient of grants from the NEA and the Guggenheim Foundation, Fraser teaches at the University of West Georgia.

Alice **Friman** has published seven poetry collections, most recently *Blood Weather*, from LSU Press. A recipient of many honors including two Pushcart Prizes and inclusion in *Best American Poetry,* she's been published in *Poetry, Ploughshares, Georgia Review, Gettysburg Review, Plume, Crazyhorse,* and others. She lives in Milledgeville, Georgia, where she was Poet-in-Residence at Georgia College. Her website is alicefrimanpoet.com.

Ángel **García**, the proud son of Mexican immigrants, is the author of *Teeth Never Sleep*, winner of a 2018 CantoMundo Poetry Prize and published by the University of Arkansas Press, winner of a 2019 American Book Award, finalist for a 2019 PEN America Open Book Award, and finalist for a 2020 Kate Tufts Discovery Award. He has also received fellowships from MacDowell, CantoMundo, Community of Writers, and Vermont Studio Center.

Margaret **Gibson**, Poet Laureate of Connecticut, has published 12 books of poems, with a new book, *The Glass Globe*, in 2021. She is the recipient of the Lamont Selection, the Melville Kane Award, and the Connecticut Book Award. She was a Finalist for the National Book Award in Poetry in 1993 and in 2016 for the Poets' Prize. As Poet Laureate, she was awarded a grant from the Academy of American Poets and edited an anthology, *Waking Up to the Earth: Connecticut Poets in a Time of Global Climate Crisis.*

Nikki **Giovanni** has published more than 20 collections of poetry and other works in a career that first began in 1968 with the publication of *Black Feeling, Black Talk*. Her numerous awards include Woman of the Year from *Ebony Magazine* (1970), *Mademoiselle Magazine* (1971), and *Ladies' Home Journal* (1972). She has also been the recipient of the Martin Luther King, Jr., Award for Dedication and Commitment to Service (2009) and the Maya Angelou Lifetime Achievement Award (2017). She is currently a University Distinguished Professor at Virginia Tech.

Beth **Gylys** is an award-winning poet who teaches at Georgia State University. She has published four books of poetry, *Body Braille* (Iris Press 2020), *Sky Blue Enough to Drink* (Grayson Books 2016), *Spot in the Dark* (The Journal Award, Ohio State UP 2005), and *Bodies That Hum* (Silverfish Review Press 1999).

Janice N. **Harrington** is the author of *Primitive: The Art and Life of Horace H. Pippin* (BOA Editions). She is also the author of *Even the Hollow My Body Made Is Gone, The Hands of Strangers,* and several award-winning children's books. She teaches creative writing at the University of Illinois at Urbana-Champaign.

Terrance **Hayes** is the author of six books, most recently *American Sonnets for My Past and Future Assassin*. His awards include the Pegasus Award for Poetry Criticism, Hurston/Wright 2019 Award for Poetry, the National Book Award in Poetry, T.S. Eliot Prize for Poetry, the Kingsley Tufts Poetry Award, and the Bobbitt National Prize for Poetry. He is a professor of English at New York University and a MacArthur Foundation Fellow.

Edward **Hirsch** published his first book, *For the Sleepwalkers*, in 1981. He is a MacArthur Fellow and has published nine books of poems, including *Gabriel: A Poem* (2014) and *Stranger by Night* (2020). He has also published six prose books about poetry, most recently *A Poet's Glossary* (2014) and *100 Poems to Break Your Heart* (2021).

Jane **Hirshfield** is the author of more than 15 books, most recently *Ledger* (Knopf, 2020), which centers on the crises of biosphere and social justice. Her work has appeared in *The New York Times, The Guardian, Poetry,* and ten editions of *The Best American Poems*. In 2019, she was inducted into the American Academy of Arts & Sciences.

Christine **Kitano** is an associate professor at Ithaca College and teaches in the MFA Program for Writers at Warren Wilson College. Her second collection of poetry, *Sky Country* (BOA Editions) won the Central New York Book Award and was a finalist for the Paterson Poetry Prize. Recent poems and prose appear in *The Massachusetts Review, Portland Review,* and *The American Poetry Review.*

Yusef **Komunyakaa** was born in Louisiana and is a member of the Fellowship of Southern Writers. He has published more than 15 collections of poetry. His awards include the Kingsley Tufts Poetry Award and the Pulitzer Prize for his 1993 collection, *Neon Vernacular* from Wesleyan University Press.

Ted **Kooser** served two terms as U.S. Poet Laureate and is a past winner of the Pulitzer Prize. He's the author of 20 adult books of poetry, memoir, and writing instruction, as well as five illustrated children's books. His most recent collection is *Red Stilts*, from Copper Canyon Press.

Dorianne **Laux** is a Pulitzer Prize finalist whose most recent collection is *Only as the Day Is Long: New and Selected*, W.W. Norton. She is also author of *The Book of Men*, winner of the Paterson Poetry Prize, and *Facts about the Moon*, winner of the Oregon Book Award. She teaches poetry at North Carolina State and Pacific University. In 2020, she was elected a Chancellor of the Academy of American Poets.

Sandra **Lim** is the author of three collections of poetry: *The Curious Thing* (W.W. Norton, 2021), *The Wilderness* (W.W. Norton, 2014), and *Loveliest Grotesque* (Kore Press, 2006). Her work has been honored with a Guggenheim Fellowship, the Levis Reading Prize, and a Literature Award from the American Academy of Arts and Letters.

Adrian **Matejka** is the author of six books. His most recent collection is *Somebody Else Sold the World* (Penguin, 2021). He lives in Indianapolis, Indiana, and is the Ruth Lilly Professor of Poetry at Indiana University Bloomington.

Airea D. **Matthews** is the author of *Simulacra*, the 2016 Yale Series of Younger Poets, which was selected by Carl Phillips. She is also the recipient of the 2016 Rona Jaffe Foundation Writers' Award and the 2020 Pew Fellowship. She is an assistant professor of Creative Writing at Bryn Mawr College.

Campbell **McGrath** is the author of 11 books of poetry, including *Spring Comes to Chicago, Seven Notebooks, XX: Poems for the Twentieth Century*, a Finalist for the 2017 Pulitzer Prize, and most recently *Nouns & Verbs: New and Selected Poems* (Ecco Press, 2019). Born in Chicago, he lives with his family in Miami Beach and teaches at Florida International University.

Dunya **Mikhail** is an award-winning Iraqi American poet and writer. Her books include *In Her Feminine Sign, The Beekeeper: Rescuing the Stolen Women of Iraq, The Iraqi Nights, Diary of a Wave Outside the Sea*, and *The War Works Hard*.

Robert **Morgan** is the author of several books of poems, including *Terroir* (2011) and *Dark Energy* (2015). He has published 10 books of fiction, most recently *Chasing the North Star* (2016) and *As Rain Turns to Snow* (2017). His works of nonfiction include *Boone: A Biography* (2007). He's been the recipient of awards from the Guggenheim Foundation and the American Academy of Arts and Letters. He is currently the Kappa Alpha Professor of English at Cornell University.

David **Mura** has published four collections of poetry: *The Last Incantations, Angels for the Burning, The Colors of Desire* (Carl Sandburg Award), and *After We Lost Our Way* (National Poetry Contest winner). His two memoirs are *Turning Japanese* and *Where the Body Meets Memory*. His newest book is *A Stranger's Journey: Race, Identity & Narrative Craft in Writing*.

Marilyn **Nelson** is the author of some 20 books. Her honors include the Frost Medal, the Golden Rose Award, the NSK Neustadt Prize, the NCTE Poetry Prize, the Ruth Lilly Prize, a Chancellorship of the Academy of American Poets, and Poet-in-Residency of the Cathedral of St. John the Divine.

Laura **Newbern** is the author of *Love and Eye* and the recipient of a Writer's Award from the Rona Jaffe Foundation. Her poems have appeared in *The Threepenny Review, Plume, The Atlantic*, and elsewhere. Her second book-length manuscript has been a finalist for the Anthony Hecht Poetry Prize and the Bergman Prize.

Annemarie **Ní Churreáin** is a poet from the Gaeltacht region of northwest Ireland. Her publications include *Bloodroot* (Doire Press, 2017), *Town* (The Salvage Press, 2018), and *The Poison Glen* (The Gallery Press, 2022). She is a recipient of The Next Generation Artist Award from the Irish Arts Council. Visit www.studiotwentyfive.com.

Alicia **Ostriker** lives and bikes in New York City. Her most recent collection, *The Volcano and After: Selected and New Poems, 2002–2019,* won the National Jewish Book Award for Poetry. Currently, she is the New York State Poet Laureate.

Frank **Paino** is the author of three books, most recently *Obscura,* published by Orison Books in 2020. His poems have appeared in a variety of literary journals and anthologies. Frank has received a Pushcart Prize, the Cleveland Arts Prize in Literature, and an Individual Excellence Award from the Ohio Arts Council.

Sara **Pirkle** is an identical twin, a breast cancer survivor, and a board game enthusiast. Her first book, *The Disappearing Act* (2018), won the Adrienne Bond Award for Poetry. In 2019, she was nominated for Georgia Author of the Year in Poetry. She is the Assistant Director of Creative Writing at the University of Alabama.

John **Poch** is a Paul Whitfield Horn Distinguished Professor at Texas Tech University. He is the author of seven books of poems, most recently *Texases* (WordFarm 2019). His poems have been published in *Yale Review, Poetry, The Nation, Paris Review*, and many other journals.

Paisley **Rekdal** is the author of ten books of nonfiction and poetry, including *Nightingale* and *Appropriate: A Provocation.* Her work has received the Amy Lowell Poetry Traveling Fellowship, a Guggenheim Fellowship, an NEA Fellowship, Pushcart Prizes, and various state arts council awards. She teaches at the University of Utah and is Utah's Poet Laureate.

Alberto **Ríos** has published more than 15 books, including *Not Go Away Is My Name,* preceded by *A Small Story about the Sky, The Dangerous Shirt,* and *The Theater of Night,* winner of the PEN/Beyond Margins Award. A finalist for the National Book Award and recipient of the Western Literature Association Distinguished Achievement Award, he has taught at Arizona State University since 1982.

Tim **Seibles** is the author of six collections of poetry and the former Poet laureate of Virginia. He is a professor of English at Old Dominion. As well, he teaches workshops for the Cave Canem Foundation and at Stonecoast MFA Program in Creative Writing. His most recent collection is *One Turn Around the Sun.*

Vijay **Seshadri** has published four collections of poetry, including *3 Sections,* which won the 2014 Pulitzer Prize. His other awards include the James Laughlin Prize of the Academy of American Poets and the Bernard F. Conners Long Poem Prize from *The Paris Review.* He has received grants from the John Simon Guggenheim Memorial Foundation and the National Endowment for the Arts.

Patricia **Smith** is a visiting professor at Princeton University and a distinguished professor for the City University of New York. She's been the recipient of the Kingsley Tufts Award, the *LA Times* Book Prize, and the NAACP Image Award. *Shoulda Been Jimi Savannah* was the recipient of the Lenore Marshall Prize from the Academy of American Poets, and *Blood Dazzler* was a National Book Award finalist. She's the author of *Incendiary Art* and a finalist for the Pulitzer Prize.

Virgil **Suárez** was born in Havana, Cuba, in 1962. At the age of 12 he arrived in the United States. He is the author of eight collections of poetry, most recently *90 Miles: Selected and New*, published by the University of Pittsburgh Press. His work has appeared in a multitude of magazines and journals internationally. When he is not writing, he rides his motorcycle up and down the Blue Highways of the Southeast, photographing disappearing urban and rural landscapes. *The Painted Bunting's Last Molt* is forthcoming.

Mai Der **Vang** is the author of *Yellow Rain* (Graywolf Press, 2021) and *Afterland* (Graywolf Press, 2017), winner of the Walt Whitman Award of the Academy Poets. She is an assistant professor of English in Creative Writing at Fresno State.

William **Walsh** is the author of seven books, including *Fly Fishing in Times Square*. The director of Reinhardt University's undergraduate and graduate creative writing programs, he is also known for his many literary interviews, which include Czesław Miłosz and Joseph Brodsky. His debut novel, *Lakewood*, was published in 2022 by TouchPoint Press. In 2023, his new novel, *Haircuts for the Dead*, will be published by TPP.

Afaa M. **Weaver** has published 15 books of poetry, the most recent of which is *Spirit Boxing*. In 2023, Red Hen will publish his next collection, *A Fire in the Hills*. His poetry has been translated into Arabic and Chinese. He is a professor emeritus at Simmons University, a member of the MFA faculty at Sarah Lawrence, a Guggenheim fellow and a Cave Canem Elder.

Artress Bethany **White** is a poet, essayist, and literary critic. White is the recipient of the Trio Award for her poetry collection *My Afmerica: Poems* (Trio House Press, 2019) and author of the essay collection *Survivor's Guilt: Essays on Race and American Identity* (New Rivers Press, 2020). She is an associate professor of English at East Stroudsburg University.

Carey Scott **Wilkerson** is a poet, dramatist, and opera librettist. His most recent works include a collection of the poetry, *Cruel Fever of the Sky,* and the libretti for *The Heart Is a Lonely Hunter,* an opera based on the classic Carson McCullers novel, and *The Rescue,* an operatic retelling of the Orpheus myth. He is an assistant professor of creative writing at Columbus State University and is currently working on a portrait opera about the famous African American abstract expressionist painter, Alma Thomas (1891–1978).

William **Wright** is the author or editor of more than 20 volumes of poetry, poetics, and prose, including *Grass Chapels: New & Selected Poems* (Mercer University Press, 2021), and a novel, *Blight* (Iris Press, forthcoming). His recent book, *Specter Mountain* (with Jesse Graves), won the Appalachian Book of the Year.

Jenny **Xie** is the author of *Eye Level* (Graywolf Press), which was a finalist for the National Book Award, and a recipient of the Walt Whitman Prize. She is on the faculty at Bard College as well as New York University. Her chapbook *Nowhere to*

Arrive won the 2016 Drinking Gourd Chapbook Poetry Prize and was published by Northwestern University Press.

Monica **Youn** is the author of *Blackacre* (Graywolf Press 2016), which won the William Carlos Williams Award of the Poetry Society of America and was short-listed for the National Book Critics Circle Award and the Kingsley Tufts Award. Previously a finalist for the National Book Award, she has been awarded the Levinson Prize, a Guggenheim Fellowship, a Witter Bytter Fellowship from the Library of Congress, and a Stegner Fellowship. Her fourth book *FROM FROM* is forthcoming from Graywolf Press in March 2023.

Credits and Permissions

Kim Addonizio: "Cigar Box Banjo" from *My Black Angel: Blues Poems and Portraits*, SFA Press. Copyright 2014 by Kim Addonizio. Poem and essay are reprinted by permission of the author.

David Baker: *"Nineteen Spikes"* first appeared in *Poetry* (November 2020) and is reprinted by permission of the author. "Writing in Peril" is reprinted by permission of the author.

Aliki Barnstone: "Scripture for Coronavirus" and "On Writing 'Scripture for Coronavirus': E Pluribus Unum" are reprinted by permission of the author.

Erin Belieu: "With Birds" from *Slant Six*. Copyright © 2014 by Erin Belieu. Reprinted with the permission of The Permissions Company, LLC on behalf of Copper Canyon Press, coppercanyonpress.org. "Notes on 'With Birds'" is reprinted by permission of the author.

Richard Blanco: "Looking for The Gulf Motel" from *Looking for the Gulf Motel*. Copyright © 2012 by Richard Blanco. Reprinted by permission of the University of Pittsburgh Press. "Memory as Homeland" is reprinted by permission of the author.

David Bottoms: "Under the Vulture-Tree" from *Armored Hearts: Selected & New Poems*. Copyright © 1995 by David Bottoms. Reprinted with the permission of The Permissions Company, LLC on behalf of Copper Canyon Press, coppercanyonpress.org. "Under the Vulture-Tree on the Wakulla River" is reprinted by permission of the author.

Earl Sherman Braggs "Sandy Columbine Hook Parkland" and "What We Come to Know, What Comes to Know Us" are reprinted by permission of the author.

Fred Chappell: "The Departures" and "They" are reprinted by permission of the author.

Chen Chen: "The School of Night & Hyphens" first appeared in *Tin House* then *poets.org*. "The School of Night & Hyphens" and "Telling the Truth About Love" are reprinted by permission of the author.

Marilyn Chin: "Bamboo, the Dance" from *Portrait of the Self as a Nation*. Copyright © 2018 by Marilyn Chin. Used by permission of W.W. Norton & Company, Inc. "Poetry of Necessity" is reprinted by permission of the author.

Ama Codjoe: "Burying Seeds" © 2020 by Ama Codjoe. Published 2020 by Northwestern University Press. All rights reserved. "On Composing 'Burying Seeds'" is reprinted by permission of the author.

Stephen Corey: "History of My Present" first appeared in *Shenandoah*. "History of My Present" and "The History of 'History of My Present'" are reprinted by permission of the author.

Chad Davidson: "Putting In" and "The Tricky Business of Elegies" are reprinted by permission of the author.

Denise Duhamel: "Recession Commandments" from *Blowout*. © 2013 is reprinted by permission from the University of Pittsburgh Press. "Lies I Told Myself" is reprinted by permission of the author.

Camille Dungy: "One Night in 1888, as the French steamboat Abd-el-Kader powered from Marseilles to Algiers, news reports proclaim *the sky became quite black with swallows*" first appeared in *Orion* and "One Night in 1888" (essay) are reprinted by permission of the author.

Index